Quilt Winders and Pod Shavers

Other books by Hugh Barty-King

SUSSEX IN 1839
SCRATCH A SURVEYOR
ROUND TABLE, THE SEARCH FOR FELLOWSHIP
THE BALTIC EXCHANGE, THE HISTORY OF A UNIQUE
  MARKET
A TRADITION OF ENGLISH WINE
FOOD FOR MAN AND BEAST

Quilt Winders and Pod Shavers

The History of Cricket Bat and Ball Manufacture

Hugh Barty-King

MACDONALD
& JANE'S
LONDON

Who wind the quilt, who shave the pod,
Come Duke, come Twort, come Small, come Odd.
Who heart and soul and hand engage,
Come Clapshaw, Nicolls, Wisden, Page.
In crafts now part of cricket lore,
Come Surridge, Gradidge, Gunn snd Moore.
They're working still, they're at it yet,
The likes of Cobbett, Dark and Pett.

To Jenny

ISBN 0 354 08547 6

Designed by Judy Tuke

Published by Macdonald and Jane's Publishers Ltd,
Paulton House,
8 Shepherdess Walk,
London, N1 7LW

Set, printed and bound in Great Britain by
Fakenham Press Limited, Fakenham, Norfolk

Contents

Acknowledgements

I hope perhaps that this book will inspire someone more qualified and with more time than I to dig further; much of the story still lies uncovered. But for much of what I have been able to unearth I am very grateful to those who found time to talk to me, especially those still active craftsmen whose names are mentioned in the text; and Mr Stephen Green, curator of the MCC; Mr Edward Holland; Mr C. G. Howard, secretary of the Surrey County Cricket Club, The Oval; the late Mr A. H. Spink, secretary of the Federation of British Manufacturers of Sports and Games; the late Mr Len Newbery, managing director of Gray-Nicolls Ltd; Mr Bill Mepham (by whose kind permission I give extracts from the notebooks of Thomas Twort which he had carefully preserved); Mr Norman Joy; Mr John Taylor; Mr John Tipper; Mr Norman Hunt of B. Warsop & Sons (who gave me access to the Warsop archives before they left St John's Wood); Mr John Reader (who had kept the ECBMA minute book and in rediscovering it found a tin of 'gold' dust that turned out to be brass filings); Mr Leslie Adams of Alfred Reader & Co; Mr Bernard Taylor MIBE, a descendant of Aquila Clapshaw; Mr Harold Tipper; Mr Thomas Ives; Mr Thomas R. Twort; Mr H. Freeman and Mr R. H. Ellis of Lillywhite Frowd; Mr Pat Lee; Mr Fred Sayers; Mr Leslie Eade and Mrs Gowers.

I am grateful too for the information volunteered by correspondents, particularly Viscount De L'Isle VC, KG; Lord Sackville; Miss Diana Rait-Kerr; Sir Alan Lubbock; Mr R. J. L. Altham; Mr A. H. Brodhurst; Dr Felix Hull, Kent County Archivist; Dr A. E. J. Hollaender, Keeper of MSS, Guildhall Library, London; Miss Fiona Marsden, Curator of the Sussex Archaeological Society; Mr R. A. Storey, Chief Assistant Registrar, National Register of Archives; Mr John W. Waterer, FSA, FSIA, President of the Museum of Leathercraft, Brighton; Mr G. D. Copus; Mr W. J. Smith MA, FRHistS, Deputy Head Archivist, Greater London Council; Judith Whitten, Archives Assistant, The Labour Party; Rev F. J. Turner SJ, Librarian, and Michael Weld, Bursar, Stonyhurst College; Mr Ruthven O. Hall FRIBA, Bursar of Winchester College; Mr Peter Gwyn, Archivist, Winchester College; Mr J. D. Coldham, editor of *The Journal* of the Cricket Society; Miss M. E. Cash BA, Hampshire County Archivist; Mr K. C. Harrison MBE, FLA, City of Westminster Librarian; Mr H. W. Gray and Mr R. G. Blake of Grays of Cambridge; Mrs Joyce Deacey of County Sports St Neots Ltd and her son Roderick Deacey; Mr R. T. Simpson of Gunn & Moore Ltd; Mr W. Lambert; Mr R. F. Bryan; Mr Duncan Fearnley; Mr D. Bush of Harry Hayley Ltd; Mr M. Smith of Slazengers Ltd; and for the help of librarians of the libraries I visited, including the British Library, Bloomsbury, The British Museum Newspaper Library, Colindale, the Science Reference Library, the Patent Office Library, Tonbridge Public Library, Sevenoaks Public Library, and the Westminster Public Libraries – Leicester Square, Victoria and Marylebone branches.

Foreword

This story of the cricket ball and cricket bat makers of England is a work of scholarship as is rarely encountered in the literature of cricket. To cover – or rather uncover – a territory that is essentially unfamiliar and untrodden is a formidable undertaking even in the allegedly well-documented field of cricket history. The archaeology of cricket, however, with which the author in the first part of this book so closely concerns himself, is (with but one exception) notably sparse in the treatment afforded it hitherto by historians. At all events, no one has before applied himself to the archaeology and subsequent history of cricket exclusively from the point of view of the two basic implements of the game – the bat and the ball.

This is a subject that ought to have been on cricket shelves many years ago – only the thoroughly daunting nature of the effort involved accounting for its absence. Others have dabbled in the story of bats and balls, and one or two have taken the matter to respectable lengths: but it has required uncommon diligence, spread over many years, to break the back of the subject as thoroughly as Mr Barty-King has done. He has not done everything, by any means, that the subject can demand, and he is the first to acknowledge that. Indeed, his very efforts demonstrate how vast was the field that he had to tackle: though at the same time they demonstrate also how successful he has been and how much further – infinitely further – he has carried his researches than any known writer before him.

There is no doubt that this volume forms a valuable social document as well as a history of cricket ball and cricket bat making in England. The social historian will find here material that has never been at his disposal before, or at least only in a highly dispersed form. The growth of the trade into an industry is a study of much importance not only in a cricket sense. As a source of employment alone, the cricket manufactories played an important role – and are still doing so. There was, and is, healthy competition just as has existed in every trade. Though Kent (and, to a lesser extent, London) takes the lion's share in this activity, especially in the manufacture of cricket balls, there were pockets of production elsewhere: though the north of England, which has certainly produced its own bats, if not balls, in the passage of time, has been given less attention in this treatise. Little-known bodies like the Amalgamated Society of Cricket Ball Makers (with headquarters, naturally, in Tonbridge!) and the English Cricket Ball Manufacturers' Association (based, too, in Tonbridge) reflected the advance and need for collective representation in the industry. The archives of these bodies and of the individual firms in membership furnish a great deal that is of fascination in the tripartite relationship between the cricket manufacturers, the playing community, and the legislators.

The household names in bats and balls, known to every cricketer and cricket reader, have ancient traditions which have been nurtured with a careful pride through many successive generations. To have recorded their stories in such a fluent form reflects the highest credit on the author, and leaves the reader with a sense of gratitude that the job has at last been done and been done so well.

It is astonishing – as well as sad – that the intricate and fascinating crafts of bat and ball making have not been properly placed on record before: and even sadder to think that the pioneers and their successors have been all but ignored whilst all the glory has been afforded the players who have relied so abundantly on these ancient crafts for the exercise of their own special skills.

Now Mr Barty-King has attempted to set the record right. If I had to choose a man to write about the making of cricket bats and balls, I would choose one from Kent, preferably from Tonbridge. In the absence of that, I would settle for one from East Sussex, from Ticehurst, where Mr Barty-King resides – marginally over the Kentish border and as close to Tonbridge and its environs as to make no matter. Many a cricketer's eyes will be opened by this book, which is at once erudite and readable, without being oppressively technical. It is a task well done.

Irving Rosenwater

1 The Cat and Dog Link

A search for antecedents

The first cricket ball was a cat; the first cricket bat a dog. Cricket has many misty ancestors, but the one with the firmest outline in the murky pool of likely derivatives is the sport of Cat and Dog, with its shadow, Cat in the Hole. However it was a long time before cricket reached even that stage. Taking a whack with a stick at a stone, an oak apple or a tuft of grass had been an exhilarating exercise from the time man first lifted himself on to his two hind legs and found he was able to hold a stone to throw in the air with one hand while holding a stick in the other hand to hit it with. It was the start point of battledore, tennis, badminton, rackets, hockey, pelota, lacrosse, croquet, the whole group of diversions which has come down via the intermediary forms of knockabout sports like Catch Ball, Club Ball, Trap Ball, Stool Ball, Chevy Chase, Rounders, Bandy, Shinty and Hurley.

One thing to hit and another to hit it with did duty for the lot – one shape, one size, the universal ball, the universal bat, both ready-made, as far as possible, by nature. If further manipulation was necessary, it had to be minimal. Anything that fitted into the hand and was light enough to lift and wave would do for hitting with; but the thing you hit could never be as rough and ready. Nature fashioned reasonably rounded stones, and what you hit did not have to be perfectly round for these primitive pastimes, though the rounder the better. Rounded knots which grew in birch trees required no craftsmanship. The skill lay not in doing anything to them but in finding them. Cutting them away from the trunk without upsetting their natural form required a certain knack, and if you could make them rounder by shaving the edges so much the better. The knur in the old north country game of Knur and Spell was made of holly wood roughly shaped with a knife – the word 'knur' means a hard excrescence or swelling in a tree. The ball of the half-croquet, half-golf game of Pall Mall, *paile maille* (still played at Montpellier in France up to the beginning of the First World War and possibly even today), was made of the roots of boxwood growing in rock crevices and forming a knot, which was extracted and carved.

There were many versions of the hitting-something-with-a-stick-game; the common link was the 'something' being called a cat. There was a version which involved manipulating a cat through narrow hoops, another version between wider posts and yet another into holes. It was obvious that by the time the sport had achieved this degree of diversification the universal ball had had its day. Each version demanded a cat to suit its own requirements. In the case of Tip Cat it was a short piece of wood tapering at both ends, one of which the player tipped with a stick. As it sprang into the air he knocked it away into the distance. In Trap Ball the cat was a round ball which the player placed in the hollow of one end of the trap. The player hit the other end with his club and hit the ball when it lifted into the air, as the different shaped cat was hit in Tip Cat.

In *The Book of The Ball*, which A. E. Crawley wrote in 1913, he made out a case for variations in the ball creating variations in the game, and not vice versa. The first 'made' balls, he pointed out, were stuffed rather than built up – casing first, then the body inserted. The stuffing was cloth, hair or feathers. This was the universal ball of the ancients. If it had been an inflated bladder for instance, ball games would have developed differently, he claimed.

Joseph Strutt referred to this in his *Sports and Pastimes of the English People* (1801) when he described a ball game, played by the Romans with a ball of leather stuffed with feathers, called Paganica (because it was played by unsophisticated country folk). This rustic pastime he said was the forerunner of Cambuc or Goff. 'The golf ball is composed of the same materials to this day [1801]' commented Strutt, 'though I have been told it is sometimes, though rarely, stuffed with cotton.'

But as craftsmen developed skills, it seems, Crawley notwithstanding, they made a cat in whatever shape, size or weight the game dictated. Was the cat to be thrown into the air by the player or the trap? Hit against a wall or over a net? Would it be required to bounce off the ground or roll along it? Or both? The cat evolved for the along-and-over-the-ground game became the hockey ball; the cat for the along-the-ground-and-through-the-hoop game became the croquet ball.

After tortuous journeys the along-and-over-the-ground-and-into-the-hole game evolved, via Cat in the Hole, into 'goff', and via Cat and Dog into cricket.

These were both children's games invented, it seems, in Scotland. In his *Etymological Dictionary of the Scottish Language* of 1808 John Jamieson gave Cat and Dog as 'the name of an ancient sport in Angus; also used in Lothian'. In his article on cricket in the fourteenth edition of the *Encyclopaedia Britannica* Harry Altham spelt it Cat and Doug. 'An old Scottish game, apparently an early form of cricket' was how Cassell's *Encyclopaedic Dictionary* of 1909 described it. Joseph Wright distinguished two forms of Cat and Dog (or Cat and Dog Hole), in his *English Dialect Dictionary* of 1897: (a) a boy's game, and (b) a species of the game 'Trap and Ball' which he said was sometimes called Cat and Trap.

For Jamieson the cat in Cat and Dog was not a ball but 'a piece of wood'.

> Three play at this game who are provided with clubs. They cut out two holes, each about one foot in diameter and seven inches in depth, with a distance between them of about 26 feet. One stands at each hole with a club, called a 'dog', and a piece of wood of about

four inches long and one inch in diameter, called a 'cat', is thrown from the one hole towards the other by a third person. The object is to prevent the cat getting into the hole.

The cat could in fact have been a cut off the dog – four inches chopped off the end of a branch of a tree. It did not have to roll along the ground – it was thrown – so did not need to be either cylindrical or spherical. It had to be capable of falling into a foot-wide hole in the ground seven inches deep without bouncing out again, and capable of being hit by a (presumably wooden) club.

> Every time that it [the cat] enters the hole, he who has the club at that hole loses the club and he who threw the cat gets possession both of the club and of the hole, while the former possessor is obliged to take charge of the cat. If the cat be struck, he who strikes it changes place with the person who holds the other club; and as often as these positions are changed, one is counted as won in the game by the two who hold the clubs and who are viewed as partners.

This was not unlike the Stool Ball described by Joseph Strutt in 1801.

> I have been informed that a pastime called 'stool ball' is practised to this day in the northern parts of England which consists simply in setting a stool upon the ground, and one of the players takes his place before it, while his antagonist, standing at a distance, tosses a ball with the intention of striking the stool and this it is the business of the former to prevent by beating it away with his hand, reckoning one to the game for every stroke of the ball. If, on the contrary, it should be missed by the hand and strike the stool, the players change places.

Commenting on this in an article in *The Strand Magazine* of September 1895, Alfred T. Story recollects that he played such a game as a child in the East Riding of Yorkshire as recently as the early 1850s. It was played with a stool lying on its side so that the ball was bowled at the seat of the stool.

> It would usually be played in a garden path with a parti-coloured leather ball stuffed with sawdust which was purchased at the sweet-stuff shop for a halfpenny. I do not recollect what the game was called; but I know the little wooden stools that were used were called 'crickets'. They were very different from the more finished and ornamental stools, and were formed of a thick piece of wood, round or square, which constituted the seat, and three or four legs, as the case may be. They may be seen in the houses of the poor, almost anywhere in the north, and are rough, tough and very durable pieces of furniture, admirably suited for children to play with and knock about.

> It may be worth while to note, too, that I once saw a nurse-girl improvise a game of 'stool-ball' in a very peculiar way to amuse a little boy. She placed a small foot-stool, or cricket, upside down, laid a comb across from one leg to another like a wicket bail, rolled up a rag ball, and gave it to the boy to bowl with, while she defended her odd wicket with a hair brush. She held the bat until the little bowler knocked down the comb, when she took the ball and the youngster handled the hair-brush bat.

This mezzotint is by R. Thompson RA in 1808 and called *Trap-Ball*

In fact, Stool Ball originated in Sussex. For John Jamieson, Cat and Dog more nearly resembled Club Ball, an ancient English game also described in Strutt's *Sports and Pastimes*. 'It seems to be an early form of cricket,' said Jamieson. It was a kind of rounders.

When he came to describe the second form of Cat and Dog, 'a species of the game Trap and Ball,' Jamieson said the ball in that game was substituted by 'a piece of wood' of box or yew 'and when laid on the ground and smartly struck at either end, it will rise high enough for the striker to hit it away from him as it descends. The "dog" is the stick with which it is struck.'

A four inch long 'piece of wood' but described this time as being *pointed at each end*, featured also in the Tip Cat described by William Bolland in his *Cricket Notes* of 1851. He had the information, he said, from a manuscript which was once in his family's possession and was sold in 1840. This piece of wood was placed by the player inside a marked circle 'rather larger than a boy's marble ring'. The player 'strikes the end of the piece of wood causing it to ascend and while in the air he strikes it again as far from the circle as may be'. If one of the fieldsmen caught the wood, the striker was out. If the cat (the wood) was not caught it was tossed back into the circle. Again there seemed to be no rolling requirement. When struck by the dog the cat presumably spun round in the air and fell dead to the ground without moving further. If the fieldsman managed to lob the cat back so that it fell inside the circle, then the striker was out, and another took his place.

'And from this rude sport of children,' says William Bolland, 'we propose to trace cricket. The similarity is obvious. We have the circle as the wicket, the wood as the ball, and the stick as the bat. We establish at once the innings, the hit, the catch, and make an approach to bowling. We introduce also fielding, forming together, no slight foundation whereon to raise a structure.'

Tip Cat, he said, was chiefly played in the outskirts of old London – particularly Lincoln's Inn Fields. The authorities allowed only part of the fields for public sports so as many people as possible crowded into one game, and sides had to be chosen. 'The crowded contests led to double base Tip Cat; a very important change as it was clearly the type of double wicket in the double game and it was necessary for the striker to change ends or bases. Whenever therefore the cat was struck, the players ran across, and here we recognise the Tip and Run of our boyish days.' Bolland reckoned that the players crossing each other from wicket to wicket as they ran in the double Tip Cat game gave rise to it being called 'Cross Wicket' – 'which by syncope became Cricket'. He quoted similar corruptions in the English language to support his case – inn signs like Goat and Compasses becoming God Encompasses Us and Bag O'Nails becoming Bacchanals. Thus the abbreviation from Cross Wicket to Cricket, he claimed, was 'no monstrous conclusion to reach'. Few however agreed with him.

Joseph Strutt considered the cat in Tip Cat was a piece of wood 'about six inches in length and an inch and a half, or two inches, in diameter, diminished from the middle to both ends, in the shape of a double cone'.

He saw the cat being used in a different way to that described by Bolland. The players mark out a ground, he said, consisting of a circle of four to eight holes and 'one of the opposite party who stand in the field tosses the cat to the batsman who is nearest him and every time the cat is struck the players are obliged to change their situations and run once from one hole to another in succession'. He described a second version in which the striker stood in the middle of a ring creased into the turf and had to hit the cat as far out of the ring as he could. If he missed the cat and it landed in the ring, he was out. If he hit it he judged with his eye how far he thought it had travelled in terms of bat lengths and 'calls for a number to be scored [i.e. notches carved in his stick] towards his game'. The number of actual bat-lengths was now measured, and if his guess was over-optimistic he was out.

The cat was the same for both versions – a double cone which could be easily flipped into the air and would not have needed much skill in the making. It was not required to roll or be caught. Yet for the game which

1 2
3 4
5 6 7
8 9

From W. W. Read's *Annals of Cricket* 1896: 'The Evolution of the Cricket Bat' greatly resembled Strutt's 'rounders' version of Tip Cat, though not Bolland's, players did use a ball, and the cat, in *Alice Through the Looking Glass* fashion, assumed the shape of the dog. For the piece of wood which players had to place in the base in the game of Cat in the Hole was an elongated form of the four or six inch cat of Cat and Dog – in fact a cat with a handle. In Cat in the Hole there were two contenders for a place in the hole which, as in Cat and Dog, was the base to be guarded, and there was only room for one. One contender was a cat wielded by a player by means of the long handle attached to it; the other was a *ball* wielded (thrown) by the player who alone, as in Cat and Dog, had no 'club'. Thus the cat in Cat in the Hole had a dual function: getting into the hole first and keeping its rival, the ball, out by blocking the entrance or hitting it away. The implement had become the 'piece of wood' and the 'club' of Cat and Dog all rolled into one, a cat dog. It was probably a branch of a tree initially, with perhaps a hook like a crochet needle, a stick with a crick or crook at one end, which could be said to be the cat element of the composite tool and therefore more easily popped over the lip of the hole. This cricked end enabled a player running full tilt at the hole to stretch out his arm, clasp the rim and pull himself towards the hole. Cat in the Hole was a more complicated game than the three a side Cat and Dog, and it was a question of not merely one base (a hole) or even a double game of two holes opposite each other, but of six holes or more, in a circle, in the manner of rounders, baseball and Strutt's Tip Cat. It was, said Jamieson, a game played by boys 'common in Fife [the county of St Andrews of course] and perhaps other counties'.

> If seven boys are to play, six holes are made at certain distances. Each of the six stands at a hole with a short stick in his hand; the seventh stands at a certain distance holding a ball. When he gives the word ... all the six must change holes, each running to his neighbour's hole and putting his stick in the hole which he has newly seized. In making this change the boy who has the ball tries to put it into an empty hole. If he succeeds the boy who had not the stick (which is called the cat) in the hole to which he had run, is put out and must take the ball. There is often a very keen contest whether the one shall get his stick or the other the ball first put into the hole. When the cat is in the hole, it is against the laws of the game to put the ball into it.

The use of the word 'ball' as opposed to 'a piece of wood' denotes something round which rolls – a 'globular body'. There is no mention of throwing it in the air; the putting or popping of the ball in the hole indicates rather a lobbing action or trundling it along the ground, in which case it had to travel evenly and in the direction in which it was bowled. There are no true spheres in nature, so the fashioning of a wooden ball made from box or yew to meet the requirements of the rules of Cat in the Hole would have called for a certain degree of skill which would not have been needed for the stick whose function was more blocking – keeping the ball or cat out of the hole – than striking.

But sooner or later, as W. South Norton has suggested, the players of Cat and Dog must have found they could get more fun from playing the game with a ball, like Cat in the Hole, which would have to be rolled along the ground rather than lobbed in the air. He is at pains to show that these cat pastimes for boys and girls were a separate breed from the game which became 'regulation' cricket. Cricket without stumps he calls them. 'WS cricket' was not 'cricket' – though one at least of these children's games was *called* 'cricket'. 'The evidence seems to show that there may have been more than one so named long before our present cricket was thought of – although the latter took the title when it was invented. The same word being used to describe earlier sports, as well as the later cricket, has caused confusion and error.'

It is indeed confusing. What was the game referred to in the Guild Merchant Book at Guildford in 1548 in which a witness at an inquest testified that he knew a piece of wasteland where 'he and several of his fellowes [of the Free School at Guildford] did runne and play there at Crickett'? What had John Florio in mind when in *A Worlde of Wordes Most Copious and Exact* published in London in 1598 he gave the English for *squillare* as 'to make a noise as a cricket; to play cricket-a-wicket and be merry'? or Sir William Dugdale when he gave as an instance of the dissolute behaviour of the young Oliver Cromwell (born 1599) the fact that he was 'famous for football, cricket, cudgelling and wrestling; a roysterer'? What was the 'cricketing' reported to have taken place between the Weald and Upland near Chevening in 1610? What was Randle Cotgrave thinking of when he defined the French *crosser* in 1611 as 'to play at cricket'? What were those six parishioners playing at who were prosecuted for desecrating the Lord's Day at Boxgrove in Sussex in 1622? What sort of game was it that Robert Matthew was saying the 'men' of Winchester College were playing on St Catherine's Hill in 1637? How formalised was the disorderly pastime which the erstwhile roysterer's commissioners proscribed in Ireland in 1656, what did the sticks and balls look like which he had burned by the common hangman? Just what were those English residents up to in Aleppo in 1676 who were reported to be passing the time with 'duck hunting, fishing, shooting, hand-ball krickett, scrofilo'?

No one knows the answers to these questions for certain, but it is safe to assume that by the beginning of the seventeenth century the cat games which were purely cat, the cat games which were half-cat half-cricket, and the games which were set on the path to becoming 'regulation' cricket, had begun to sort themselves out. It had been a long evolutionary journey. A principal feature had been the increase in the length of the pitch, a change which had a marked effect on the character of both what was struck and what was used to strike it with.

At twenty-six feet the hole was easily discernible, but as the nine yards became twenty-two (the agricultural chain) it became more and more difficult. So to mark it they put the stump of a tree in it – like the pole with the flag on it in golf. But the stump got in the way, and they replaced it with two stumps, one on either side of the foot-wide hole, bridging them with a small stick. With six inches clearance on either side, the two stumps were some two feet apart. This little structure, at first only a foot high, could easily be seen from twenty-two yards away and no longer hindered the entrance of the ball or the cat – or the dog. Shepherds who passed the time with their version of the cat/cricket game on the uneven surfaces of the Downs found it impractical to make their mark a hole in the ground, so they used the hurdle gate in the sheep

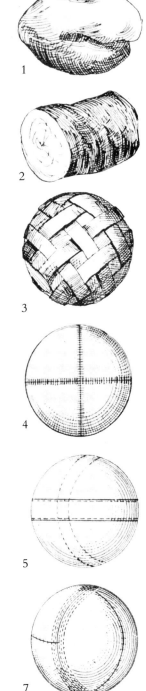

From W. W. Read's *Annals of Cricket* 1896: 'The Evolution of the Cricket Ball'

pen. This consisted of two uprights with a crossbar resting on their slotted tops. This was known as a wicket, after the Anglo Saxon word *wican* meaning to give way – the place where the pen yielded to let the sheep in. Florio certainly knew the word – 'cricket-a-wicket'.

The hole remained beneath the wicket, but as the game came to involve more people, as has been seen in the case of Tip Cat on Lincoln's Inn Fields, the game developed in such a way that it was not only for the bowler to dismiss the striker, by popping the ball or cat directly into the hole, but for any of the other players to do so, particularly the one behind the hole – the 'second bowler'. It came to be that a striker's innings could be terminated in two ways: bowled out and what would now be called 'stumped'. The latter would be achieved by the second bowler behind the wicket, who retrieved the ball which had passed the striker and also missed the hole. A struggle ensued between the man with the dog/bat and the man behind the wicket who now had the cat/ball. The first bowler had missed his chance of bowling the striker out, and now it fell to the second bowler. The striker with his crooked, wooden dog thrashing away at the hole, and the wicket-keeper impetuously thrusting his unprotected hand with the ball into the same small pit, must have led to many broken knuckles and considerable loss of temper. The remedy seems to have required the wicket-keeper still to attempt to pop the cat into the hole if he got it, but the striker was allowed a very much larger 'hole' into which he had to place his bat if he were not to forfeit his innings. He was given the area round the hole, or rather in front of it – like the circle which was the mark in Tip Cat. The most forward safe point of this area was marked by a line indented or creased into the turf. The wicket-keeper still had to pop the ball into the actual hole, but for the striker the 'hole' into which he had to pop his bat was the complete space between the wicket and this 'popping crease'. This was the new and safer form of 'stumping'.

This was taken a stage further when it was decreed that a striker was out if, after hitting the ball away and exchanging places with the other striker, he failed to return to his place in time to put his bat over the popping crease before the wicket-keeper had put the ball in the hole. He was 'run out'.

Yet another stage was reached when the wicket-keeper was no longer required to pop the cat/ball into the hole but, with the cat in his hand, to knock the wicket down. This led to the first bowler, too, no longer being required to lob the cat directly into the hole but to knock the wicket down which, to make a better target, was made taller and less broad.

Obviously the piece of wood that would best be popped into a hole was likely to be different from the one which best knocked a tallish wicket down. With the marker of the hole and not the hole itself becoming the target of first and second bowler, the Cat game was well on the way to becoming 'regulation' cricket, and the cat a cricket ball.

Evidence for evolutionary stages such as this is to be found in *The Young Cricketers Tutor* which John Nyren wrote with Charles Cowden Clarke in 1833. He quoted from a small manuscript furnished him by William Ward 'written some years since by an older cricketer containing a few hasty recollections and rough hints to players'.

From the authority before me, it appears that about 150 years since [1683] it was the custom, as at present, to pitch the wickets at the same distance apart, namely 22 yards. That the stumps (only 1 ft high and 2 ft wide) were surmounted with a bail. At that period, however, another peculiarity in the game was in practice and which it is worth while to record. Between the stumps a hole was cut in the ground large enough to contain the ball and the butt-end of the bat. In running a notch [the method of recording a 'run' was by carving or scoring a notch in a wooden stick], the striker was required to put his bat into this hole, instead of the modern practice of touching over the popping crease. The wicket keeper in putting out the striker when running was obliged, when the ball was thrown in, to place it in this hole before the adversary could reach it with his bat. Many severe injuries of the hands were the consequence of this regulation; the present mode of touching the popping crease was, therefore, substituted for it. At the same period, the wickets were increased to 22 inches in height [in fact a *reduction* from 24 inches] and 6 inches in breadth, and instead of the old custom of placing the ball in the hole, the wicket keeper was required to put the wicket down, having the ball in his hand.

This is the classical quotation which, more because it bears the authority of the much respected William Ward, the greatest cricketer of his day, the Director of the Bank of England who saved Lord's Cricket Ground and the MCC from extinction, than because of John Nyren's sponsorship, establishes the link between regulation cricket and the Cat and Dog game of earlier times.

But at this point the story can stop groping in the dark and clamber on to the firm ground of the well-documented, early form of the game which was Stonyhurst Cricket.

A twentieth century reconstruction of early cricket as played at Stonyhurst College near Blackburn in the eighteenth century with the only surviving stone wicket seventeen inches high and thirteen inches wide. Fossilised for two centuries in France, 'Stonyhurst Cricket' – a single wicket game – was brought back to England in 1794 and played by the boys until 1884

2 The First Professionals

Bat and ball craftsmen of the 18th century

At a time when those who wished to continue practising the 'old religion', and to educate their children in its principles, found it increasingly difficult to do so, a Jesuit priest conceived the idea of establishing a school for the sons of Roman Catholic Englishmen in the realm of His Most Christian Majesty the King of France.

Father Robert Parsons founded his English grammar school at Eu in Normandy in 1582, and, when his patron, the Duke de Guise, was murdered some seven years later, he gathered them together again at 'The English College of St Omers' (St Omer), with a preparatory school for younger boys at Watten. There were thirty-three boys by 1593 and forty years later there were two hundred. When the French Parlement proscribed the Society of Jesus in 1762, the English College moved to Bruges (which they called Bridges) in the Austrian Netherlands; and when in 1773 the Jesuits were suppressed by the Pope, the pupils moved to Liège. Here the English College remained until it was chased out by the French Revolutionary armies of 1794, when it settled in an estate in England, donated by an old boy, some fourteen miles north-east of Preston in Lancashire, called Stonyhurst Hall.

Robert Parsons had been anticipated in his anxiety to outwit the designs of Elizabeth I to suppress the old religion by William Allen, a former Fellow of Oriel College, Oxford, and Principal of St Mary's Hall, and from 1587 a cardinal. In 1568 he opened an English College at Douai, not for boys but for English Catholics wishing to train for the priesthood. This, too, survived until the French Revolution when the scholars and senior members thought it best to come to England, where in 1804 they found a home at Ushaw, Northumberland.

The ketch *John of Yarmouth* which brought the young Roman Catholic gentlemen of the English College at Liège from the Meuse to the river Hull that July day in 1794 carried in its hold as part of the schoolboys' luggage a number of oddly shaped clubs about three feet long, round at the top and an inch in diameter, and a number of leather balls, with which the boys were used to playing a game called cricket.

It was a game the boys had been playing term in term out ever since the first of their number had crossed the channel to join Father Parson's

pioneering school at Eu two hundred years before. 'It would appear
very probably to have represented,' as John Gerard wrote in his ter-
centenary history of Stonyhurst College in 1894, 'the rudimentary form
in which the game was played in England, when in the days of Elizabeth
the founders of the college had to take themselves and their institutions
away from their native land.'

From the rules on games in general drawn up in the very earliest
period of the settlement at Stonyhurst, certain pastimes were dismissed
as 'trifling' and officially frowned on. The tradition of playing these
came across the channel together with the tradition of playing what
became known, to distinguish it from London Cricket, as Stonyhurst
Cricket. Among these 'trifling games' was Tip Cat which seems to have
differed from one of the officially condoned games which was called
simply, Cat. Attached to the rules about games in general was a list of
approved pastimes appropriate to each season. Football began in the
Great Vacation and continued till Easter. 'Then Cricket, which is only
to last the Easter Vacation, Cat, Trap & C. Top [spinning tops?] begins
with the Great Vacation and ends with the retreat.'

Here then is a game called Cricket and a game called Tip Cat and
another called Cat all existing side by side. They were all bat and ball
games, and one kind of ball seems to have done for all of them. The rules
included an injunction that at the school balls 'are not to be made too
hard'. If Stonyhurst Cat was a form of the Angus Cat and Doug, the fact
that a universal ball was used for all the bat and ball games bears out the
contention that in time the four inch long 'piece of wood', which was
the cat in Cat and Dog, became a ball. Trap was presumably the Trap
and Ball which Jamieson described as being similar to Cat and Dog, but
with a ball as a substitute for the 'piece of wood'. Father Gerard says
Trap, whatever it was, had certainly been played at St Omers, but adds
surprisingly that Trap and Top 'did not flourish on English soil, as we
find no record of their subsequent existence'. Trap and Ball may have
faded out later, but it certainly seems to have been in fashion for some
time in England – though perhaps it was not the same as Trap.

Stonyhurst Cricket was played at the school in England, as it had
been by the exiles on the continent for two hundred years, from 1794 to
1860 when it was displaced by London Cricket – the 'regulation' game
played according to the laws of the Marylebone Cricket Club. Father
Gerard wrote:

> We are told that the Ushaw games of Cat and Battledore were
> transported by Cardinal Allen from sixteenth-century Oxford to
> Douay. About the same period there is clear evidence of the exist-
> ence of Cricket in some form and there is nothing improbable in
> the supposition that this was in like manner taken over sea. On
> French soil it would naturally be fossilised, none of the influences
> which combined to develop the game at home affecting its course,
> while school tradition would rigorously preserve its original fea-
> tures. However this may be, certain it is that the primitive
> Stonyhurst game, the nature of which was regulated by a minute
> and complex code of rules, combined with the essential features of
> Cricket much that was altogether different from what is com-
> monly called by the name.

This Stonyhurst College boy of 1979 holds one of two surviving Stonyhurst Cricket bats. Some three feet two inches long and four-and-a-half inches wide, weighing about two pounds, these were made by college servants at nearby Hurst Green

The base to be guarded was neither the hole nor the circle of the Cat games but a stone of the size of a small milestone. A bowler – one of a team of five – bowled one of the not too hard balls underarm along a thirty yard pitch on a smooth, hard, gravel playground in the direction of the stone, with the object of hitting it and bowling the batsman out. He bowled twenty-one balls at the batsman as fast as he could, one after another, never having to mind whether the batsman was ready or not. One of the rules was 'A Batsman cannot be bowled by a full-pitch or first-bounce unless he offers.'

What is meant by 'unless he offers' is not clear, but it is evident that the ball was basically required to be of a size that fitted a boy's hand, that would roll along hard gravel ground and was capable of being hit a distance by a wooden bat.

All the balls used in Stonyhurst Cricket were partly made by the boys themselves. They made the interior which consisted of a core of list – cloth, that is – tightly covered with worsted soaked in glue which was then rapidly dried before a fire. In latter days they made the core with a nucleus of hard 'india-rubber', as it was then always called. The core, which had been made by the boys in this way, was then passed to the school shoe repair shop, where trained shoemakers covered it with two half-circles of thick, hard leather, the edges of which, with their inner surfaces laid together, were stitched through and through with wax-end – thread coated with cobbler's wax. The seam thus formed made a raised belt round the ball, like the ring of the planet Saturn. One of the rules was 'A bowler must bowl as fast as he can, and always with the seam' – which meant *on* the seam. Apart from being bowled out, a player could be caught out by one of the other three fieldsmen or the 'second bowler' who, as seen, was what would now be called the wicket keeper, who crouched a yard behind the stone. This raised seam all round the ball made catching it extremely tricky.

Presumably the ball, which the boys of the continental English College, later Stonyhurst College, made for their cricket, changed in form between 1594 and 1794. Similarly others who indulged in the

Stonyhurst Cricket First Match Higher Line (senior) bats were branded '999', Second Match Higher Line '888' and so on. The '555' on the bat on the right means it was a First Match Lower Line (junior) bat. These matches were played every day. A game played only when the boys felt inclined was termed a 'Free and Easy Match', and the bats used were branded '000' – though the third '0' seems to have been omitted from the bat on the left. The leather covered ball sits in the only surviving wooden mould below the last mallet with which Stonyhurst cricket balls were hammered into shape by school cobblers

different Cat/Club Ball pastimes in England experimented with different techniques in order to arrive at a ball with which the latest version of the game could best be played. Rules and ball evolved together. The first cricket balls, made by those who played the game, were solid wood affairs which could have been carved by almost anyone who possessed a knife. Some would have been covered with leather. Later the solid wood core gave way to a combination of cork and wool like the 'list' of the Stonyhurst ball. Such mixed cores became known as 'quilts'. The skill of the village shoemaker and saddler, accustomed to the working of leather, would be enlisted for the cover, but as John Waterer, liveryman of the Saddlers Company and author of the standard work *Leather in Life, Art and Industry*, points out, the stitching of a cricket ball has no parallel in either the saddlery or any other leather trade.

The requirements of the game led to a degree of standardisation throughout cricket-playing England. The ball had to be round for rolling along the ground and it had to be resilient for hitting. It had to respond to the stroke of a wooden club, so needed a density corresponding to that of wood. It settled down to between five and six ounces in weight, though at first it was probably on the small side. As it was not required to bounce off the pitch it did not also need to have resilience appropriate to turf. As soon as the striker was no longer required to concentrate on keeping the cat out of the hole, and the lip of the hole he had to defend had been extended to the popping crease, the game became more of an offensive than a defensive one, and the ball essentially one for hitting. Who was responsible for the first of these 'made' balls?

In the autumn of 1811 (the year the Prince of Wales was proclaimed Regent) a distinguished artist and art connoisseur took the two o'clock Sevenoaks Stage Coach from London to spend a six-week holiday in Kent with a friend of his called William Wells, a rich shipbuilder with a fine collection of pictures. This was Joseph Farington, a member of the Royal Academy, who made drawings of all the pictures at his home, Houghton Hall in Norfolk, and then sold the lot to Catherine the Great of Russia for £40,555 – an act which appalled Horace Walpole. Shortly afterwards he sold the house, too, and moved to London (1780). A hundred years after his death in 1821 the manuscript of his voluminous diary was found in an attic, and in 1922 the *Morning Post* began to publish extracts from it.

At Sevenoaks that 27 September 1811, Farington found his friend Wells waiting for him in his carriage, and drove with him the seven miles to his house on Redleaf Hill just outside Penshurst, the village dominated by Penshurst House (now called Penshurst Place), the ancestral home of the Sidneys. After he had been there a month he was persuaded to pay a visit to the cottage next door and witness for himself the activity taking place there which must have been the topic of many a mealtime conversation. His diary entry for 21 October reads:

> I passed the morning in study – drawing and walking to make observations on the landscape of the country. – The weather has hitherto been so favourable that we have not had fires till the evening. – I called upon —— Duke, a person who resides near Red

Nine generations of the Duke family are said to have been born and to have died in this house, The Paddocks, on Redleaf Hill, Penshurst, Kent (far right). In the little workshop opposite (right) they made cricket balls from 1760 until 1841 when they moved to Chiddingstone Causeway

Leaf and is remarkable for making Cricket Balls of the best quality. He has only one Competitor in England for the reputation of making the best Balls. He told me that His family had been famous for this art for 250 years past. The great secret of it is to wind the thread round an *octagon* piece of cork which forms the Kernel of the Ball. This art He does not disclose but to His own family & now had a Son, a lad, working with Him. When the Ball is perfectly formed with Cork and thread, He delivers to men who work in a room adjoining and they put on the Leather cover which is made of *Bull Hide*. The weight of a Ball, according to the rules of the game is not to be less than 5 ounces and a Half or more than 5 ounces and Three quarters. – The price of a Ball of the best kind is Seven Shillings. – He showed me the rules of the game. The wickets are to be pitched at the distance of 22 yards.

F. S. Ashley-Cooper in the potted biographies in the Register of Kent County Cricketers 1792–1906 section of the *History of Kent County Cricket* devotes eight lines to a Joseph Wells who, he says, 'was born at Redleaf Penshurst on 14 July 1828, and played cricket seven times for Kent in 1862 and 1863. He was a very fast round-armed bowler.' At the end of his note Ashley-Cooper adds 'He was a nephew of Timothy Duke who played for Kent from 1823 to 1828, and father of Mr. H. G. Wells the novelist.' But confusingly there were two people with the name 'Joseph Wells' and they were no relation.

In *Experiments in Autobiography* (1934) H. G. Wells wrote: 'My father Joseph Wells was the son of Joseph Wells who was head gardener to Lord de Lisle at Penshurst Place in Kent. My father was one of several brothers and sisters, and although he bore his father's name he was the youngest of the sons. There were uncles and cousins in the district, so that I suppose the family had been in Kent for at least some generations. The aunts and uncles were all, as far as I can ascertain, of the upper-servant, tenant-farmer class, except that one set of my father's first cousins at Penshurst, bearing the surname of Duke, had developed an

industry for the making of cricket bats and balls, and were rather more prosperous than the others. My father grew up to gardening and cricket, and remained an out-of-doors, open-air man to the day of his death. He became gardener at Redleaf, nearby, to a Mr Joseph Wells who in spite of the identical name, was no sort of relation, and in the summer, directly the day's work was over, my father would run, he told me once, a mile or more at top speed to the pitch at Penshurst to snatch half an hour of cricket before the twilight made the ball invisible. . . . He played for the West Kent Club from 1857 to 1869, and bowled for the County of Kent in 1862 and 1863. On June 26 1862 he clean bowled four Sussex batsmen in four successive balls, a feat not hitherto recorded in county cricket. Moreover his cousin, John Duke, at Penshurst, whom he had once got out of danger when they were swimming together, let him have long and considerate credit for a supply of cricket goods that ousted the plates and dishes from half the shop window.'

This seems to be the connection between the two families:

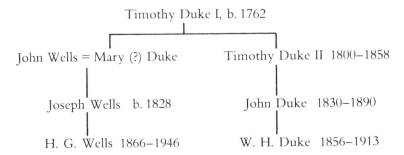

To supplement his earnings as a professional cricketer Joe Wells in 1855 took over a china shop in Bromley which belonged to his cousin George Wells. 'Behind the three panes of the front window and under the centre display stand' [at Atlas House, 45 The High Street, Bromley the 'China,

Glass & Staffordshire Warehouse' of the Master China Dealer] wrote
Norman and Jeanne Mackenzie, Wells's latest biographers in *The Time
Traveller* (1973), 'the crockery was pushed aside to make room for the
cricket goods which Joe found a more congenial line. When a new
delivery came in from Duke, his cousins at Penshurst who made cricket
gear, bats and balls were even stacked in the parlour behind the shop.'
They quote one of his advertisements in the *Bromley Record*:

CRICKET!   **CRICKET!**   **CRICKET!**

Joseph Wells has an excellent selection of all goods requisite for the
noble game, are of first class quality and moderate prices. His
cane-handled Bats specially selected by himself are acknowledged
to be unsurpassed in the trade.
Youth's bats of all sizes, &c &c at his

OLD ESTABLISHED CHINA AND GLASS WAREHOUSE
High Street, Bromley

Ashley-Cooper credits Joe Wells with founding the Bromley Cricket
Club in 1856, but the Mackenzies say he merely 'helped to revive it'. In
1877 he broke his leg which put paid to his career as a cricketer. He was
not a good tradesman and during the early years of H. G. 'Bertie' Wells,
who was born in Bromley in 1866, the family was always on the verge
of insolvency.

The link between the cricket ball maker and the writer is as fascinating as it is unexpected. If the '—Duke' was in any way accurate in the
'250 years' which Farington noted in his diary, it would trace his
family's activity back to 1560 and the Cat and Dog era. Certainly they
are the oldest family of ratepayers listed in Penshurst parish records.
Tradition has it that nine generations lived in the cottage on Redleaf Hill
which Farington visited in 1811. The building, with its long, sturdily
built wooden outhouse, still stands. It is called The Paddocks. Up to
forty years ago it was occupied by the bailiff of Penshurst Place, John
Sturgess, whose father was bailiff before him. The Paddocks was the
Penshurst Place estate office from the 1850s to the 1930s, and may well
have been for many years before.

Were the cricket ball manufacturing Dukes also bailiffs and did they
occupy The Paddocks in this capacity? There was certainly a man
named Duke bailiff to Viscount Lisle (the then Sidney occupant of
Penshurst House) in 1612. He could well have lived in the cottage now
called The Paddocks, and, like those who came after him, have made
cricket balls at the same time.

There is no evidence that he did, only for his existence. On 20 April
1612 a certain F. Goldynge wrote to Viscount Lisle 'I have caused the
Bailiff William Duke to put out all the horses that were in the Town
Llandes in James his occupation, and charged him to look unto them
and to the Brewhouse Croft which must serve to receive my Lady's
cattle if there chance to come a flood.' (Historical MSS Commission 77,
De L'Isle and Dudley Manuscripts Vol V) The will of a Richard Duke of
Sevenoaks made in 1689 is in the Kent Record Office in Maidstone.

William Duke is unlikely to have been making cricket balls profes-
sionally in 1612, but by 1660, which is one hundred and fifty and not
two hundred and fifty years before 1811, his son or grandson might well

have been, along with several others in various parts of Kent. A member of the Duke family would almost certainly have taken part in the village cricket games which attracted the attention of the aristocrat who had retreated to Penshurst House during the Commonwealth. To recruit a fast scorer to the household as gardener or gamekeeper was only commonsense; and if there was a cricket ball maker among them – well, make him your bailiff!

But perhaps this is attempting to account for what may well have been a slip of the tongue, or, as the noted cricket historian G. B. Buckley thought, simply misreporting. Buckley considered Farington must have heard Timothy wrongly, and that what he said was not 'two hundred and fifty years past' but 'two and fifty years past'. This is an attractive theory since, if he said this, all he was wanting to convey was the year in which his father had decided that the market justified his putting his cricket ball manufacture on a more businesslike basis and adopting the style 'Duke & Son', if not actually drawing up a partnership. This was 1760 – just about fifty-two years before 1811.

When Ashley-Cooper quizzed the Duke management of 1900 about this date, he was told that this was the year in which the manufacture of cricket balls was begun as a separate business, the demand for balls for the first time justifying such a step. Significantly it was the year the famous Hambledon Club was formed to which players of the game looked for a lead and for further 'regulation'. Up to 1760, Ashley-Cooper was told, the Duke family had combined leather bootmaking with cricket ball making.

The head of the family who made this move, the father of Timothy Duke I, may have been either the Richard Duke who was assessed for property in Penshurst village according to the churchwardens' rate books of 1748–62; or the John Duke who was assessed for a shop there in 1762 and 1763. Though 1760 makes a nice round figure (and is memorable for being the year George III began his long reign), it is tempting to think that perhaps the actual year was 1762, for this is the date of the birth of Timothy Duke I – the son in 'Duke & Son'? Hardly able to contribute much from his cradle to the craft being so ardently pursued in the outhouse across the garden, he would however have given a proud father with a sense of humour enough cause to link his firstborn with the enterprise which now needed a designation to mark its separate existence, and the dropping of the dreary leather footwear which took up so much room.

The kind of cricket ball this Richard or John Duke was making on Redleaf Hill in 1760–62, and his father and grandfather before him, was probably not far removed from that which Joseph Farington saw being made in 1811. In the hundred years 1660–1760 'regulation' cricket had come into being.

With the one-time roysterer's closure of the court, and his disapproval of frivolity in general and gambling which was their prime source of entertainment in particular, the nobility had escaped from Puritan austerity into their country houses and were soon looking round for some local source of amusement. Something which seemed to be diverting their bailiffs and gardeners so greatly on the village green was this sport they called cricket.

Soon the exiles from the London court in the counties surrounding the metropolis – Kent, Sussex, Surrey – men like the Duke of Dorset at Sevenoaks, the Earl of Egremont at Petworth, Viscount De Lisle at Penshurst – 'adopted' cricket as a highly entertaining diversion to supplement stag hunting and shooting, and gave the regulation of the game a new impetus. They wanted something a bit more pulled together and exact, particularly if the game was to become a new and intriguing medium for gambling. Articles of Agreement were drawn up for each major match so that the parties concerned were quite clear what it was they were laying their bets about. Though these were quite apart from the laws which regulated the playing of the game, the latter tended to be tightened up in the process, and with them the nature of the implements employed. The quality of the ball to be handled by the likes of the Rev Lord Frederick Beauclerc (great, great grandson of Nell Gwynn and Charles II) and Lord Sackville, needed to be somewhat higher than that which passed muster on the village green. It was a stimulus to the few craftsmen who, by the time the monarchy was restored, had come to the fore in the Commonwealth period as specialists in the craft of making cricket balls, now in demand as never before and from discriminating customers.

Parish cricket became club cricket – although the knockabout game continued alongside it in its Cat form for some time. It was no longer a game played solely by teams of village players on local pitches, but involved 'matches' of the kind advertised in a *Post Boy* of 1700 as going to take place on Clapham Common between two sides of ten gentlemen.

From this time on similar matches for so many guineas a man were commonplace. The first county match proper took place between Kent and London in 1709. In the 1720s cricket matches were being played 'in Penshurst Park, the seat of the Earl of Leicester' (as the current Sidney had become). A Sevenoaks team was playing London on Kennington Common in 1731, though the famous Vine Cricket Club was not formed till later. The cricket being played by boys at school – the first perpetrators – by now conformed to a more regular pattern, though one might not have thought so from Horace Walpole's remark that when he went to Eton in 1726 'playing cricket as well as thrashing bargemen was common at that time there'.

The process of systemisation took an important turn when in 1736 occurred the first recorded match behind the high walls of the Artillery Ground in Finsbury Square, London, and in 1744 the London Club who played here made a first attempt to codify the rules. For the framer of these laws, incidentally, a cricket ball was of the female gender.

Laws for the Strikers or Those that are in.

... If the striker touches or takes up the ball before she is lain quite still, unless asked by the bowler or wicket keeper, it is out ... He must neither strike her nor touch her with his hands.

Whatever her sex, the cricket ball used in 'matches' was now without doubt no longer a wooden affair, but, since the beginning of the eighteenth century, an altogether more elaborate confection with a core and a leather cover. This is clear from the much quoted Latin poem

written by William Goldwin in 1706, *In Certamen Pilae*, in which he writes of the *coriaceus orbis* which H. A. Perry in his 1922 translation calls 'the leathern orb'. Later on Goldwin talks about the *pila lubrica viribus acta/Carcere prona fugit* – 'urged with might/Speeds the greased ball in level flight'. 'Greased' refers to the practice of greasing the leather with what was probably deer fat. 'Level flight' means along the ground.

The bowler is about to trundle a ball along the ground towards a very low, wide two-stick wicket behind which a wicket keeper (or second bowler) kneels expectantly. These players form part of a decorative border, *The Arms of Shrewsbury*, 1739

In the laws of 1744 the ball was specified as having to be between five and six ounces – if it was under weight it would be soaked in water to make it heavier – but apart from that it could be of any colour, diameter or circumference, of any material or shape.

As far as colour was concerned, from early days it seems to have been red. In his poem 'Sevenoke' of 1753, inscribed to the Duke of Dorset, William Harrod writes:

> From nervous arm, with force impulsive, see
> The crimson ball attack the destin'd mark,
> The Youth's disastrous, short-liv'd, luckless chance
> Prompts his successor to avenge his cause.

Faltering verse, but firm evidence.

As far as material was concerned, the point of having a leather cover was to give a nice texture for friction and grip. Even if the texture was not all it might be, the fact that there was a separate layer from the rest of the ball made a great difference. The covering damped over-resilience, and gave an artificial homogeneity to the cork strips and twine which formed the core.

A Duke might have made Goldwin's *coriaceus orbis* of 1706 but it is unlikely. If he had been operating then, he would not have been the only cricket ball maker. To what extent then was he a pioneer? He would not have been the first to clothe a wooden ball with leather; many village cobblers would have been doing this for the games on the village green. Neither did he conceive the idea of the cork core. Yet Ernest Ward, 'the well-known writer on cricket', who wrote a footnote to the entry in Farington's diary when it was published in 1927, edited by James Greig, refers to this *Ur*-Duke as having 'invented' the cricket ball.

This is a reference to the 'treble sewn' ball with the two cups of leather sewn together over the core with three seams, a process which could be said to be the 'invention' of the Duke & Son craftsmen of Penshurst, if it were not for Father Gerard's story of the 'two hemispheres of thick hard leather . . . stitched through and through with wax end' with which the school cobblers finished the ball used in Stonyhurst Cricket. He might have been describing the process employed in 1860 when the game was abandoned, and not that in 1794 when the game was brought to England. Duke's seam was not of course as pronounced as that on the Stonyhurst ball which rolled along the hard gravel pitch on it; and it was probably the fact that there were *three* seams which gave it its unique character and planted it firmly in the Duke legend.

When increasing debts forced him to close Carlton House his London residence in 1785, George III's eldest son and heir, George Prince of Wales, moved to Brighton, accompanied by his illicit bride of the previous year Maria Fitzherbert. At Brighton he encouraged the playing of cricket, which he found a favourite sport of the local nobility, and in 1791 he gave the town the cricket ground which became known as Ireland's Garden. It was to this royal patron of the Noble Game, when a boy of thirteen (he was born in the same year as Timothy I), that Duke & Son in 1775 presented their first treble sewn cricket ball. This was the year after the tolerance for the weight of the ball had been reduced to between five-and-a-half ounces and five-and-threequarters ounces. When the royal cricketer, after being Regent for his mentally afflicted father for nine years, eventually ascended the throne as George IV in 1820, he granted Duke & Son the royal warrant.

This presentation of the first treble sewn cricket ball to the Prince of Wales is the most evident feature of Duke history – though some say it took place in 1780. When, a century later, John Duke was questioned by Frederick Gale he expressed candid uncertainty about this, and every other aspect of what had come to be regarded as tradition. 'We have no record of the earliest date at which the present style of cricket balls was first made,' he said. 'Our great-grandfather, we believe, made and presented the first treble sewn ball to the Prince of Wales, and our family have been in the trade considerably over 100 years.'

But of course in 1870 Joseph Farington's diary was still lying undiscovered in that attic.

The era of players of local teams being the only makers of cricket balls, and purely for their own use, had ended. Reputations of good craftsmanship spread as the playing of the game spread from the closed circuit of inter-village contests, neighbour against neighbour, to the wider operation of matches between strangers. A club from one part of England played against a club from another part; ideas were exchanged, and innovations discussed. In this way reputations travelled – and not only for making runs but making implements.

A reputation made in Hampshire, which in the eighteenth century spread at least as far as Kent, was that of John Small of Petersfield, born in 1737, who became one of the greatest professional cricketers of his day. His name is linked with the famous Hambledon Club. He was for a long time gamekeeper at the manor of Grantham and Foley owned by someone who liked to be known as Madame Beckford. He regularly began every day with a seven-mile round tour of the estate with his gun under his arm. He followed hounds on foot up until four years before his death at the age of eighty-nine. In the winter when ice covered Petersfield Pond he demonstrated his agility as a skater. He sang in the

John Small's gravestone in the churchyard of Petersfield parish church. A linen draper by trade, he began playing cricket aged eighteen in 1755, and then took to making cricket bats and balls for Hambledon Club players until his death in 1826

choir of Petersfield Church for seventy-five years and played the tenor violin 'without spectacles' which seems to have impressed his admirer Arthur Haygarth, who wrote very fulsomely about him in his *Memoirs of the Old Cricketers*. He also taught himself the double bass. Tough John Small senior was said to have been returning from a party one night, where he had been entertaining the company with his playing, when he encountered a hostile bull which he charmed into docility, so the story goes, by a tune on his fiddle. The incident was immortalised by Andrew Lang in his *Ballade of Dead Cricketers*:

> And Small, that would like Orpheus, play
> Till wild bulls followed his minstrelsy?

When the Duke of Dorset heard of John Small's musical talent, he sent him as a present a handsome violin and, chronicled John Nyren whose father Richard kept the Bat and Ball Inn at Hambledon which the club used as their headquarters, 'paid the carriage'. 'Small, like a true and simple hearted Englishman, returned the compliment by sending his Grace two bats and balls, also paying the carriage.'

It was a gesture the third Duke would have appreciated, for:

> His Grace for bowling cannot yield
> To none but Lumpy in the field . . .
> He firmly stands with bat upright
> And strikes with his athletic might;
> Sends forth the ball across the mead
> And scores six notches for the deed.
> (Gentlemen's Magazine, 1773)

John Frederick Sackville, 3rd Duke of Dorset (1745–99), was a member of the Hambledon Club and of the committee which drew up the original laws of cricket. He had played in the open field near White Conduit House in Islington in 1784 and often thereafter. Out of the White Conduit Club grew the Marylebone Cricket Club with its head-quarters at the ground Thomas Lord established in 1787 in Dorset Square with the encouragement of the Duke of Dorset, the 8th Earl of Winchilsea and Charles Lennox, later Duke of Richmond and Viceroy of Canada. When Dorset was British Ambassador to France at the time of the French Revolution, he arranged for an English eleven to come over and play in Paris, but then violence broke out in the streets of the capital and he thought it wiser to cancel the fixture.

Lumpy was fat Edward Stevens who ate a whole apple pie at a sitting at a Hambledon Club dinner, and was the leading bowler of the day. If the Duke was considered second to Lumpy he must have been good, and in sending John Small a violin he was probably angling for a return present of the kind that he in fact received. For John Small's renown was as much as a maker of cricket balls as a player. Arthur Haygarth considered his cricket balls 'matchless'. When Small was eighty years of age, he recalled that he sold the last half-dozen balls he ever made to E. H. Budd from whom William Ward afterwards wished to pur-chase them at a guinea apiece.

John Small was making cricket balls for most of his forty years as a player – from shortly after his first game as a youngster of eighteen in 1755 to his last when, at the age of sixty-one, he turned out for Hampshire against the Marylebone Cricket Club at Lords in 1798 – and for much of the time that was left him until his death in 1826. Indeed the House of Small is probably the House of Duke's 'one Competitor in England for the reputation of making the best Balls' cryptically referred to by Farington in his diary, though this may have been 'one named Clouts a famous cricket ball maker' of Sevenoaks. In his diary John Baker of Horsham records visiting Clouts in June 1773 when he came to watch the Hambledon Club play All England on the Vine (Sussex Archaeological Collections, Vol LII, p. 55).

There is little record of John Small's activity as a cricket ball maker at Petersfield, but the methods are likely to have been similar to those described at Stonyhurst in 1794. Small is often said to have had early training as a cobbler, but in fact he was a linen draper. His shop on the north side of Petersfield square remained a draper's, latterly as 'Norman Burton', until it was burnt down in the 1960s. But he would have learnt something of leathercraft from his father who was a saddler with a workshop off Edgware Road in London.

The early records of the Hambledon Club provide little information about the club's activities beside members' consumption of food and drink at meetings and their appointment of officers. But entries in their account book between 1791 and 1795 show they were making purchases from Small's workshop after he had ceased playing for the club.

> 13th June, 1791. Paid Small as p. Bill 90. £2 – 6 – 0
> 18th June, 1792. Paid Small's Bill for 91. £2 – 3 – 0
> 26th July, 1793. Paid Small for Batts and Balls. £3 – 7 – 0
>   June, 1794. Paid Small Bill 93. £2 – 12 – 6
> 21st October, 1795. Small his bill for the last year. £1 – 17 – 0
>   Ditto for this year. £1 – 14 – 0

When he died he was widely mourned.

> Here lies, bowled out by Death's unerring ball,
> A Cricketer renowned, by name John Small.
> But though his name was Small, yet great his fame,
> For nobly did he play the noble game;
> His life was like his innings, long and good,
> Full ninety summers he had death withstood,
> At length the ninetieth winter came, when (fate
> Not leaving him one solitary mate)
> This last of Hambledonians, old John Small,
> Gave up his bat and ball, his leather, wax and all.
>   (from Richard Daft's *Death's Doings*)

His son, John Small junior, also a notable player, who had been trained in the making of cricket balls, inherited the business and continued it.

Frederick Gale wrote: 'John Small the younger son of the Small recorded by Nyren, who was ball maker to the old Hambledon Club, lived at Petersfield and exhibited a rough notice on his premises,

> "Here lives John Small
> Sells bats and balls
> And will play any man in England."'

It looks from this as if perhaps he was only selling and no longer making. Be that as it may, John Small senior handed on the secrets of his craft to someone who was in a position, at the centre of cricket, to make sure that the tradition and standards were maintained and propagated.

It is Arthur Haygarth who, in *Cricket Scores and Biographies of Cele- brated Cricketers from 1744 to 1826*, published in 1862, told how Robert Dark 'bought when a young man the tools and knowledge of cricket ball making from John Small senior of Petersfield, Hampshire and of the far fam'd Hambledon Club'.

This Robert Dark was born in 1802, the younger brother of the James Henry Dark (born about 1795), cricketer and umpire, who in 1836 became proprietor of Lord's Cricket Ground by purchasing the remainder of the lease from William Ward and sold it to the MCC in 1864 for £12,500, when twenty-nine years still remained. For many years Robert Dark was money taker at the gate of Lord's which his brother had joined as a boy helping to look after the ground in 1804.

It is significant that Robert Dark did not purchase John Small's cricket bat business too, for John was as much, if not more, renowned, as cricket bat maker. Cricket ball making however had always been more difficult than bat making, which had never required the same degree of skill and attention. As H. J. Henley has said, 'even after the game had progressed beyond its most primitive stage and was known by the name of cricket, many years passed before the bat was anything better than a small branch of a tree roughly shaped and its size was not governed by the rule until 1774.' But from the first, careful attention was given to the ball, presumably, he said, on the grounds that while the article with which to strike could be conveniently left to individual choice, it was necessary for the ball to be reasonably rounded and neither too heavy nor too light.

Again, it was a question of the demands made on the bat in terms of the rules of the game which determined its shape, size, weight. Did it have to tip, strike or block? And what did it have to tip, strike or block? An irregular cat or a spherical ball? A hard ball or a soft ball? Would the ball come at the bat through the air or along the ground? Would it be propelled by another at a distance or by yourself the length of your arm away? And would the bat be held in one hand (because the other held the ball) or two?

Early forms of cricket bats and balls are illustrated in this document in the Bod- leian Library at Oxford. The figures are playing an early version of Club Ball. Joseph Strutt reproduced this document in his *Sports and Pastimes of the English People* (1801)

What kind of an instrument had the cricket bat and its antecedents been in these years of evolution up to 1774?

Joseph Strutt's researches took him back to the Club Ball of the thirteenth century and he unearthed the drawing reproduced here from a genealogical table of the kings of England made in the reign of Henry III (1216–1272) whose family the Plantagenets (*Planta Genista*) derived their name from the yellow broom which gave us the word for the implement with the handle, not wholly unlike a cricket bat, used for sweeping. Here the ball which the striker himself threw in the air was huge – a foot in diameter? – and his bat had a broad end for hitting with and a thin handle to hold with. This comes from a manuscript in the Bodleian Library dated 1344.

Strutt bracketed Trap Ball with these and other bat and ball games of the thirteenth and fourteenth centuries, and implied that it was still being played (1801). Compared with cricket it was a childish pastime, but he had seen it played in Essex in a different way from the game practised near London, and requiring more dexterity. 'For instead of a broad bat with a flatted face, they used a round cudgel about an inch and half diameter and three feet in length, and those who have acquired the habit of striking the ball with this instrument rarely miss their blow but frequently strike it to an astonishing distance.'

The same kind of bat he considered was used for his version of Tip Cat, already described – a 'cudgel or bludgeon resembling that used for trap-ball'. A similar instrument was used in hurling (a mixture of football and hockey). 'About the year 1775 the hurling to the goals was frequently played by parties of Irishmen in the fields at the back of the British Museum, but they used a kind of bat to take up the ball and to strike it from them; this instrument was flat on both sides and broad and curving at the lower end. . . . The bat for hurling was known and probably used in England more than two centuries ago, for it is mentioned in a book published in the reign of Queen Elizabeth and is there called "a clubbe" or "hurle batte".'

South Norton considered the dog in Cat and Dog 'must at first, I think, have been of the same pattern as the "cricket staffe" of Cotgrave, i.e. the "goff stick" or "bandy" of the hockey type which I assume to have been used by Cat and Dog batsmen in front of the holes'. In his Dictionary of French and English of 1611, already referred to, Randall Cotgrave gave the English of *crosse* as 'a crosier, a bishop's staffe; also a cricket staffe or crooked staffe wherewith boys play at cricket'. Bandy legs were bowed or crooked; so were bandy staffs. In Edward III's reign (1327–1377), says Strutt, the Latin name of *Cambuca* was applied to the pastime of goff 'because of the crooked bat or club, also called a bandy, from it being bent and so in English often called Bandy Ball'. Incidentally, that monarch issued a proclamation prohibiting Club Ball and Cambuca because they engrossed too much of the leisure and attention of the populace and diverted their minds from pursuits of a more warlike nature.

The clubs which were bandied or crooked or cricked were so formed because they were required to lift a ball off the ground. The generic term for such a piece of wood was a Crickett. The etching by Hollar, done in 1646, depicting a riot in St Giles's, Edinburgh, has the legend 'The arch-prelate of St Andrews in Scotland reading the new service-books in his pontificalibus assaulted by men and women with Cricketts, Stooles, Sticks and Stones'. (It has already been noted that the word 'cricket' also applied to a stool – written 'crickett' says Joseph Wright in his English Dialect Dictionary, 'a small, low stool with either three or four legs serving as a footstool, milking stool or a child's seat, mostly in Yorkshire'. Arthur Story corroborated this in the *Strand Magazine*.)

Like the first cricket ball, an early cricked club or bat would have been of solid wood, the handle and hitting surface, which at this stage hardly warranted the name of 'blade', all in one. The wood would have been of any kind the player who made his own bat could lay his hands on; the exclusive use of willow came much later. In most instances it would have come up to the elbow, but there was no restriction on height, weight, width, shape. Once the game which was to become 'regulation' cricket separated itself from the various Cat games, and the hole which had been the original base had been replaced by the wicket which once merely marked its position, the role of the dog, to be popped into the hole before the cat, acquired a more offensive character, with the prime, though not the sole function of hitting the cat (now a ball) as far away as possible. The writers of the 1830s who seemed to be unaware of what the design of the cricket club owed to its Cat and Dog function of hole plugging, deplored its unsuitability for defensive play. 'The long pod [blade] and curved form of the bat as seen in the old paintings,' observed Rev James Pycroft in his *Hambledon Club and the Old Players* of 1833, 'was made only for hitting, and for ground balls too.' Unaware of the origin of the hole plugger design, John Nyren, also writing in 1833, was concerned for unfortunate players of the old days for whom the curved form made it ill-adapted for the purpose of blocking or defending a *wicket* other than by striking. Moreover such hitting as there was 'could neither have been of a high character nor indeed safe, as may be gathered from the figure of the bat at that time, which was similar to an old-fashioned dinner-knife, curved at the back and sweeping forward in the form of a volute [a spiral curve] at the front end! With such a bat, the system must have been all for hitting; it would be barely possible to block.'

The old dog element in cricket bat design had outstayed its welcome and lived on into an era when it restricted the game's development. Yet the design of cricket bats rested with the players who after all made the rules – and made bats to suit them.

From what was probably a spoof news item in *Read's Weekly Journal* of 17 August 1723, it seems that by the 1720s the stage had been reached when players who were particularly adept at making cricket bats for themselves had begun to make them in addition, firstly for acquaintances who admired their handiwork and wished to own a bat of that quality themselves, and second for stock – in the expectation of orders from outside his immediate circle. By 1723 it seems one could buy bats.

> Rome, July 29, N.S. There was lately imported hither a great number of Batts and other utensils for Cricket-playing, being a present from Sir Humphrey Wildair to the Chevalier who last week began to Exercise himself in that Diversion in a spacious Green behind his Palace: but the Chevalier being of a *weakly*

Constitution soon gave it over and contented himself with being a *Seeker-out* [fielder]; which an arch wag was heard to say was the fittest for him, *he having been a Runner from his Cradle* and having withal *a light pair of* heels highly qualifies him for considerable an Employment.

Though fairly transparently an anti-Jacobite smear on the 'pretended Prince of Wales' in exile, son of the James II who had vacated the throne of England in 1688 and fled to the continent, the report was probably founded on the fact, known to contemporaries, that the Old Pretender ('the Chevalier') was a cricketer. Who knows, he might have included in his wanderings around Europe a visit to his young Catholic confrères at St Omers and received coaching which whetted his appetite for the more orthodox style of cricket practised by the sharers of his exile who formed his 'court' in Rome. Thomas Lord, founder of Lord's Cricket Ground, is after all known to have been a Scot with Jacobite leanings who sought sanctuary in London.

What kind of bat would the Old Pretender have played with, if he ever did, on that spacious green behind his palace in Rome? Only one cricket bat of the 1720s is known to have survived, the one by an unknown maker weighing two pounds two ounces and marked 'J.C. 1729' in large letters on the side which belonged to James Chitty of Knaphill. It belongs to the Surrey County Cricket Club, and can be seen in the pavilion of The Oval at Kennington. A photograph of this can be found on page 37.

Another bat which may belong to this period or to an even earlier age is the one brought over by the English Catholic schoolboys from Liège when they ended their two-hundred-year exile on the continent in 1794. It would have been earlier than 1794 in design, for the form of the bat, like the game itself, had become 'fossilised'. Father Gerard described it as having:

> A handle about two feet long, round at the top and an inch in diameter. This handle became gradually flatter, finally terminating in an oval head, some four and a half inches wide at its broadest part, and sloping outwards with a gentle curve on the striking side to a maximum thickness of nearly two inches; the approximate length of the whole being three feet. The striking side of the head had its edges rounded. As a general rule, this portion was made of alder wood, and was spliced with strong twine to the handle; but there were also bats of a single piece of ash, which were much affected by some players.

In footnotes to the above Father Gerard stated the dimensions he had given were for a full-sized 'Higher Line' bat; there were smaller implements for smaller boys. A specimen of the spliced alder bat and the single piece ash bat, he said, were preserved in the school museum but were poor examples of their kind and not of the largest size. In the centre of his text on page 180 was a photograph of these lying on their side with a ball. The caption read: 'Stonyhurst Cricket Bats and Ball (one bat marked 00 has belonged to a "Free-and-Easy Match").' They were still there ninety-five years later and were re-photographed in 1979 – see page 22. The twine on the handle of the bat marked 00 hides a splice; the 555 bat is all of one piece and of ash.

This bat marked 'J.C. 1729', the property of the Surrey County Cricket Club and kept at The Oval, is probably the oldest cricket bat in existence. It belonged to James Chitty of Knaphill

Father Gerard gave no clue as to how these bats were made, or who made them. Presumably the boys themselves, who had made the cores of the balls, or the school carpenter. They were designed to pick up a leather ball with a protruding seam, delivered underarm along a hard gravel pitch, and knock it as far away as possible, at the same time defending a stone wicket seventeen inches high, thirteen inches wide and eight inches thick at the bottom, which perhaps resembled the proportions of a wooden wicket of the early seventeenth century.

The date of the Stonyhurst bat can only be conjecture, but a firmer claim to be the second oldest bat to have survived belongs to the curved, humped club-type implement at Winchester College bequeathed in 1931 by Miss Ellen Mary Miles of Eastleigh. In 1979 this was to be seen on display in Hunter Tent, the school cricket ground pavilion. It belonged to Miss Miles's great grandfather John Osmond Miles who, according to tradition in the Miles family, used it in the first match played on Broad Halfpenny Down by the Hambledon Club. Winchester are the owners of Halfpenny Down. There is a ball with no maker's name stamped on it, as well as the bat.

The notice in the display case with the bat and ball says, 'The Hambledon Club, according to oral tradition, was founded about 1742. The bat is undoubtedly of the type used at that date and the ball may well belong to the same period. Only one older bat is known, a bat which belonged to John Chitty of Knaphill, dated 1729, now in the pavilion at Kennington Oval. Unfortunately there are no records of the earliest Hambledon matches or players. The first mention in the press of Hambledon is in 1756, and of Broad Halfpenny Down in 1767, and the names of the Hambledon eleven are given for the first time in 1768. We cannot produce written evidence to support tradition about J. O. Miles, and his fame must rest upon legend. The letters J.O. on the back of the bat probably stand for John Osmond. The blade of the bat is covered with grey paint; the initials 'J.O.' are embossed on the hump of the non-hitting side. The handle is bound with black cord within two inches of the top.

This may have been the 'bat of 1743' which Frederick Gale, a Wykehamist, mentioned among the relics of cricket which he had seen, in his book *The Game of Cricket*, though obviously not at Winchester College. He was at the school in 1839 and his book was published in 1887 – and Miss Miles's bequest did not arrive till fifty years later. He may have seen it at Eastleigh. The photograph reproduced here shows its shape.

In *The Game of Cricket* Gale referred to the 'narrative' of an actor called William Woolgar who acted with Edmund Kean and played cricket while he was on tour. According to this narrative, he says, a Mr Rogers, a surgeon of West Meon near Hambledon, still retained as family relics two of the stumps, a ball and a bat of the oldest period. Gale did not say that he ever saw the bat and ball Mr Rogers kept as family relics, but perhaps he was referring to these in his earlier passage and not the Miles bat.

'The bats which have been preserved,' commented Gale, 'and the oil picture at Lord's of the date 1743, belonged to the "swells" who were adopting the game with better materials than those used in purely country districts for village cricket.'

Only the Chitty bat and the Miles bat can demonstrate their shape in the round, but the prints of the 1740s show exactly how these clubs looked: that decorative border for the Arms of Shrewsbury of a Youth Playing at Cricket; Francis Hayman's picture of the match in Marylebone Fields showing bats with string round the handle; and the famous 1743 print by Benoist of the game in Artillery Fields in which the bat was aptly considered by Eric Parker to resemble 'an enormous antenna of a butterfly' and had no string on the handle.

Everyone had their pet way of describing this characteristic curve. Gale considered 'the end took the shape of a nautilus and was flat like a cutlet, about an inch and a half in thickness; it must have been some-thing like a New Zealand war club.'

The 1743 print is thought to have been a sketch for a larger painting by Francis Hayman and William Hogarth for a decoration at Vauxhall Gardens. Indeed the wicket keeper behind the two low stumps is thought to be Hogarth, who in 1743 would have been forty-six.

The bats which figure in these pictures were certainly made by their owners, but who were the players whose superior skill as turners and wood-workers distinguished them from all the others who made their own utensils? Who were these first suppliers of a market which the growing popularity of the game, and its transition from parish to club, was slowly expanding? How did they set about their business?

Very few names have come down to us of those who in the eighteenth century stood out from the run of the mill 'rough shapers' of wood, and had any pretensions to calling themselves 'cricket bat makers'. There is even less information on the nature of their activities. The first ones would certainly have been located in the southern counties of England which cradled the game which was to become regula-tion cricket, and framed the first unofficial laws – Kent, Surrey, Sussex, Hampshire, Middlesex (which included 'London' apart from the City).

The name that must stand at the top of such a list has already been

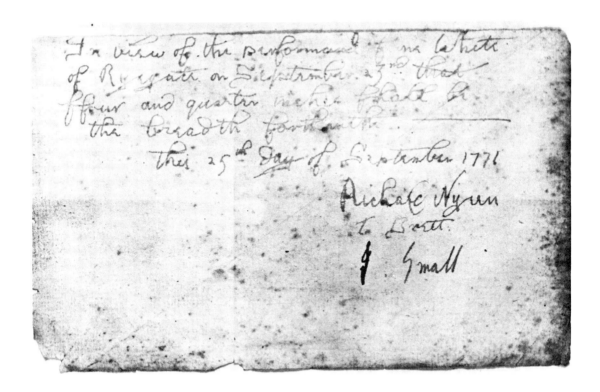

mentioned – John Small senior, the first known professional cricket bat maker. As has been seen, he started to play cricket seriously at the age of eighteen in 1755. At first he would have made bats for his own use, to suit his own height and strength, with a handle to fit his hands. A left-handed player had to give his bat curves in the opposite direction to a right-handed bat.

When Small started playing in the 1750s the ball came at him along the closely cropped grass and he would have to have been able to lift and hold the bat he made for himself above the horizontal 'at the ready' (as in the old prints) and come down on the ball with the greatest force he could muster and hit it away to the farthest corner of the field. But soon he and his fellow bowlers and strikers became increasingly bored with the limitations imposed by having to trundle the ball along the ground, and agreed that bowlers could lob it in the air and make it bounce a few times before reaching the popping crease. Introduction of this 'length bowling', as it was called, was attributed to the Hambledon bowler David Harris (1754–1803), a potter from Odiham, who in his latter days was badly affected by gout and had an armchair brought on to the field in which he sat down after each delivery, 'in his own calm and simple grandeur' as John Mitford put it. It was still underarm, but as a high tossed lob it presented greater opportunities to the striker for a greater variety of strokes both in hitting out and in defending his wicket. Length bowling soon developed into full length bowling which pitched the ball right up to the wicket. The fashion demanded not only a new style of batting but a new style of bat. John Nyren wrote:

Cricket authorities have given sparse attention to the specification of the game's tools. Here is an early, and rare, ruling minuted by the committee of the Hambledon Club, on 25 September 1771, that 'in view of the performance of one cricketer of Ryegate on September 23rd that four and quarter inches shall be the breadth of a bat forthwith'. It is signed by Richard Nyren, T. Brett, and J. Small, who were reacting to the tactics of 'Shock' White who walked on to the pitch with a bat wider than the wicket

Tradition has it that John Osmond Miles used this bat in the first match played on Broad Halfpenny Down by the Hambledon Club in 1742. Miles's initials J. O. are embossed on the back of the blade.

> When the practice of bowling length balls was introduced, which gave the bowlers so great an advantage in the game, it became absolutely necessary to change the form of the bat, in order that the striker might be able to keep pace with the improvement. It was therefore made straight in the pod; in consequence of which a total revolution – it may be said a reformation too – ensued in the style of the play. . . . Some years after this the fashion of the bat having been changed to a straight form, the system of stopping or blocking was adopted.

John Small was the innovator who set the pace, in spite of having reached an age when he would have been expected to have become set in his ways and resisted change. 'When he first began cricket of course,' pointed out Arthur Haygarth in *Memoirs of the Old Cricketers*, 'the crooked bat and scraping style of play must have been in use, and therefore more credit is due to Small in being able, when about 38 years of age, to change his play to the straight and defensive system!'

The mark to be defended in the 1750s and 1760s was still the wicket consisting of two low, widely spaced stumps and the normal width of the bat used for defending it put the striker at a distinct disadvantage *vis-à-vis* the bowler. It was 'normal' only because the players found it was the best form for hitting with, but there was nothing in the 'rules', published by Reeve in 1755 and drawn up by the Duke of Dorset and others in London and the southern counties, which forbade a player to come in with a bat of any width he wanted.

> Although 'straight in the pod' the bat was still very wide; and when the blocking system became popular and batsmen found that with ordinary skill they could keep their places at the wicket a long time, the form of the bats gradually grew wider; and as there was no law in those days restricting the bat to any particular width many cricketers came to the wickets with bats as broad as scavengers' shovels.

(An Old Cricketer, *The Cricket Bat: and How to Use It*, 1861)

Indeed there was nothing to stop a striker playing with a bat which was wider than the wicket if he saw fit.

At a match between Hambledon and Chertsey during the season of 1771 one Thomas 'Shock' White of Reigate did see fit, and strode to the crease carrying a monster of a bat which was in fact wider than the wicket, and shocked everyone into acknowledging the absurdity of there not being a ruling to prevent it. The Hambledon Club were far from amused, but they got the message, and at the September meeting of their committee passed a resolution limiting the width of a cricket bat to four and a quarter inches. The minute recording this decision is reproduced on page 39. John Small, their ace cricket bat maker, was probably asked his advice – he signed the minute with Richard Nyren, the Hambledon captain, and T. Brett. He may have been the one to suggest having an iron gauge made for testing the widths of bats in future. The ruling of the Hambledon Club was embodied in the laws revision made by the representatives of the five counties in London in 1774.

In his *English Cricket* Neville Cardus put the whole incident into admirable perspective.

The crooked bat became straight out of sheer expediency; wit and not morality was the cause. A curved bat, with the weight concentrated at the bottom, was necessary as a counter to the ancient underhand bowling, quick and along the ground, almost 'grubs'. As soon as Hambledon men bowled a length and used the air and caused the ball to rise sharply from the ground, a hockey stick sort of defence was of no avail, and so the shouldered narrow blade was evolved. Even this most hallowed of symbols of cricket, the straight bat, was not given its fair and narrowish rectitude by some categorical imperative issued from conscience and ethic; oh dear no! In the beginning no bound was put by law on the width of a blade. One day a cricketer of Reigate came into action with a bat broader than the wicket. It is pleasant to imagine the scene in which this great opportunist of Reigate prepared his new weapon; the quiet kitchen in his cottage in the village; and while he smoothed and polished his handiwork with sandpaper until it glowed in the candle-light, he chuckled to his admiring wife: 'Hey old lady, but this be an artful device, and a march forward of the Intellect.' Alas for vision that overeacheth, a rule was brought in enforcing a four and a half inch limit. None the less the Archimedes of Reigate – 'Shock' White to his intimate friends – had his hour and it became immortal.

These players are equipped with the no 1 type bat of 1743 depicted in the eight bat line-up of W. G. Grace's *Cricket*

Four years later the incident involving John Small occurred, which had a second important influence on the character of the cricket bat. It was during a single wicket, five-a-side match between Hambledon and Kent on the Artillery Ground in Finsbury Square London on 22 May 1775. John Nyren recounted what happened.

A cricket bat similar – except that it has a slight horn-like curve – to the mediaeval club depicted in the drawing of Club Ball in the Bodleian Library document, is being wielded by the defender of the two-stick wicket in this sketch of 'Thomas Lord's Cricket Ground, Dorset Square' ascribed to Thomas Rowlandson (1756–1827)

In this painting by Francis Cotes RA owned by Lord Brocket, the fifteen-year-old Lewis Cage seems thoroughly at ease with his curved cricket bat on which is written his name, that of the artist and the date, 1768. Eric Parker reckoned that the bat must have weighed four pounds. The two-twig wicket indicates a still primitive form of the game – and far from padding his shins he bares a knee

When Small went in, the last man for fourteen runs and fetched them, Lumpy [Edward Stevens] was the bowler upon the occasion; and it having been remarked that his balls had three several times passed between Small's stumps, it was considered to be a hard thing upon the bowler that his straightest balls should be thus sacrificed; the number of stumps was in consequence increased from two to three.

The match had been for £50 a side, and naturally enough those that had backed Hambledon to win were irked by the superior skill of their star bowler Lumpy – he was basically a Surrey man, being gardener to the Earl of Tankerville at Walton-on-Thames – going unrewarded. It was as if an archer had found the bullseye, but the centre of the target had been omitted and the arrow had passed through.

The trendsetters of Hambledon took immediate action, but for some time later, at Sevenoaks anyway, they were still using two stumps. In the entry for his diary of 26 June 1776, Richard Hayes of Cobham wrote:

I set off about seven in the morning to Sevenoaks Vine to see Hambledon play with All England at cricket. The Duke of Dorset bowled the first four balls ... The Duke was bowled out after getting about six runs. I heard him say if he missed a ball he was sure to be out. The Hambledon men were in between five and six hours. They beat us in guarding their wickets and in standing out too. N.B. They talk of having three stumps. By their playing with very broad bats and playing all the blocking short play, so that it is a very hard matter to hit a wicket.

Not only on this occasion had the players not followed Hambledon's adoption of three stumps, but neither had they apparently taken much attention of the Hambledon restriction on 'very broad bats' following Shock White's *reductio ad absurdum*. Perhaps when the fixtures were on the home ground in Hampshire they could insist on the 'new style' cricket; but when they were playing away had to be a little more tolerant. Certainly three stumps were not used on the Sevenoaks Vine until 1777. A report in the *Kentish Gazette* of 4 June of that year stated:

On Sevenoaks Vine on Wednesday 18th June instant will be played the first match for a thousand guineas. Hampshire against All England. The wickets to be pitched at ten-o-clock and to be played with three stumps to shorten the game.

The reason given for using three stumps was an interesting one, for a main objection to the introduction to having a third stump was that it would become too easy to bowl batsmen out and the game would be over too soon. Here however was an extra stump being put down *in order* to do that very thing.

John Nyren considered the objections on this score were groundless. All that would result, he said, was that the striker would redouble his care 'knowing the danger of missing one straight ball which every loose hard hitter would learn to stop and play as safe a game as possible'.

The debate gradually lost its momentum, three stumps became the universal practice and, in 1785, the 'law'. Lord Winchilsea introduced a

four-stump wicket, two inches higher than standard. 'The game is thus rendered shorter by easier bowling out,' commented the *Hampshire Chronicle*. But no one followed suit.

The picture 'A Game of Circket circa 1790' in the MCC collection at Lord's shows better than any words how the effect of length bowling and the introduction of the three stump wicket, as Diana Rait Kerr has observed, took the hockey stick curve out of cricket bats and gave them instead a backwards arch.

The man responsible for introducing the blade with the square shoulders to meet the requirements of this undoubted revolution was John Small, and the first of the new style bats would have been bought by his fellow players at Hambledon and other Hampshire cricketers. In distant Kent however, as master of Knole and owner of the Vine, the Duke of Dorset, though a member of the Hambledon Club, felt a stronger allegiance to the Sevenoaks cricket bat maker who already, like John Small, was making more than a local reputation – William Pett.

There had been Petts in Sevenoaks for four hundred years or more. They probably derived their name from the village of Pett beside Fairlight on the coast north of Hastings. A Thomas atte Pette was a tithing man in 1414 who in 1429 was fined 4d because he was 'a common victualler and charges excessively'. In 1425 a Thomas Pette was agent of William Sevenoke. Within a hundred years the family had attained a new affluence and social standing. In the sixteenth century the wealthy Richard Pett owned an estate on Riverhill, land at Quakers Hall, property in Westerham and a shop in Sevenoaks. His grandson John Pett was one of the 'fathers' of Sevenoaks School – an assistant (governor) from 1560 to his death in 1593. In his book *The Pleasant Town of Sevenoaks* Sir John Dunlop tells of a William Pett who 'far back in Tudor times' was one of a group of Sevenoaks townsmen who bought twelve acres of land near the Vine as an endowment for Sevenoaks School to provide an annual income from letting for agriculture (not as playing fields). These School Lands were sold to the Sevenoaks Urban District Council in 1910 and in 1974 were Holly Bush Lane Recreation Ground. A Mr Pett was the Shipwright member of the Navy Board responsible for Chatham Yard in 1662, an associate of Samuel Pepys who became the scapegoat after the Dutch attack on the Medway.

By the eighteenth century the family seems to have lost its grip on the social heights attained by the Tudor generation of Petts, and the William Pett, cricket bat maker, who was born in the town in 1709 was of an altogether humbler breed and calling. His father was Thomas Pett of West Malling and his mother, née Ann Evernden, Tom's second wife, came from the same village. It is known that he made the Duke of Dorset's bats from a bill for some of them which he presented to his Grace on 12 June 1766, reproduced on page 45. As can be seen, it was for no less than eleven 'crickett batts' at half a crown each, plus two cricket balls, which he may or may not have made, at three shillings and sixpence each. The difference of cost reflected the greater degree of craftsmanship which went into a cricket ball. The Duke seems to have paid at once and the receipting of the account by son Thomas Pett 'for Father William Pett' is dated eight days later.

Father William Pett used this draw knife to make cricket bats for the Duke of Dorset at Knole and members of the Vine Cricket Club at Sevenoaks, in whose pavilion it is now on display

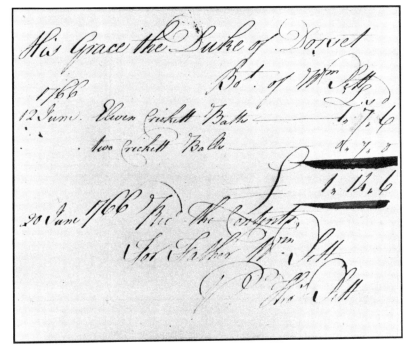

This receipt 'For Father Wm Pett' of Sevenoaks signed by his son Thos Pett for £1–14–6 from the Duke of Dorset for cricket bats and cricket balls, dated 20 June 1766 is from the Sackville MSS in the Kent Archives Office

William Pett would have been the main supplier of cricket bats to members of the Sevenoaks Vine Cricket Club, as John Small had been to Hambledon Club members. Precisely when the Vine came formally into being is not known. A team representing Sevenoaks was playing London on Kennington Common in May 1731 and again in July 1734, when the twenty-four-year-old William Pett might well have first supplied at least some of the Sevenoaks side with their heavy, curved bats for defending their low two stump wickets and scooping up the sneaks that came at them underarm along the turf.

Also in 1734 there was a match on 6 September at Sevenoaks between the Gentlemen of Kent and the Gentlemen of Sussex, and it is unlikely that it was played anywhere other than on the open field by the Vine Inn, though there is no specific mention of the Vine Cricket Ground as such till a few years later. A replica of the style of bat used by strikers in this match was made for the bicentenary celebration of what was

Charles Budd of Emsworth, Sussex, made this bat on the back of which is inscribed 'W. Capron Moor, near Midhurst, 1792'.

considered the first known match to be played on the pitch. Teams captained by Lord Sackville and Capt Viscount Gage, descendants of the two men who led the original sides, restaged the 1734 event in the dress of the period and employing 1734-type 'utensils'. In the absence of a member of the Pett family still making cricket bats in 1934, they went for the replica cricket bat to Duke & Son who by then had turned to bat as well as ball making. It hangs in the Vine pavilion.

Whatever might have been the exact date of the first use of the Vine cricket ground, it is obviously older than the Vine Cricket Club. In his pompous poem 'Sevenoke' of 1753, William Harrod was referring to the ground and not the club when he wrote:

> Thou, Vine, for pleasure and for sport design'd,
> Where lively activeness strings ev'ry nerve.

Fred Lillywhite reckoned the club was formed between 1750 and 1760; most others say later. The earliest report of a meeting to have survived is dated 15 May 1788.

By the 1770s William Pett must have been making cricket bats on a reasonably large scale, for they seem to have been readily available for purchase in retail shops in London and probably elsewhere. In her diary the young Fanny Burney, the contemporary of Jane Austen and writer of similar novels, quoted a letter from her friend in the west country, Mrs Rishton, requesting a favour. It is dated 6 June 1773.

> Mrs Rishton begs Miss Burney [who would have been 20] to buy Mr Rishton two cricket batts made by Pett of 7 Oaks. You will get them at any of the great toy shope, the maker's name always stamp'd upon them. Ask for the very best sort which costs 4s or 4s 6d. each. Let them weigh 4 lb and a quarter or 4 lb and a half each. Send them by the Exeter post coach.

Actually Mrs Rishton, who must have been as vague about her weights and measures as her spelling, had put 'oz' instead of 'lb', but unless she was wanting it for Mr Rishton's dolls it must have been a slip of the quill, though at four pounds they would have been heavy bats. But she was not making a mistake about telling Fanny to go to a toy shop. The sports outfitter had not arrived. Even as late as 1851 a stockist who thought it worth taking an advertisement on the back of 'Bat's' *Cricketers Annual* of that year, H. Farley of 31 Fleet Street, described himself as Toyman.

But for the weight and dimensions of a typical William Pett bat of this period there is no need to rely on the scatter-brained message of Mrs Rishton from Exeter, for one of them has survived. Sevenoaks Vine Club members heard of its existence in the 1930s and wrote off to Messrs Turner Brothers, cricket and lawn tennis outfitters, of Oxford who had it on display in their window. It had the maker's name stamped on it just as Mrs Rishton had said – on the bottom: PETT 7 OAKS Kent. Its length was three feet one inch, being two feet to the shoulder. At the upper end it had a circumference of eight and a half inches, broadening at the lower end to ten and a half inches. It had no splice and no symmetry; and it weighed two pounds two ounces. (Perhaps Mrs Rishton was writing about balls and *had* meant ounces?) It was black (tarred?) and wormed, so it was impossible to see what kind of wood it was made of. The handle was roughly bound with cord and on one side was stamped the name 'Bancalari', that of a well-known family of Oxfordshire cricketers. It was thought to date from 1780.

Dr Gordon Ward, the Sevenoaks local historian, asked Mr L. H. Turner if his firm was prepared to sell it to the Vine, but received a dusty answer. Eventually however the bat did find its way to Sevenoaks, and in 1979 it had pride of place in a glass case on the wall inside the Vine pavilion. A photograph of it is reproduced here. Here however the bat is labelled as dating from 'about 1755'. William Pett may also have made the other old bat in the Vine pavilion signed across the front 'Richard Mitchel 1745', but there is no evidence that he did.

William Pett died in 1786, and his grave is in the graveyard of the parish church of St Nicholas in Sevenoaks. His cricket bat manufactory was carried on by his son Thomas, the offspring of his marriage to Mary Taylor of Seal in 1735. There is a deed extent dated 1789 in which Thomas Pett is described as a cricket bat maker, but he never achieved the fame of Father William. He was basically a 'turner'.

There was a Thomas Pett who was a member of the Amicable Society of Sevenoaks and was one of four people by whom the accounts were 'seen and allowed'. This was mainly a drinking club which held quarterly meetings at the Chequers Inn and Blackboy (still standing, both of them) and at the Dorset Arms, a friendly activity crowned with an annual 'feast'. There were fines for swearing which upset the amity, and the proceeds went towards the expense of visiting members when they were sick and their funerals when the jollity got the better of them. In the accounts for the last quarter of 1780 however there is an entry which makes one think that perhaps the Amicable Society Thomas Pett is not the cricket bat maker.

Paid Thomas Pett one week & visiting	8s 0d
Paid his funeral	£4 – 0 – 0
Paid stewards for attending it	4s 0d

For Gordon Ward, the authority on Sevenoaks history, gives 1801 as the year in which Thomas Pett bat maker died, though of course he may have been mistaken. All his effects were sold that year, he says, including a library of some fifty or sixty books of which one alone – on gentlemen's recreations – could be said to have indicated any association with the noble game with which the family name is always connected. There was no sign of any cricket bats either, 'only a bag of chair legs in the garret to remind us that in his younger days he had been accustomed to the use of a lathe'.

Father and son Pett were not without rivals in Sevenoaks. William Staples is known to have made and sold cricket bats in the town at about the same time, but no record has remained of his activities or any example of his craftsmanship.

In the same county and not very far away was a Thomas Rhodes who according to G. D. Martineau was making cricket balls in Maidstone in 1796, and perhaps made bats as well. Also mentioned in his *Bat, Ball, Wicket and All* were J. B. Bentley (1786) and Charles Budd of Brighton.

For years Harry Altham, the cricket historian and coach, had a cricket bat made by Charles Budd hanging on the wall over the door of his

This old bat made *circa* 1755 by William Pett (1709–86) and sold for 4s 6d, belongs to the Vine Cricket Club in whose pavilion in Sevenoaks it is displayed

study when he was housemaster of Furleys at Winchester. When he died it came into the possession of his son R. J. L. Altham who in 1979 had it at his home near Hitchin. The bat has 'C. Budd, Emsworth' stamped on the top of the handle and the bottom of the blade. Emsworth is a Hampshire village near the coast on the Sussex border. Budd may have been operating in Brighton earlier – or later. The Local History Section of Brighton Reference Library has no record of his activities.

Handwritten in a flowing style in ink along the back of the bat is 'W. Capron Moor, near Midhurst 1792'. It is thirty-eight inches long and four-and-a-half inches wide tapering to three-and-threequarters inches at the top. It has a wedge-shaped profile, being one-and-a-half inches at the top widening to just over two-and-threequarters inches at the bottom. It weighs two pounds four ounces. Apart from a certain amount of woodworm, the bat is in very good condition, as is the binding on the handle covering rather more than threequarters of its length. Dick Altham has no idea where, or from whom, his father obtained the bat.

It would be nice to think it was one of the bats used at Winchester. Cricket was certainly being played at some public schools in the eighteenth century. It was played at Eton in Horace Walpole's time as has been seen; the scores of matches played as early as 1793 are extant, and there are still earlier records of matches played by old Etonians. In 1796 Eton sent an eleven clandestinely to play Westminster on Hounslow Heath. The *Gentleman's Magazine* of October 1756 contains a poetical 'Exercise at Merchant Taylor's School' on cricket. But of cricket at Winchester, in the days when Hampshire was the home of the game and Hambledon Club was supreme, there is no record, though doubtless it was played in some form or another, and someone would have made the bats and balls for it. As A. K. Cook wrote in the quincentenary volume *Winchester College 1393–1893*, the Hambledon Club had its poet, the Wykehamist George Huddesford. Yet Huddesford did not connect cricket with Winchester life; it was 'on immediate approach of holidays' that he asked Whitsuntide to:

> 'With thee bring
> Cricket, nimble boy and light
> In slippers red and drawers white.'

Not even the elegance of its costume, apparently, could thoroughly naturalise cricket among Wykehamists. It was possible in the summer of 1770 for a Winchester commoner to write long letters to a brother and schoolfellow invalided home, to declare that news 'is very scarce and very difficult to be met with', yet to make no allusion to a game for which the modern [1893] schoolboy claims, and can often command, the attention of his whole home circle.

In the Wisden Museum of Historic Cricket Bats, which had one hundred and sixty-nine of them at Wisden's Great Newport Street, London, shop, was what John Hadfield in his book *A Wisden Century 1850–1950* described as 'the oldest bat in existence, a long scoop-like, shoulderless implement which is dated 1750'. From the photograph he reproduces it is undoubtedly old, but if 1750 is its date it is not the oldest. He gives no clue as to the maker. The collection is now in the possession

This *Boy in Blue* is obviously finding it awkward to hold this strange shaped cricket bat

of Mr G. K. Medlock of Stockport. But what has happened to that other great cricket bat collection which Sir Julian Cahn Bt of Nottingham bought in 1931 from Charles Pratt Green of Great Malvern, who died in 1950 aged ninety-eight? J. N. Pentelow made a catalogue of these one hundred and forty-nine bats, now a rare collectors' item. Some went no doubt to Sir Julian's private cricket ground at West Bridgeford in Nottingham. Part of Pratt Green's collection consisted of twenty-eight curiosities which had once graced a Mr Farrant's public house in Putney. One of these was a cricket bat made from the wood of a tree which grew over Napoleon's grave at St Helena. Did Notts CCC inherit what was left of the Cahn Collection when Sir Julian died in 1944? They were busy stocktaking at Trent Bridge at the end of 1978, and no one seemed to know the answer. Perhaps it was dispersed between Lords, Trent Bridge and Old Trafford?

A bat in the old museum at Lewes, Sussex, made in 1952 by N. Cochrane, local cricket bat maker, is labelled 'Replica of a mid-eighteenth-century cricket bat; a copy of the earliest extant bat in Wisden's Museum'. (N. incidentally stood for Nellie.) There are probably plenty of others propagating the same error.

An eighteenth-century cricket bat maker of which a little more is known than Charles Budd's bears a name still in the trade in 1979. This is Aquila Clapshoe – or Clapshaw, as it was to become. Individual members of the Clapshoe family were known to have been making cricket bats in Surrey at the beginning of the eighteenth century – according to Bernard Taylor, managing director of the firm in the 1970s whose mother was a Clapshaw, there is evidence that the first members of the family were making cricket bats in 1700. The Aquila Clapshoe, who was born at Froyle in 1714 and married Mary Blanchard in 1738, was probably a cricket player who made his own bats, as did everyone else, but whose expert craftsmanship put him in a class of its own. Certainly the fifth child of this Aquila Clapshoe, who was born at Froyle in 1751, who was also baptised Aquila and who married Ann Mills in 1775, is likely to have been the one who first put the family wood-working skills on to a commercial basis and established the Aquila Clapshoe workshop at Turnham Green in Surrey in 1780, the year in which he is known to have become a master carpenter. The firm probably made furniture and cabinets, with cricket bats as a sideline. The Turnham Green firm today is the direct successor to the 1780 workshop, possessing several Clapshoe bats of this period.

It was only natural, with the popularity of the game in Finsbury Square, that a cricket bat maker should set up shop in London. The first known craftsman here was Christopher Thorn of Thorn's Cricket Bat, Turnery and Patten Warehouse, at the Bee-hive and Patten John Street, Oxford Market (now Oxford Circus). A curved, left-handed bat thought to have been made by Thorn in 1750 is in the museum at Lord's. Sir Ambrose Heal showed his trade card of 1764 in his book *The London Furniture Makers* and commented that no earlier maker of cricket bats in London has been recorded. George Wheeler of Whitechapel, another patten maker, was a contemporary of Thorn, and one of his bats of 1750 is also at Lord's, beside another of the same date by Thomas Edmonds.

Geoffrey Medlock holds what for many years was displayed in the Wisden Museum of Historic Cricket Bats at the Great Newport Street showroom as 'the oldest cricket bat in existence'. Since it was thought to date from 'about 1750' it is certainly not this. The James Chitty bat at The Oval and the J. O. Miles bat at Winchester College are both older

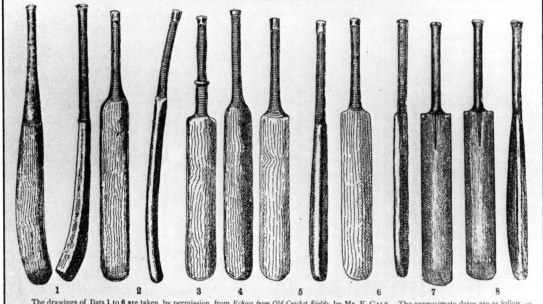

The drawings of Bats **1** to **6** are taken, by permission, from *Echoes from Old Cricket Fields*, by Mr. F. GALE. The approximate dates are as follow :— No. **1**, *1743* ; No. **2**, weighing 5 lbs., *1771* ; No. **3**, *1790*—this is a double-handed bat, and belonged to Robinson, a man with a crippled hand, who wore an iron strapped on to his wrist ; No. **4**, marked on the back *1792*, and named " Little Joey," belonged to Ring of Dartford, an old Hambledon man, to whose style of play is attributed the origin of the law l-b-w ; No. **5**, weighing about 2¾ lbs., *1800* ; No. **6**, marked on back with brass brads *1827*—belonged to John Bowyer, and weighed about 2¾ lbs. ; Nos. **7** and **8** are in my possession, and are of present date : they weigh 2 lbs. 5½ ozs., and illustrate the plan of splicing, No. **7** in addition showing the whale-bone. Figures **1, 2, 5, 6,** and **8**, show the front and edge of bat, and figures **3, 4,** and **7**, front only.

BATS—OLD STYLE AND THE NEW.

This drawing of eight cricket bats appears in W. G. Grace's *Cricket* (1891). The first six were taken from Frederick Gale's *Echoes From Old Cricket Fields*. Bats no 7 and 8 belonged to Dr Grace

A drawing of the bat made in 1792 and for some reason nicknamed Little Joey, was printed by Frederick Gale in his *Echoes from Old Cricket Fields* (and reproduced by W. G. Grace in *Cricket*), and the bat itself stands in the pavilion at Lord's. Little Joey belonged to an old Hambledon player called Ring who came from Dartford. It was his style of play which originated the leg before wicket (lbw) rule.

The oldest bat in the Gale/Grace line up reproduced here, the one on the extreme left, is merely dated 1743 in the original caption, without further details. It is probably the J. O. Miles bat at Winchester College. There are three late eighteenth-century bats in the Lord's collection; a bowed bat by W. Pawley of 1780; another of 1790 by Durtnall of Ickham, Kent; and one stamped E. Bagot, with the date 1793. As noted, in the 1930s Stonyhurst College had five of the bats used in Stonyhurst Cricket in the years following their resettlement in England in 1794, but in 1979 there were only two left.

Six-foot tall Robert 'Long' Robinson (1765–1822), the Surrey player, was not just left-handed but had only three fingers on one hand and for him someone had to make a very special bat. Two of the fingers of his right hand had been burnt off as a child, which earned him the nickname 'Three-Fingered Jack'. He had to wear an iron strapped to his wrist. The bat he had made for him was double-handed, as other bats, but as can be seen from no. 3 of the line-up of eight bats reproduced by W. G. Grace, it was not as other bats in any other respect. The handle was grooved to fit his stunted fingers. 'He once had the legitimacy of his bat called in question,' recalled the Author of the Cricket Field in *Cricketana* (1865), 'and shaved down to the proper measure [presumably the iron gauge recommended by the Hambledon Club] while he stood angry by.' The objection seems to have been to the width of the bat which perhaps Three-Fingered Jack had purposely asked to be over-broad to compensate for his deformity.

John Nyren corroborated the story. 'Barker [?] had known an instance, years since, at Lord's, when a man was sent down to the bat shop to have his bat shaved. When Mr Budd saw Robinson's bat treated equally unceremoniously with someone's pocket knife, Robinson was very angry and vowed he would do his best to serve them out for spoiling his bat and actually hit about the field with a vengeance and made one of his largest innings.'

Nyren added: 'As to the length of the bat, there was no limit assigned till 1816' [in fact the thirty-eight inch limit was introduced in 1835], which shows the objections to Robinson's bat must have been to its width. In any event, the bat in question has survived and can be seen, grooved handle and all, in the upper case on the wall of the pavilion at Lord's. William Hazlitt eulogised Long Robinson in his famous essay *Merrie England*.

With the close of the eighteenth century, the work of the pioneers came to an end, with standards set and techniques established, ready to hand on to the next generation of craftsmen. John Small played his last match in 1798, but, as noted, continued to make bats up to 1825, though in this latter period, in spite of that 'selling bat and ball' notice, his son was probably in charge. In fact Frederick Gale was at pains to apportion the major contribution to the latter. 'The *younger* Small,' he wrote in *The Game of Cricket*, 'had the credit of inventing the first bats with a

George Wheeler's trade card. One of his cricket bats dated 1750 is in Lord's pavilion

Five different shapes from the collection at Lord's: (left to right) an eighteenth-century curved bat of unknown origin; 'Little Joey' which belonged to the old Hambledon player, Ring, who came from Dartford and whose style of playing originated the leg before wicket (lbw) rule; an E. Bagot 'skyscraper' bat of 1793; the one-off bat made specially for Robert 'Long' Robinson who was not only left-handed but three-fingered; and a bat used by W. G. Grace

shoulder, much of the present form as regards face; and the bat became so popular that the orders poured in upon him and he could hardly make them fast enough.' At the same time Robert Dark was being trained to bring the Petersfield tradition to the inner sanctum at St John's Wood. Father William Pett saw the century out and handed over to son Thomas. Aquila Clapshaw had founded his dynasty.

The experimental era was over. The heavy, curved club was old-fashioned and the straight blade/square shoulder design of the Smalls had come to stay.

3 Kent and London

Cricket ball craftsmen of the 19th century

Handicapping striker or bowler in an effort to make the game fairer or more entertaining, or both, was a thankless task. The lawmakers juggled frantically with the size of the wicket in the early part of the nineteenth century to achieve acceptable dimensions – twenty-two inches high and six inches wide in 1814; twenty-six inches high and eight inches wide between 1814 and 1817; twenty-seven inches high and eight inches wide in 1818 – but almost anyone could make a stump and make it any size he liked, and even the making of a one-piece bat did not require any great skill. But the making of a cricket ball was in another category altogether. To those who had played the game it had an air of mystery and sophistication which did not belong to the making of a bat. For this reason probably, apart from an injunction to watch its weight and stipulating tolerances, the specification of the ball was let well alone.

It cannot be that Duke and Small were the only firms making cricket balls in England when the nineteenth century dawned. There would have been others, but no names have survived save that of William Martin who is known to have begun making them at Hadlow and nearby Tudeley, which lie to the east of Tonbridge, in 1808. The site of this activity however has never been pinpointed, nor are there any details available of the craftsman in question. But he bears a name which recurs throughout this story with fascinating regularity.

The composition of Duke, Small and Martin cricket balls, and those of their unrecorded competitors, are likely to have been similar and to have remained so for many a year. Even in 1927 Ernest Ward felt able to write (in the Farington Diary footnote already quoted), 'while the style and shape of the original cricket bat has changed, the ball played with to-day is in weight and size precisely as it was constructed by Duke 200 years or more ago'. Certainly the cricket ball of 1820 in Lord's pavilion which once belonged to William Ward bears this out.

And this in spite of the ball (as a result of the revolution in the style of bowling in the 1820s) being required to perform very differently from the way it had been doing throughout the years of underarm trundling and lobbing.

Around 1788 a Kent player, Tom 'Old Everlasting' Walker, thought cricket could be livened up by having the bowler swing his arm around

William Lillywhite, born in Goodwood in 1792, the Non-Pareil Bowler, from whom the cricketing Lillywhites were descended. In 1849 his third son Fred founded Lillywhite's Guide to Cricketers (pre-dating the Almanack of his partner John Wisden); the last issue was published in 1900. Fred Lillywhite joined John Wisden to open a Cricket and Cigar Depot off Piccadilly Circus in 1855. When the partnership was dissolved in 1858 he set up his own business with brothers John and James Lillywhite, founding in 1863 the Lillywhites sports shop which still flourishes

his body and then letting go of the ball so that it came at the batsman very much more smartly than it came from the hand of an underarm bowler. The law then was that the ball must be delivered 'under handed, not thrown or jerked, with the hand below the elbow at the time of delivering the ball'. The umpire would call No Ball 'if the arm be extended straight from the body or the back part of the hand be uppermost when the ball is delivered, or the hand horizontally extended'.

In 1792 Tom Walker demonstrated what he had in mind in a match against David Harris the perfect length innovator, but he overdid the pace and the cricketing fraternity shied away. But twenty years later, an amateur player called John Willes of Sutton Valence in Kent, who had been a lad of seventeen at the time of Walker's demonstration, was encouraged to make another attempt to introduce the faster style, after his sister had impressed him with her skill at *throwing* the ball at him during practice games at their home near Canterbury. He taught his dog to field the ball for him, and the wits of the day said Willes, his sister and his dog could beat any eleven in England. In spite of the MCC ruling against jerking and throwing Willes practised what he preached by bowling 'round arm' on every occasion. When he did so at Lord's in 1822 however he was no-balled, whereupon he dropped the ball, jumped on his horse and declared he would never play again. But he had already given enough demonstration of the enlivening effect of the new style to enlist a nucleus of round arm fans and ensure its eventual substitution for the underarm, though not without a struggle. Between 1823 and 1830 most players found 'throwing' thoroughly objectionable and strongly opposed it. The Rev Lord Frederick Beauclerc retired from cricket when he found it being tolerated. John Nyren devoted several pages of his 1833 classic to protesting against 'the modern innovation of throwing instead of bowling the balls' which had been defended on the ground that matches were taking too long and three day matches could be ended in one. 'If therefore the present system be persisted in a few years longer, the elegant and scientific game of Cricket will decline into a mere exhibition of rough, coarse horseplay.' He recommended weighting the odds in favour of the bowler even further by giving him four stumps to knock down instead of three, as Lord Winchilsea had once advocated before him.

But three stalwarts lent their authority and prestige to Willes's campaign – James Broadbridge of Kent, William Lillywhite of Sussex and G. T. 'Gallant' Knight of Kent. And in May 1828, when more bowlers were bowling round arm than 'old-fashioned' underarm, the MCC felt the time had come to legalise it. It was considered altogether more sophisticated. 'Gallant' Knight who, apart from bowling round arm on every occasion, wrote about its advantages at great length, was described by a contemporary versifier:

> As a bowler first-rate, as a bat far from vile
> And he bowls in the new march of intellect style.

Tom Walker's unsuccessful pioneering effort was little remembered – he himself lived to see the vindication of his stand, he died in 1831. And when John Willes died in 1852 his tombstone in Sutton Valence church-

yard bore the inscription: 'He was a patron of all manly sports and the first to introduce round-armed bowling in cricket.'

The new MCC rule of 1828 permitted the hand to be raised as high as the elbow and the arm to be extended outwards and horizontally. In 1835 came a further compromise: the hand delivering the ball could be raised as high as the shoulder. In 1838 the circumference of the ball was limited to between nine and nine-and-a-quarter inches.

In spite of Nyren and the Old Guard, the 'new' fast round arm form of attack soon became the rage. 'For 30 years to come,' wrote Neville Cardus in *English Cricket*, 'this bowling set the general technical stamp and provided the most important bridge passage in cricket's symphonic progress; it was cultivated to the highest possible potency by Alfred Mynn, Lillywhite and Caffyn. Here was the beginning of "modern" cricket.' In these thirty years (till 1864 when 'overarm' bowling was recognised) bowlers raised their hand higher and higher – in defiance of what was 'the rule'.

But apparently no one thought it necessary to modernise the cricket ball, and to modify it so that it became more suitable as the fodder for the cannonade which the new, fast round arm bowlers now pounded down unkempt pitches throughout the country. It remained as hard as it had ever been. The batsman had to face the hard, leather-covered ball which used to be lobbed at him, being thrown at double the pace, and to do so as manfully and elegantly as he could.

Even lobbing had had its casualties. For had not Frederick, Prince of Wales, George II's son, died of the effects of a blow received in the side from a cricket ball in 1751, which seemed to have caused the break up of the London Club (the MCC of the time), and the temporary cessation of great matches? The story may be apocryphal however; Smollett had it that the Prince 'in consequence of a cold caught in his garden at Kew was seized with a pleuritic disorder and after a short illness expired in his 45th year'.

The hard, though happily resilient, ball was also a threat to spectators – or rather those at the side of the ground who were unable to keep their eyes on the play, occupied as they were with other duties essential to the enjoyment of the game, such as the serving of ginger beer.

In a match played at Ticehurst in Sussex in August 1825 the ball from the bat of Thomas Cooper, perhaps the first proprietor of the Coopers Stores which still stands, was caught on the point of a knife which a woman named Stapley, who was running a ginger beer stall on the ground, happened to be holding in her hand at the time. 'Her hand was much cut by the involuntary feat,' reported *Bell's Life*, 'and the ball was so deeply perforated that some little force was found necessary to draw the knife from it.'

Alfred Mynn, protagonist of fast round arm bowling, was himself an early victim of it at the wicket. At a game at Leicester in 1836 between North and South, Mynn was knocked down and severely injured by a ball from Samuel Redgate which hit his unpadded leg. He could not rise from the pitch. He was carefully lifted on to a stretcher packed round with splints, and placed on the roof of the stage coach. On reaching London he felt unable to continue the journey to his home in Kent, and was taken to Bart's Hospital where he was examined by surgeons who told him they would have to amputate his thigh at the hip. They had second thoughts however, and after an absence of two years Mynn returned to the cricket field and played as well as ever.

Pads were not first experimented with till 1836 – unmanly? – and not widely adopted until the 1860s. Even then they were no protection against a ball that bumped high off a far-from-perfect pitch. Richard Daft the Nottingham player always held his bat high up on his chest for this reason. He recounted how at Lord's a batsman called George Summers was struck on the cheekbone by a rising ball from Platts causing concussion from which he died three days later. The fiery John Jackson was notorious for hurling a fast ball full toss at the head of any batsman who repeatedly hit his bowling to the boundary. He boasted that when playing for the North he took nine of the South's wickets and lamed the last player – 'so that was as good as ten, eh?'

Jackson became a joke. Richard Daft had a print by John Leech showing a cricketer on his way home with a black eye and a damaged leg and arm. 'Good match, old fellow?' asked a friend meeting him. 'Oh yes, awfully jolly.' 'What did you do?' 'I had a hover of Jackson. The first ball hit me on the arm, the second had me on the knee, the third in my eye, and the fourth bowled me out.' One of the less constitutional Kings of Cricket. William Lillywhite, the *nonpareil* of round arm bowling, cautioned would-be adherents of the cult against putting faith in the high pitching ball:

> Try every manoeuvre to make the ball twist and shoot after it touches the ground – one such ball will often do more service for you than a hundred well-delivered *rising ones*, however true, even to the bails. By holding the ball slightly askew, with the thumb well across the seam, you will find by working the wrist as the ball leaves the hand, it will assist it to cut and rick [twist] at the wicket; such balls are very troublesome to stop, or get rid of.
>
> ('Hints to Bowlers', *Lillywhite's Illustrated Hand Book of Cricket*, 1844)

And cricket balls remained not only hard but red. When in 1843 Charles Dickens wanted to use an image everyone would recognise in *Martin Chuzzlewit*, he described the ledgers of the Anglo-Bengalee Disinterested Loan and Life Assurance Company as having 'red backs like strong cricket balls beaten flat'.

But in spite of its danger – perhaps because of it – cricket grew in popularity. The first county cricket club, Sussex, was formed in 1839. The demand for new cricket balls increased to such an extent that the scale of production at the little Duke manufactory, established on Redleaf Hill to supply the local needs of Penshurst and neighbouring village teams, had become utterly unrealistic. Quality was up to standard, as ever, but quantity was well behind.

With the manufacturing process and the specification of the end product remaining constant, the level of skilled craftsmanship, handed from one generation to another, and in most cases from father to son, had consolidated itself, and production on a bigger scale merely meant more hands. But by 1841 there was no room in that wooden outhouse in the garden of The Paddocks for any more craftsmen.

It is likely that by 1841 Timothy Duke I, who had spoken to Joseph Farington thirty years before, was no longer running the business. Though the year of his death is not known, in 1841, if still alive, he would have been seventy-nine. His son, Timothy Duke II, who, born in 1800, would have been forty-one, was probably then in charge. Timothy Duke II was a keen cricketer and maintained the old tradition of the craftsman-player in the manner of John Small. He played for Kent between 1823 and 1828, and was noted as a fast underarm bowler.

Whoever was running Duke & Son in 1841, the firm moved out of The Paddocks in that year to the factory some five miles away which they had built themselves at Chiddingstone Causeway near Penshurst railway station.

Cricket was booming and things soon began to hum in the new premises. In May 1848 they announced they were extending their operations to include the making of cricket bats, stumps, leg-guards and gauntlets (*Bell's Life In London*, 7 May 1848). In 1851, the year Timothy II's son John attained his majority, Duke & Son won their first prize medal – in the Great Exhibition which opened in London's Hyde Park that year. They were to win five more in the next twenty-five years.

> Cricket now takes precedence amongst existing sports from its adaptation to the means and wants of all, while the spirit of emulation which it educes is in exact accordance with the habits and feelings of a true-born Briton. Within the sea-encircled land of his birth, cricket was brought into existence; it was nursed in its tender days by the sons of the British soil, and now that it is matured, Englishmen are justly proud of their offspring.
>
> Advice from 'Bat' in his *Cricketer Manual* (1851)

It was a sentiment which Prince Albert himself could not have expressed better, and one into which the truly English craft being practised at Penshurst under the shadow of the Sidneys well fitted. On the cricket field, continued 'Bat', rank left its pedestal, men of all shades congregated.

> There senator and peasant, artizan and peer, the employer and the employed jostle together, and no alloy creeps in to mar the general holiday ... Tottering senility contrasts with elastic youth. Folk of all ages meet, from the furrowed brow and channelled cheek, down to the plump and ruddy face of cherub size. The Radical finds himself alongside the Conservative and each recognises his political opponent with that degree of courtesy which is reserved for peculiar occasions ... It possesses all the charms that rustic emulation and hilarity can desire.

Cricket had come a long way since the gambling days of a century before when (in 1748) the court, asked to rule whether cricket was a lawful game within the meaning of the Statute of 9th Anne against gaming, held 'Cricket is (to be sure) a manly game and not bad in itself, but only in the ill use that has been made of it in this case by betting more than £10 on one match; that is bad and against the law'. Robert Southey (1774–1843) had not considered it was a game for gentlemen in the middle of the eighteenth century, and to support his case quoted an article in the *Connoisseur* of 1756 in which Tony Bumper's vulgarities

were enumerated as 'drinking purl in the morning, eating black pud-
dings at Bartholomew Fair, boxing with Buckhorse; and also that he
was frequently engaged at the Artillery Ground with Faulkner and
Dungate at cricket'. 'Bat's' eulogy was the very reverse of the *complaint*
of a reader of the *British Champion* of 1743 who wrote to say how *odd* it
was to see lords and gents, clergy and lawyers associating themselves
with butchers and cobblers in pursuit of their diversions.

In 1861 on the other hand 'An Old Cricketer' was eager to point out
in *The Cricket Bat* that cricket had many charms to soldiers and was of
essential service not only in development of muscular activity and
vigour but also in promotion of good feeling in the ranks, with con-
tentment and health. It was the 'chosen recreation of the soldier during
wearying campaigns; the delight of every British tar when he obtains a
liberty to run ashore'.

The late Duke of Wellington had remarked in the House of Lords,
said 'Bat', that his success in arms was owing in a great measure to the
manly sports of Britain in which in his youthful days he said he freely
indulged; and one sport above all – cricket.

With such a sponsor the commercial suppliers could not fail. The
boom was almost too overwhelming, but thoroughly respectable.

> Then welcome the sober enjoyment that flings
> Such witchery round the spot where it lives!
> The bud in the heart, to the sunlight that clings,
> Will bloom in the pleasure that cricketing gives.

And if there was perforce a bit of knockabout, it was unintentional. It
was purely a matter of being prepared in the manner prescribed by the
player who called himself Felix because his difficult German sounding
name (Wanostrocht) might have jarred amid all this Englishness.

> Provide yourself with a box large enough to contain two bats, two
> or three balls, stumps and a complete change of dress. It should
> have a small till-box to hold your watch and jewellery. And do not
> forget to have a phial of sweet oil at hand; of all the things that I
> have ever used, this has been the best. Some rub the bruise with
> vinegar and brandy; others use the first thing that comes to hand;
> but oil, oil is the 'sovereign'st thing on earth for an outward bruise'.

When Timothy Duke II died in 1858, aged fifty-eight, John (born at
Penshurst in 1830) took over. In a whimsical dialogue between cricket
historian Frederick Gale and the Spirit of Christmas about the activities
at Duke's cricket ball factory at Chiddingstone Causeway in the
nineteenth century, he asks, 'But who is this Duke, spirit?' He is told
that Duke is 'supposed to be a representative of the oldest of the many
cricket ball factories in England' (1882).

'And I suppose he is,' muses the Spirit, 'as their firm gave the first
treble-seam ball to George IV when Prince of Wales and a boy, such as
you see him in Gainsborough's picture of him with an old spoon bat in
his hand at Lord's; and he cannot count with accuracy the number of his
great and great-grandfathers who preceded him; and I don't think the
family have sustained much loss by each in turn having gone into the
factory as a youth, with his sleeves tucked up and his apron on, and
putting his own hands to the work – for mark you, there is no steam or

By tradition this 'Young
Cricketer' painted by
Thomas Gainsborough
(1727–88) is the Prince of
Wales, to whom, at the age
of thirteen (in 1755) Duke &
Son presented the first of
their new treble-sewn cricket balls. When he became
King George IV in 1820, he
granted Duke & Son the
royal warrant.

machinery, but it is all done by hand, and all the labour of the various workmen is useless if the finished ball does not pull the scale true.' (From 'About An Old Cricket Ball' in *Baily's Monthly Magazine*, November 1882, by 'F.G.'.)

That was John Duke he was talking about. He was not to die until 1890 at the age of sixty, when he was succeeded by W. H. Duke who was born in 1856 and died in 1913.

The Spirit of Christmas takes his mortal questioner round the works, after pointing out how grateful we should all be to the cow for letting us have her hide, after we have milked her dry and eaten her, to say nothing of tripe and cowheel. 'Well! come on, Mortal, or you will miss your train,' continues the Spirit. 'Well, as you said, there were the raw hides; now turn in here. There is a pile of the tanned and prepared hides, hard and white and shiny like the outside of a cavalry soldier's shoulder-belt. Now look at that man with a pot of stuff like red paint? he is laying on the dye – which, mind you, is intended for hard wear and will not come off with wet, like the beautiful (?) colour on some ladies' cheeks. There is stage "one" of the cover; and how would you like to work all day in that room, amidst that atmosphere of ammonia? So much for him. Now come here and see that man with a shoe-maker's knife cutting out the four quarters, like the four quarters of the skin of an orange. There is not much art in that, you say? Very well, wait for my final remark; and you are thinking the same about the work of that man who is sewing two of the quarters together; any cobbler could do that, you say. Think for one moment what that ball has to do; perhaps it has to be hammered by men with strong arms and quick sight, such as Mr. C. I. Thornton, or Mr. Bonnor "the Australian Baby", as that genial giant has been styled (in love, and not in derision); and beyond the ordinary rough usage of a ball, may have to drop on chimney-pots or roofs or on hard roads outside the ground, and mind you, that ball must keep its shape, and the stitches must hold. Now look at that man, who having put the quilt inside, sews the two cases together. Look at the quilt and the two cups; why the jacket, as we will call the leathern cover, does not fit by a quarter of an inch! How can the sewer manage it? Watch him now, putting on those cases – either outside fitting into a vice – the receptacle for the ball being two iron cups. See the veins swell in his arms and forehead as he screws up that vice; the pressure is so great that sometimes the screw breaks. He has done it, and the two edges are more than brought together: and now is his opportunity for making the first row of "holding stitches", which have to bear the greatest strain; and it is done. What an ugly thing that ball is when it is released from the vice with her first row of stitches, and the edges pouting like a sulky girl's lips! Look at the once rough seam now, after the ball is released from a second press which flattens the stitches! None of the stitches have given in the least and in the place of that seam is a smooth surface, and the edges of the two cups have been united as firmly as an evangelical old maid's lips, when a gospel-speaker has turned on the blue fire with an eye to the destruction of those who differ with him.

'That young fellow marking and pricking the holes for the other seams has a quick and true eye. If you doubt me, take up any one of those finished balls and see how true the stitches are, and how even the line of stitches go round. The old gentleman with his shirt-sleeves tucked up is putting a finish to the work, and does the outside seams; he has just finished one. You see he is not excited, as you seem to be; it is his daily work, and he has done his best; he simply hands it over, and the ball is weighed, and if it is true, and is neither under $5\frac{1}{2}$ ounces nor over $5\frac{3}{4}$ ounces in weight, the ball is now handed to the stamper, who puts it in a press, down comes the brand "J. Duke, Penshurst", and it goes forth to the world with an unknown fate before it. If it is given as a present to a small boy, other boys are sure to join him, to show him how to play with it, and if they should be boys of low morals, a case of "lost ball" occurs, and some pirate finds it and sticks to it. Sometimes it passes through the dignity of an "All England Match", and afterwards becomes a "bowler's ball", and gets soaked with rain and baked in the sun, and grows into an "old pudding", and eventually some village boys get hold of it, and take off the leathern cover, and net a cover for it and play hockey with it, and at last it gets too ragged and old for hockey and it joins the majority of old cricket-balls and gets into the unknown world of its class – wherever that may be – and sometimes, as you see, it has the good deeds of the last possessor recorded on it, and preserved as a treasure, as that ball of old Lillywhite's is. Now look at that brand new ball, Mortal, and does it not give the world as much pleasure as any toy ever created?'

The answer was assuredly 'Yes'.

Both floors of the Duke cricket ball factory, wrote F.G., were filled with workmen, young and old, 'many of them having succeeded to their father's or grandfather's vacant seats who had joined the majority, after passing a lifetime at ball-making winter and summer. The view of waving trees and the song of the birds which came in merrily through the open windows made the place look the *beau ideal* of the birthplace of a cricket ball. A very good cricket ground is situated close to the factory, and the factory turn out a very good eleven of their own.'

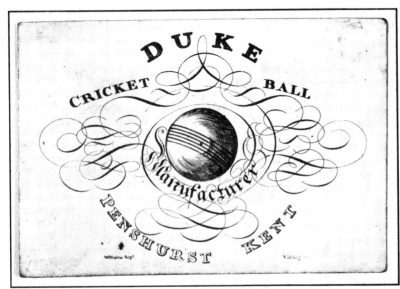

Duke & Son's trade card. Oldest of the English cricket ball makers, Duke & Son's business has been centred on Penshurst in Kent for more than two hundred years

Timothy Duke, one of the four members of the family running Duke & Son in 1897, is the man on the left of the middle row of this group of cricket bat craftsmen at Chiddingstone Causeway

The Duke family obviously had a well developed sense of public relations. It was shown not only in the encouragement of pieces like this but in the lengthy popular song they sponsored, *Willow the King* '(the music will be forwarded free on application to Duke & Son, Penshurst, Kent)'. *Willow the King* was published by Cassell as 'Harrow School Song No 7' and no 10 in their 'Gaudeamus Songs for Colleges and Schools'. It was dedicated to Hon R. Grimston and Hon H. Ponsonby 'than whom even among Harrovians King Willow had no more loyal friends'. The words were by E. E. Bowen and the music by John Farmer. The special relationship which Duke (and other cricket bat makers) seem to have had with Harrow School, manifested in 'harrow' being the word applied to an intermediate size of cricket bat, which it still is today, is indicated here, but not explained. 'Willow King' was the brand name of one of the bats they began to manufacture in 1848. Two of the verses were:

Willow King Willow thy guard hold tight;
Trouble is coming before the night;
Hopping and galloping, short and strong,
Comes the Leathery Duke along;
And down the palace [players?] tumble fast
When once the Leathery Duke gets past,
    So ho! So ho! may the courtiers sing!
    Honour and life to the Willow King.

'What of the Duke?' you ask anon,
'Where has his Leathery Highness gone?'
O he is filled with air inside—
Either it is air, or else it is his pride—
And he swells and swells as tight as a drum,
And they kick him about till Christmas come.
    So ho! So ho! may the courtiers sing!
    Honour and life to the Willow King.

Duke cricket balls won medals in London in 1851, in Adelaide in 1881, in Sydney in 1879, and in Melbourne in 1880.

There were four members of the family running Duke & Son in 1897, W. H. Duke, T. Duke, A. Duke and H. Duke. A patent specification they filed in 1895 (no 13,384) was 'abandoned' but on 27 February 1897 they filed no 5337, relating to the covers of both cricket and hockey balls, which had always been of a similar construction. 'The covers of cricket and hockey balls are formed of chrome leather preferably made by treating the pelt with potassium bichromate or chromic acid, and then oxidising in a bath composed of hyposulphite of soda and hydrochloric acid. The cover may have a lining of cork, felt, fabric, kamptulicon [a floor cloth composed of a mixture of india–rubber, gutta percha and cork on canvas] or asbestos, instead of or in addition to the usual inner leather lining.'

Duke's famous 'Willow King' cricket bat promoted in their 1909 catalogue

Cricket Bats.

Duke's "WILLOW KING."

IMPROVED COMPOSITION RUBBER HANDLES, AND
BLADES OF FINEST SELECTED WILLOW,
GOOD DRIVING POWER,
PERFECT BALANCE,
PLENTY OF TIMBER AND WELL SEASONED—
WARRANTED.

The "WILLOW KING" Bats are suitable for Private use and Leading Club Cricket, the difference of price from our "Royal" Bats being in the grading of the blades, and the construction of the handles.

They are Specially Good Value and are recommended for English and Colonial Cricketers who require high-class bats.

Men's Size	. .	.	.	.	each.
Harrow School Size		.		,,
Youths' No. 6 Size	.	.		,,
,, No. 5 ,,	.	.	.	,,
,, No. 4 ,,	.	.	.	,,

Best Red Rubber Handle Covers, smooth or rough, included.

Rubber Handle Covers on the above are a great improvement, giving a better grip and balance to the bats.

Postage on single Bats   each.

The cricket ball with which Platts concussed George Summers at Lord's Cricket Ground had not come from the Duke factory, for though, since their move to Chiddingstone Causeway in 1841, the Dukes remained the doyen of cricket ball makers and the reputation of their produce had never been higher, the Leathery Duke had never been able to penetrate the holy of holies at St John's Wood. Here the monopoly of John Small's pupil, Robert Dark, was complete.

Just when Robert Dark, the youngest of the three Dark brothers, was apprenticed to John Small senior at Petersfield is not known, but it would have been between 1817 when he was fifteen and 1829 when Small died. Throughout the season of 1845 he took a classified advertisement on the front page of *Bell's Life in London & Sporting Chronicle* which is reproduced on the opposite page. It was a trump card he played for all he was worth for the next twenty years. In 1862 he was advertising in a rather more bold, displayed fashion:

By Special Appointment
to HRH the Late Prince Consort   HRH the Prince of Wales
and the Marylebone Club

ROBERT DARK
Manufacturer of Cricket Balls etc.

Dark's Cricket Balls

The Members of Cricket Clubs, Merchants and others
are respectfully informed that they can be supplied
with the above celebrated articles on liberal terms.
They are the only balls used by the Marylebone Club,
and in all the Grand Matches at Lord's, therefore
they need no guarantee.

Certainly only Dark balls were used at Lord's, but it is open to question whether the Duke or Dark produce was chosen for the ice cricket match played on skates by members of the Sheffield Skating Club on the frozen pond at Chatsworth Park, the Duke of Devonshire's seat (by kind permission of Mr Paxton) one cold January day this same year of 1845, reported in the 'Cricketing' columns of *Bell's Life*. It would surely have needed something rather special to rise from this hard pitch of ice six inches thick with the surface 'as transparent as glass'. But rise it did, for runs were made by both sides after the appropriately named E. Skidmore had opened the game with a fine twenty-six before being run out – not skidding enough presumably. Large bonfires were lit around the pond to keep the waiting batsmen and spectators warm, and when it was all over there was 'figurative' skating and the dancing of Payne's Quadrilles.

'Robert Dark,' wrote Arthur Haygarth in *Cricket Scores and Biographies*, 'the noted glove, leg-guard and ballmaker at Lord's (he never had the bat business, as some supposed) died at Holyrood House, St John's Wood Road, London, 10 March 1873 aged 71. He was the younger brother of James Henry Dark and was (besides the above business) for many years money-taker at the gate of Lord's on a grand

CRICKET, under PATRONAGE of the MARYLEBONE CLUB.—ROBERT DARK, sole inventor and manufacturer of the Tubular India Rubber Gloves and the Improved Leg Guards, respectfully informs the lovers of the game of Cricket that he has a large supply of these essential articles, in addition to his celebrated Cricket Balls (no others are used in the great Matches on Lord's Ground) always ready. Spiked soles for cricket shoes. The Laws of Cricket, as authorised by the Marylebone Club, Scoring Papers, &c. Foreign and provincial orders, accompanied by a Post Office Order or a reference in town, punctually executed. An allowance made to clubs, and the trade supplied.— Robert Dark being the manufacturer of the various articles which are here enumerated, and therefore assured as to the excellence of the quality of the different materials with which they are constructed, can with the greatest confidence recommend them to the cricketing world. A list of prices forwarded.—Tennis Court, Lord's Cricket Ground, St. Marylebone.

match day. The ball business was purchased by Mr Frank Dark on the death of Robert Dark, and the bat business he had also from his mother Mrs M. Dark.'

Before selling out to Frank, Robert Dark spent much of his active life passing on his knowledge to the next generation of craftsmen. One of these was Thomas Twort.

Thomas Twort was born on a farm at Speldhurst near Tonbridge at midnight on 30 April 1828, but he always kept his birthday on 1 May. Tworts had been living in this part of Kent since the sixteenth century, though then they spelt their name Tort and Turt and Tourt. It was a Norman name – Tourte – and there are Tourte families in France today. Armand Tourte was a famous maker of violin bows which today fetch large sums. Frant Manor Court Rolls record the death of a Katherine Turt at Brenchley in 1539; Tourts were tanners at Horsmonden in the seventeenth century; in 1701 William Tourt the Elder married Ann Austin at Canterbury, who was a first cousin of William Austen of Tonbridge, grandfather of Jane Austen.

Thomas's father was William Twort, born at Speldhurst in 1795. He apprenticed Tom to a saddler in Tunbridge Wells, one William Razell, to whom he paid £10. Tom stayed there four years and eighteen weeks and learnt the art of stitching leather with small, neat stitches. Though he grew in understanding of this intricate craft, he failed to grow in height – he was never more than five-and-a-half feet tall, a cheery, dumpy man, as his photograph on page 66 shows. His cheeriness was self-generating; he rejected all forms of alcohol and became an ardent crusader in the case of temperance, even to the extent of opposing the offering of fermented liquor at Holy Communion. When he grew up he became a familiar figure at local fêtes in a high Derby hat and white pocketed apron selling soft drinks from a table in front of a large placard reading 'Samson Drank Water And Revived'. He hoped that those who had over-exerted themselves at the coconut shy or tug-of-war would emulate that distinguished man of muscle and buy from his rather than the devil's beer tent round the corner. He made merry in his own way – letting off fireworks of his own devising, for which he was called before the beaks for not having a licence, and walking for miles across the fields

Thomas Twort

for a day's fishing. When he was a lad of fifteen and had just begun his apprenticeship Tom bought himself a cheap notebook and in it recorded the cost of his pet rabbits:

16 Nov 1843	Two rabbits cost	0 – 3 – 3
17 Nov	For a half a bushel of bran	0 – 0 – 5
	Bushel of turnips	0 – 1 – 0
	Gallon of oats	0 – 0 – 5

The outlay was amply rewarded, for on 16 December he was able to record with some satisfaction:

Sandy rabbit littered 7 young
Black   ,,   ,,   7 ditto

Four years later when his pets had doubtless multiplied to an excessive degree and he had completed his apprenticeship, he was able to turn his mind to more serious matters and felt justified in calling himself:

Thomas Twort
Saddler
Harness and Colter Maker

for thus he headed a paper bound notebook, dated 'March the 1 1847' in which he jotted down measurements of the harness, bridle and other items he had learnt about at Tunbridge Wells. His masters had evidently failed to impart much knowledge of spelling, but a firm grasp of phonetics enabled him to express most of what he wanted to convey. Typical entry under 'Bridle':

	ft	in
Cheale of the Bridle		9
The Billett left out	1	0
Nose piece in short	1	2
Do. piece to go all round	2	6
Headpiece	1	10
Frunt in Clear	1	0
Winker stays	1	6
Throat lash made	1	8
Forred piece made	1	6

There were the measurements of Riding Rain, Gig Rains, Carriage Round Rains, Waggon Harness, Trace Harness, Cupling Rain, Quiler Harness, Poney or Donkey Harness, Ox Harness, Head Stol Holters, Calvers Holters, Tandum Harness, Goat Harness, Nea Caps, Cart Collers, Saddle Pads – these last three with neat drawings. He made a note of a harness maker's tools which included The Spoke Shave, The Screw Vane, Five Coller Needles, Five All Havs, The Eging Oirn, The Pipe Loop Vane, the Seat Ale and Have. There was a section on Antigropelos (leather gaiters) with illustrations of three styles at £1 1s, £1 8s and £1 0s 5d a pair.

For three to four years he must have practised as a journeyman, probably at Razell's saddlery in Tunbridge Wells. But in 1851 or earlier

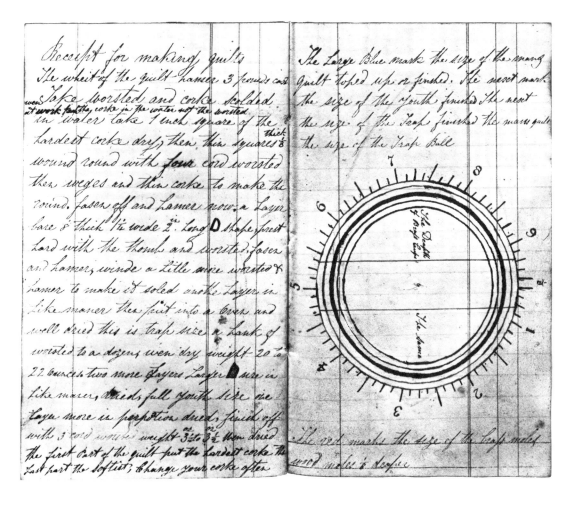

he decided to turn his hand to cricket ball stitching, and it must have been at this time that he went to learn the craft from Robert Dark at Lord's. He was perhaps spurred in this endeavour by the success of the Lion Cricket Ball Works which Leonard Woodhams had set up in Southborough, which lies between Tonbridge and Tunbridge Wells, in 1845. For a notebook of Thomas Twort has survived, bound in white leather of the kind used for making cricket ball covers, dated 1 December 1851.

Thomas Twort learnt cricket ball making from Robert Dark of Lord's and set up his own workshop in Southborough near Tunbridge Wells in 1853. Here is his 'Receipt for Making Quilts' – still the same one hundred and twenty-five years later

Cricket Ball Stitching
Settled up 26 May 1851
19 Dozen & 10 Treble   £9   5   0

Taking in stitching of leather covers for other makers was a common practice continued late into the next century. For Thomas Twort I (as he must be called) it served as an introduction to setting-up as a full-dress cricket ball maker, which he did in 1853 by joining forces at the age

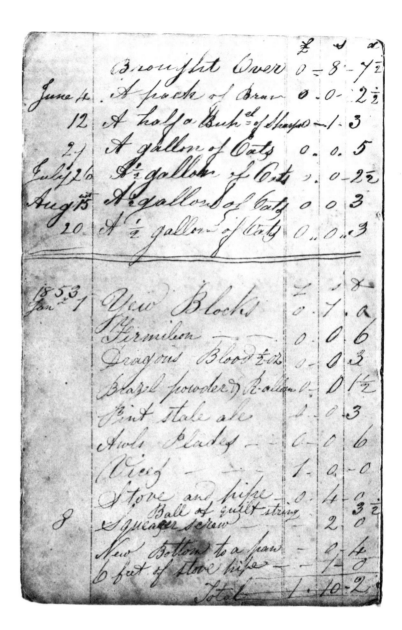

A cricket ball maker's earnings and expenses in the mid-nineteenth century – Tom Twort's accounts, 27 January 1853

of twenty-five with another young man of his acquaintance, John Martin, and acquiring a workshop in Southborough where Woodhams was already established. This was at 37 and 39 London Road which extended to Draper Street at the back. This fine terrace still stands in 1979. No 37 became, and remains, Geo Green's chemist shop – brass aprons below the window sills still carry the engraved legend 'Medical Hall'.

Tom remembered the notebook, of which only a few pages had been used to note progress on the rabbit front, and, not wishing to incur unnecessary expenditure, used it as the account book for his new venture. The first entry was dated 'Jan 1 1853'. A selection of items listed throws an interesting light on the raw materials which went into a cricket ball of the period.

	£	s	d
Yew blocks		7	0
Vermilion			6
Dragon's blood			3
Brazel Powder and Rock Alum			1½
Pint of stale ale			3
Ball of Quilt String			3½
½ lb of candles			3
Hide of wite leather		15	0
2 wood moulds turned			6
1 oz cochineal		1	2
1 oz of Termeriac			3
One hundredweight of best serklers		3	0
3 hanks of spinel		2	6
½ gallon of brown oats			3
Alum, termeriac and hops			11½
A ball of home made hemp			5
¼ lb of lard and ½ lb of suet			3
One pound of rosin			2
½ lb of dear suet			
For a 7 ft deal		3	0
Ran thread		1	6
For cricketz ball	2	2	0
carriage		7	0
Expenses to London		12	6
4 lb 11 oz of worsted		7	6
For Beas mole and Cups		8	3
2 dozen of printed papers		2	0
½ lb candle composition			8
for Painting and Riting a sine		7	6
1 Parcell of Balls to Windsor		1	0
Part on the Stamp		3	0
Corke & other expenses		15	0
Carriage for Cricket Balls		1	6
for Circlers money		5	6
Money for leather	1	4	0
Altering vise irons and brass		3	6
for an iron nut and plates		1	6
½ oz of Brissels			11

Buying two guineas worth of 'cricketz ball' which needed seven shillings for their carriage, suggests he bought a crate of the finished article to split asunder – perhaps from Dark – so that he had a pattern to follow in those pioneering days of going it alone.

At Dark's he noted the various processes he was shown which played a part in the making of cricket balls such as this 'receipt' for dressing white leather:

> For to dress one Bullick's Hide take two gallons of Lime in a quantity of cold water sufficient to cover the Hide kept moved

once every day for 8 or 9 days, afterwards unhardened flesh. Then put into water and then Bran, about a pack, with warm water covered about 4 days, and then after Being worked well on the Beam put into salt and alum Liquors, as hot as the Hide will bear 10th of Salt and 4th of alum moved well and left with Liquor four or five days hung in the shade, dried, cut up in slips 5½ in wide, washed, dried and straiked, dried and colored.

For the latter he had a 'Receipt for Making Red Colour':

Two quarts of water; ¼ lb Brazel Chips; 1 teaspoonful of Brown Indies Lake; 1 oz of Termeriac; one piece of Alum (size of walnut); a few hops; all to be boiled up together for one hour.

The mixture which would take stain from red leather and brighten the colour 'to be used cautiously' was a 'solution of muriate chloride of Tin; use a few drops, rub it on with a small piece of linen'. Oxalic acid he noted was the stuff for cleaning brown leather, but hot water must be added, and the solution shaken.

'Cricket Balls Sold and Money Received' 20 April 1853, by Thomas Twort of Southborough

He recorded with illustrations how Dark had taught him to make the all–important 'quilt' or core, his first observation being 'the wheit of the quilt hammer 3 pounds cast'.

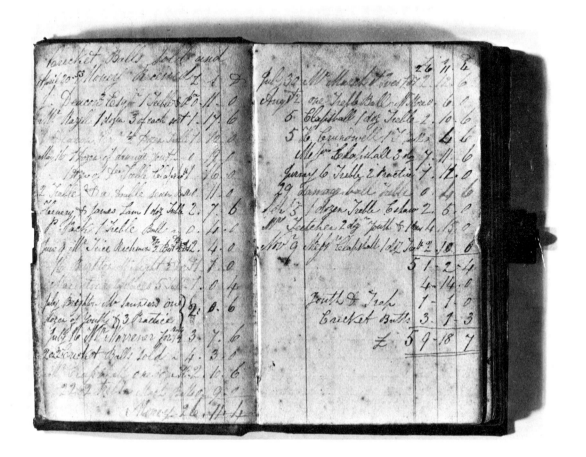

Take worsted and corke scolded in water; take one inch square [i.e. cube] of the hardest corke dry, then thin squares ⅛ thick wound round with four cord worsted, then weges – thin cork to make the round, fasen off and hammer now.

For good measure he wrote into this notebook all kinds of other information he picked up which might help him survive the rigours of life of mid-Victorian rural England, such as this Remedy for the Bite of a Mad Dog.

A Saxon forester by name Castell now of the venerable age of 82 unwilling to take to the grave with him a secret of much import to mankind has made public in the Leipzic Journal the means which he had used for 50 years and wherewith he affirms he has reserved many fellow beings and cattle from the fearfull death of hydrophobia. Take immediately warm vinegar or tepid water, wash the wound clean therewith and dry it; pour then upon the wound a few drops of muriatic acid because mineral acids destroy the poison of the saliva by whose means the evil effect of the latter is neutralised.

For children's broken out faces, take one pennyworth of the best tar, stand it under a fat mutton chop roasting by the fire about half an hour; keep it stirred. To cure the jaundice: 'one pint of gin, one ounce of termeric; three pennyworth of saffron and a small handfull of Rue; put it into a ½ pint glass bottle, shake it up and let it stand 24 hours. N.B. The gin is supposed to preserve the herbs. Try 1 pint of good spring water.' To make a man sober: 'liquid ammonia, spirits of Hartshorn, 6 drops of each'.

He reckoned he had made seventy dozen cricket balls that first year of operation (1853), and he totted up the Cost & Profitt to be

Money for 70 dozen balls   **£150–0–0**

Workmanship for 70 dozen Balls	
one with the other	80 –0–0
Papers and journeying	39 –0–0
Winding worsted and spinell	0–18–8
Wear of tools, fire & candle	£1– 2–4

£121 –1–0

Profitt on 70 dozen   £29 – 1 – 0
                                            20
                         ───────
                   70 /581

8.3 shillings per dozen

In a third notebook he recorded his output and sales, with the names and addresses of his customers and what they paid him in places like Guildford, Hastings, Canterbury, Chelmsford, Chichester, Rugby, Worcester, Oxford, Banbury. Typical entry for 1860:

Mr James Buchanan, 215 Piccadilly,			
2 doz Best Match Balls	£5	0	0
Mr Saunders, Hare & Billett, Blackheath			
1 doz	£3	6	0

Martin & Twort flourished in London Road, Southborough, for eight years, assisted from the start by Tom's father William Twort who knew something about leather working, for there was a time when he was a tanner. In 1858 thirty-year-old Tom married Elizabeth Parker of Rye who was two years his senior. Her father Sam Parker owned a boat which he sailed between Rye and Littlehampton, and there were unproven stories of Sam's smuggling activities. Tom must have been fully occupied with orders at his manufactory for he only found time to take one day off for his honeymoon – a trip to High Rocks, Tunbridge Wells. The following year a son was born, Thomas William – Thomas Twort II.

In 1861 the partnership of Martin and Twort was dissolved, but John Martin must have continued on his own, for the Southborough Post Office Directory of 1867 shows three cricket ball makers, Thomas Twort, Leonard Woodham(s) jnr, and John Martin. On the proceeds of his eight years in London Road, plus a loan he obtained from his cousins John and William Twort of Stockland Green, Speldhurst, Thomas bought some land in a new street which was being planned to lead off London Road and designated as Park Road, though at that time its route had only roughly been laid out on the fields and there were no houses in it. On this plot he built a two-storey workshop which for some reason became known as the Coach House, in spite of it being nothing of the sort, though it seems to have been the home of the birds and rabbits which Tom still liked to keep as pets, as well as a place for practising the craft of cricket ball making. On the rest of the ground he built a large, three-storey house for himself and his family (which grew in time to four sons and three daughters). It had sixteen rooms, purposely more than he needed so that Elizabeth his wife could let out some of them as apartments in order to pay back what he had borrowed from his two Speldhurst cousins. This house he called Belle Vue because of the fine, unrestricted view he had over Southborough Common, a state of affairs however which time altered all too soon. In the garden he planted fruit trees – he was a great one for grafting – with red currant and gooseberry bushes beneath; a cob nut bush by the gate, a walnut tree by the quilt shop door and a grape vine which wandered over the workshop roof – all of which survived to be admired and loved by those who lived and worked there for eighty years to come. If ever there was a rural industry this was it. Again, father William Twort helped him at the Park Road enterprise for the first ten years of its life – he died in 1871. By 1874 Thomas Twort II had begun his apprenticeship with his father. One other of Thomas's four sons, Edwin, entered the business; he made himself an efficient quilt maker and seamer. The other two, Albert and William, went into Inland Revenue. Thomas Twort II had no children, and the line was continued through Edwin Twort.

By the time Tom's two sons had joined what then became Thomas Twort & Sons, two more cricket ball makers had settled on the other side of London Road, Southborough: John Sales in Holden Park Road and Parker & Mercer in Taylor Street, who advertised themselves significantly as 'from the late R. Dark of Lord's Ground' to emphasise that Tom Twort was not the sole depository in the area of the Dark secret. Henry Parker was on his own by 1882, by which year it was John

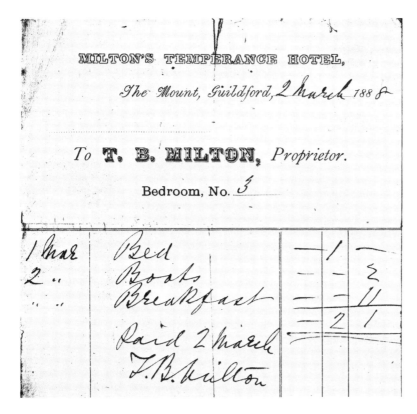

It was cheaper in 1888 – Tom Twort's bill for a night away from home

Martin & Son. Ten years later (1891) it was *William* Parker at 71 Taylor Street and *James* Sales at Modest Corner, with a newcomer George Avery at 9 and 11 Charles Street. When Thomas Twort I died in 1898, Leonard Woodhams was still operating at 123 London Road, but John Martin had gone. It is difficult not to think of him as some kind of relation of the William Martin who started making cricket balls at Hadlow in 1808, but there is no evidence that he was.

Farther north a member of the Clouts or Clout family was still making cricket balls in Sevenoaks in 1829. This was James Clout, presumably a descendant of the 'one named Clouts a famous cricket ball maker' whom John Baker of Horsham called on in June 1773 after the Hambledon Club versus All England match had finished early. It may have been the same man still working in his eighties. According to a 1829 Sevenoaks directory he coupled the activity with that of a druggist. The name was a familiar one in Sevenoaks. After the death of the cricketing 3rd Duke of Dorset at Knole in 1799 two of the three-man team who went to the house to make an inventory of his grace's pictures and furniture, which doubtless included a cupboard full of Pett cricket bats and maybe some Clout cricket balls, were Thomas Clout and James Clout.

By the 1860s there were no cricket ball makers in either Sevenoaks or Tonbridge, and even Kelly's Post Office Directory of 1882 listed only one in Tonbridge – Kingswood & Son of Great Bridge.

Thomas Twort set up his first cricket ball workshop with John Martin in 1853 at the back of no 37 London Road – The Parade – Southborough, Kent, seen here unchanged since those days. The house is now Green The Chemist, the last shop on the left with the blind down

Two names which appeared alongside Buchanan and Saunders in Tom Twort's notebook of customers were Mr J. Wisden of Coventry Street, London, and Mr W. Wisden of Duke Street, Brighton.

Brothers John and William Wisden both came from Brighton. John, the more famous of the two, was born there in 1826, in the house in Hampden Place where his father Thomas Wisden ran a building business. On the death of his father he went to live with a cricketer, Tom Box, in another part of Brighton. This legendary wicket keeper who played for Sussex for twenty-four years on end between 1832 and 1856 injected his enthusiasm for the game into the young Wisden with such success that in 1845 when only nineteen his protégé was chosen to play as a professional for Sussex against Kent. He continued to do so until 1863.

John Wisden was only five feet four inches tall and weighed seven stone, which naturally enough earned him the name of The Little Wonder, as soon as his reputation for fast and accurate bowling spread. He won a place in the All-England Eleven which had been formed by William Clarke in 1846 to tour England by railway and coach. Later, rebelling at Clarke's officiousness, he raised a breakaway team which he named the United England Eleven.

But merely playing cricket was not exercising the energies of the Little Wonder to the full, and in 1849 he persuaded another player called George Parr to join him in opening a cricket ground at Leamington which led in the following year to the formation of Parr and Wisden's Cricket Club which arranged fixtures with the MCC and the famous I Zingari touring club which had been formed in 1845.

Not content with this he launched a shop in Leamington in which he sold cricket bats and balls. The success of this encouraged him to join forces with an equally famous player and fellow member of the United England Eleven, Fred Lillywhite, third son of William Lillywhite the Nonpareil bowler, and the two of them took premises in London at no 2 Coventry Street off Piccadilly Circus which from 1855 they ran as a 'cricket and cigar depot'. The next year brother William opened his shop at no 3 Duke Street, Brighton, and W. Wisden & Co still trades as a sports outfitter in Duke Street to this day (could the name of the street have anything to do with the Penshurst cricket ball makers?) A Postal Directory of 1867 lists W. Wisden as a 'cricket bat maker and archery outfitter residing at 33 Ship Street' – probably his private residence, his shop being in Duke Street.

Fred Lillywhite dissolved the partnership in 1858 to go and set up a cricket bat making business with his brother John at 10 Seymour Street, Euston Square, with which William's eldest son James later also became associated. Indeed it was trading as James Lillywhite that the three of them opened in 1863 the sports shop in London which still flourishes in Piccadilly. In the 1890s there was a James Lillywhite operating from Queens Circus, Cheltenham, and a James Lillywhite & Frowd from Newington Causeway, Borough. This was the James Lillywhite who was a cousin of William. In 1893 the firm in the Borough took over the firm in Euston Square, and moved their West End showroom from 18 Cockspur Street to 24 Haymarket.

Diminutive John Wisden, cricketer and founder of the Almanack, whose London sports emporium John Wisden & Co sold cricket bats and balls along with a variety of other sports equipment. He died a bachelor in 1884, and his business was bought by his manager Henry Luff who took Wisden's into manufacture as well

"THE LITTLE WONDER"
from an old print in the possession of the Company

A tattered cover of a John
Wisden catalogue of 1894

John Wisden had an accident while playing rackets in 1863, when he was only thirty-seven. Since this put an end to his cricketing career, in spite of his former partner Fred having already pipped him to the post with his *Lillywhite's Guide to Cricketers* first published in 1849, Wisden decided to bring out another *Cricketers' Almanack* – and John's has survived where Fred's fell by the way in 1900.

John Wisden & Company's sports emporium in London was purely a retail exercise which sold the cricket bats and balls and other equipment of a variety of manufacturers. In 1860, as evidenced by Thomas Twort's sales book which records an order from Mr J. Wisden, the store was buying cricket balls from the Southborough manufactory and presumably selling them as 'Thomas Twort' balls. Later it seems Wisden were contracting with Thomas Twort to make cricket balls to their specification which they then retailed at their London showroom which moved to Cranbourn Street, as 'Wisden' balls.

A Wisden price list of 1882 – 'orders for regiments, ships and clubs who have accounts with us should be authorised by commanding or other responsible officer' – stated that 'our' cricket balls contained 'the best material and workmanship of Duke's and Darke's [sic] manufacture'. 'Duke has a working arrangement with "John Wisden", the famous Cranbourne Street firm,' wrote Ernest Ward in his footnote to the Farington Diary in 1927. 'Virtually Duke-cum-Wisden has something approaching a monopoly of the output of the classic cricket ball.'

Whoever made them they were marketed as Wisden's Cricket Balls. In an 'unsolicited' testimonial George Lohmann recommended Wisden's Cricket Balls on the grounds that 'they keep their shape and do not increase in size which is a great fault in many.'

The cricket balls available in 1882 were listed as:

'Match', best treble seamed   per doz   72s
                              single ball   7s 6d.
'Practice'   60s a doz.
Patent Catgut seamed   80s a doz.
                              (7s 6d single ball)

For long there had been co-operation among the Kent craftsmen. Each had their speciality, and if they received an order for a line which was outside their range they passed it to the firm they knew could supply. For instance in July 1884 Duke & Sons 'Cricket Ball, Bat, Stump, Leg Guard, Gauntlet, Tubular India Rubber Glove and Spiked Sole Manufactory' of Penshurst wrote to Mr Twort, Cricket Ball-Maker, Southborough:

Dear Sir
  We have an order for India for 1 doz Mens Size Balls for Practice @ 30/-. This is the price we must charge them at less 7½% off. We make no Mens Balls cheaper than 44/- Pr doz. Can you please supply us with them? if so and you will send them with invoices, we will send you a Post Oᶠ order for the amount and you will much oblige.
      Yours truly,
        Duke & Sons

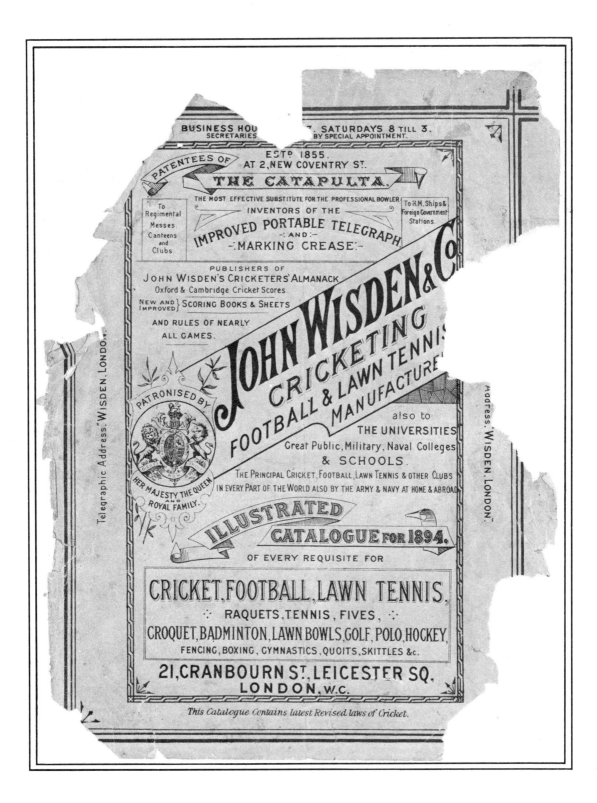

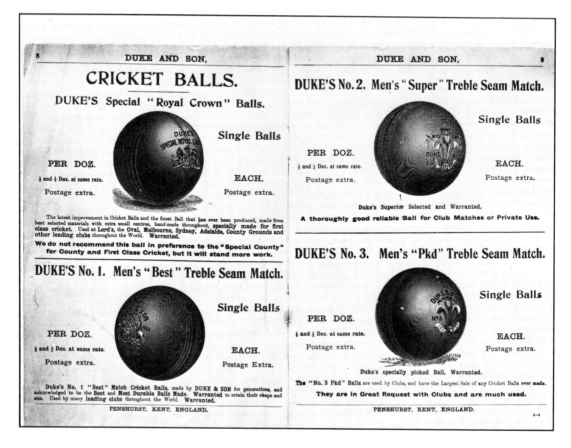

A page from a catalogue which illustrates the various grades of Duke cricket ball. When Wisden started manufacturing cricket balls on their own account, their charging tactics at their London retail showroom led to Duke & Son suing them in the High Court – and winning

It was in this year of 1884 that John Wisden died, a bachelor. With no son to inherit the business, it was bought by his manager Henry Luff. Ten years later Wisden's were selling Luff & Week's Patent 'Marvel' Ball at 7s 6d 'made on an entirely new principle, less hard than most balls while their flight and playing qualities are perfection'. Henry Luff had decided to go in for manufacturing himself. In 1896 he told Henry Edgar, a Wanstead vet who came to Cranbourn Street to buy one of Duke's well-known seven and sixpenny 'best' cricket balls, that for many years he had supplied nothing but Duke's and Dark's but two years ago Duke's were bad and Dark's very bad. He realised something had to be done about that, so started making cricket balls on his own account. In 1894, Luff told Edgar, it was a question of competition between himself and Duke; the following year he thought Duke would be left behind altogether.

Naturally Luff the retailer, now also a rival manufacturer to Duke, would feel obliged to push his own cricket balls at the expense of all others. Duke expected this and could have no objection to it so long as the competition was conducted fairly. But one day in 1896 James Phillips the Test umpire told the Penshurst firm that anyone who now asked at Wisden's London showroom for a no 1 'best' Duke ball (wholesale price 72s a dozen and retailing at 7s 6d each) was sold the inferior and cheaper no 4 ball (wholesale price 54s a dozen and retailing at 4s 6d or 5s each), and charged 7s 6d. Duke made enquiries which not only confirmed this but indicated that Wisden were systematically representing to their Cranbourn Street customers and the world at large that Duke had gone to the bad and the quality of their cricket balls had fallen off; that in particular they were too hard for county cricket – hence the 'less hard than most balls' line in the description of the Luff & Week 'Marvel' ball.

Henry Edgar had gone to Cranbourn Street on instructions from Penshurst and was able to report that the ball which Henry Luff had personally sold him across the counter purporting to be a Duke no 1 Best and charged at 7s 6d was in fact the inferior no 4 for which he should have been charged 5s. So long as Duke's name was on the ball no gentleman demeaned himself to worry about 'tradesmen's' details such as whether it was a no 1 or a no 4; it was a Duke and Duke was best. No gentleman moreover would harbour the thought that the venerated Wisden would try and trick him. Luff played on this, but when in 1898 he was sued by the Penshurst firm in the High Court before the Lord Chief Justice he protested it was all a mistake. He had acted throughout under a misapprehension, he said – in spite of the fact that William Smith, his manager of twelve years, gave evidence that during the period that he was in Luff's employ it was a regular practice to offer the inferior ball as Duke's best and charge 7s 6d for it. Luff insisted he had always ordered 'Crown' balls from Penshurst and these he understood were their first quality balls.

In fact the cheapest of the four grades which he was selling as 'the best' was clearly marked 'no 4 Match' and bore no royal arms or Prince of Wales feather. The superior ball had these and was marked 'no 1 Best'. Duke's counsel said Wisden's action over three years had hit his clients hard and was 'driving them out of the market'. They only wanted their reputation cleared. It was not a question of money. Lord Russell thereupon entered judgement for the plaintiffs, Duke, on Wisden undertaking only to sell Duke cricket balls in future under their proper denomination.

Thomas Ives was born in 1855 and was apprenticed at the age of nine to one of the cricket ball makers in the Tonbridge area, probably Duke. In 1875 having acquired *all* the skills of the cricket ball maker, he was determined to set up on his own. He turned to the man in the house next door, Charles Smith, who some say was manager for a time at Martin & Twort, though the head of the Twort family today refutes this. Whatever his previous experience, if any, Charles Smith joined Thomas Ives as partner in the cricket ball manufactory which the latter established in the workshop at the back of his house off Quarry Hill, Tonbridge, in 1875. After a few years Smith & Ives moved to a bigger workshop in Woodlands Road.

In 1896, with twenty years' profit in the kitty, the two of them decided to build a works on a really big scale, large enough to compete, as no other manufactory had yet done, with the Chiddingstone Causeway operation. They bought a site at the corner of Baltic Road and Quarry Hill Road, Tonbridge, and on it built a large, brick three-storey factory, in which they hung oil lamps from the ceiling by long wires by way of illumination. Into this prison-like structure Smith & Ives Ltd put some seventy craftsmen. It was a success from the start, and within a few months they had an order from Wisden in London for thirteen hundred dozen cricket balls.

It was the largest ever order, but its very size, which put the entire staff on Wisden work exclusively for weeks on end, led the customer to think, if such large orders were to continue, it would be more economic to have them met not by an outside supplier but by themselves. They at once offered to purchase the Baltic Road works lock, stock and barrel.

Charles Smith the business man was all for accepting the offer; Tom Ives, unwilling to let his own child be wrested from his keeping, opposed it. The two partners – and neighbours – were at loggerheads, but Ives finally relented, on condition that the factory under Charles Smith, who planned to stay on as manager under Wisden, only made cricket balls for Wisden and no one else. So it was agreed. But inevitably the time came when business was slack and Charles could not resist the temptation to take orders from customers other than Wisden, and when Tom Ives came to hear of it he was so angry with his old friend that he did not speak to him for seven years.

Ives took his share of the proceeds from the sale and with it bought himself a plot of land on the other side of Tonbridge at the end of a short row of Victorian villas in Preston Road, overlooking the railway line into Tonbridge station. Here he built, and opened – in 1897, the date is still on the wall for all to see – a cricket ball factory, Thomas Ives & Son. Tom employed some forty-five craftsmen in this sturdy two-storey building, and gave stitching and seaming to many outworkers in Tonbridge and to a small workshop in the back garden of a man who gave space for three others in Southborough.

The son in 'Thomas Ives & Son' was Tom's child Harry, born in 1879, who as a boy of fourteen sailed in a clipper to Australia with a view to joining the merchant navy, but came back to Preston Road after the one voyage and sat down to learn the cricket ball trade as his father had done.

A wing was added later to the Wisden factory in Baltic Road to give it its present L shape, but not before 1902 when Fred Sayers (who, in 1973 at the age of eighty-five, remembered the day well) joined as a lad of fourteen to learn the craft of cricket ball stitching from Bill Woolley – no relation of cricketer Frank Woolley and his brother Claude with both of whom, however, Fred had been at school. He was one of four apprentices among ninety-five craftsmen who included his uncle Sid Mathers, Jack Kingston, Charlie Apted, Dick Parmenter, Fred Wright, all closers, of whom in 1973 he was the only one left to look back and remember. 'Major' May was foreman.

Fred's father John was a nephew of the famous Sussex boxer Tom Sayers who took his only defeat in 1853, the year Tom Twort set up in Southborough, and fought his last fight in 1860 and is buried in Highgate Cemetery. The Sayers were Brighton people and Fred was born there in 1889. John Sayers was a butcher by trade who took up running, and for years was athletics coach to the gentleman cadets of the Royal Military Academy, Sandhurst.

By the time Fred Sayers had finished his two years apprenticeship at

Fred Sayers was eighty when he demonstrated his skill at hand-stitching to these lady cricketers from New Zealand who paid the Duke/Wisden cricket ball factory at Chiddingstone Causeway a visit in 1963

Baltic Road, he was averaging three dozen Best ninety-stitch cricket balls a week. Later he went on to seaming. Colin ('Charlie') Blythe the Kent cricketer recruited him into the Royal Engineers in 1914, and at Cambrai, where Charlie was killed, Fred was taken prisoner. Back at Tonbridge again after the armistice, he resumed his place at the cricket ball factory where he had already spent twelve years before joining up.

When the factory was on short time in the summer months, in order to prevent a build-up of too large stocks, the management encouraged their workforce to take jobs at cricket grounds. Fred Sayers was fifty-three years on the St Lawrence Ground, the Kent County Cricket Club's headquarters at Canterbury, and thirty-six of these as head gateman. In this period he served under seven managers. When he had done fifty years the club celebrated his jubilee by giving him a benefit. Some £400 or so was raised from four collections at the Dover, Maidstone, Canterbury and Tunbridge Wells grounds, and from fivers sent from the likes of Lord Harris and Lord Cornwallis – a mark of the respect and affection with which Fred Sayers was held in the county over all those years.

Thus the end of the nineteenth century saw three cricket ball makers in Tonbridge: John Wisden & Co at Baltic Road (though Kelly's of 1899 gives their address as The Drive which runs off Baltic Road – perhaps their offices); Thomas Ives & Son at Preston Road; and, by the bridge over the Medway, a unit which called itself the Kent Cricket & Football Manufacturing Company and was owned by Duke, which may have been the former Kingswood & Son.

In Southborough Thomas Twort & Son were still flourishing under the direction of old Tom Twort I and his two sons, Tom II and Edwin. They were making cricket balls also for Charles Lillywhite & Co, who in 1893 were advertising, from the Twort address of 28 Park Road, their Superior Treble Seamed Balls from 40s a dozen – 'Every ball is fitted with the original Hand Made Spring Quilt and is confidently recommended and guaranteed – NO MACHINE WORK.'

When in 1860 Horace Henry Hitchcock built himself a large, brick house facing the village green at Hildenborough, which lies to the north of Tonbridge on the way to Sevenoaks, his wife and family took one look at its gaunt, uninviting features and refused to live in it. It had an unwelcoming central front door, on either side of which were two echoing, high-ceilinged rooms, with two similar apartments on the floor above. It was more of a factory than a home, and a factory it became. H. H. Hitchcock bowed to his family's condemnation of his architectural tastes and, rather than knock the place down and start again, he recruited craftsmen from Penshurst and Tonbridge, and put them to work in what were planned as drawing-room and dining-room, bedroom and bathroom, to make 'Hitchcock' cricket balls. There were no 'usage' worries in those days; no need for planning permission. The business succeeded, and by the end of the nineteenth century, with the aid of Edward Harrison ('Ned') Hitchcock, Horace's son, an amateur oboeist of distinction who sat down beside his father's employees and learnt every process, it was making a useful contribution to the cricket ball output of the area. A wooden annexe had to be built out into the garden to make the original building T-shaped to house the extra craftsmen.

To the south of Tonbridge – at least in 1887 when he had an advertisement on the back of Frederick Gale's *The Game of Cricket* – J. Rudman was making cricket balls at 19 Standen Street.

But the Quarry Hill – Hildenborough – Penshurst firms did not have the field entirely to themselves. The Martins on the Maidstone side of Tonbridge had never stopped making cricket balls since William Martin had opened his workshops at Hadlow in 1808. His son Harry (H. Martin & Son) engaged in a diversionary tactic in London in mid-century, and when Harry's son Edward got a job as keeper of the Christchurch Ground at Oxford he provided what was expected of him in that role, a bat repairing service, which inevitably involved a certain amount of bat making. It seems also that he set up a cricket ball making exercise (which he knew more about), something not expected of a ground keeper.

Edward Martin was born at Brenchley in Kent in 1814 and played cricket for the county from 1845 to 1851. He went to Oxford to take up his appointment at Christchurch Ground in 1847. However long he stayed there, it is likely that the family business of cricket ball making never left Kent and continued without interruption, like Edward's appearance for its first eleven. The firm was no longer at Hadlow but at Teston, a few miles to the east, on the western outskirts of Maidstone. Cricket ball making at Oxford ran parallel to the activity at Teston.

According to local intelligence, Teston had originally been Teeson but when the railway came, a signwriter, hired to produce a board, wrote TESTON by mistake, and the company refused to waste further money by having it altered. But everyone who lived there naturally continued to call it TEESON, as they do to this day, though they and everyone else copies the signwriter's spelling.

With Edward in Oxford the Teston business was run by his son (?) Thomas, and in his name (T. Martin). Maybe before, but certainly by, the 1860s, the Martin home was the village shop/post office in the centre of Teston which they rented from Roger Leigh of Barham Court. Cricket ball making was undertaken at first in the kitchen of the house which formed part of the shop, and later, when business improved, in the single storey workshop they built out into the garden at the back, to which was afterwards added a wooden first floor.

Having to weigh out the rice and sort out the postal orders soon became a chore cricket ball makers trying to cope with an expanding market could do without, and in the mid-1860s they were looking for someone to whom they could sub-let the grocery and post office side to leave them free to concentrate on the more exciting, and exacting, exercise in the workshop behind. And along came the Readers.

The Readers were East Enders who came to Kent every autumn for the hop and fruit picking. Alfred Valentine Reader's parents liked it so much they decided to move their household from dark smoky mid-Victorian London to the light and air of the Kentish countryside, to the little village of Loose just to the south of Maidstone. Alfred planned to

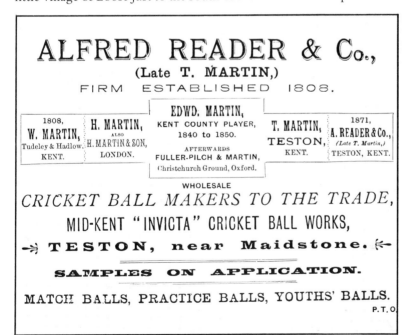

seek employment with the brewing fraternity and succeeded in getting a job with Fremlins. But he found it increasingly difficult to reconcile his religious views with his dependency on a trade which caused large-scale drunkenness of which he could not fail to be a daily witness. To Alfred Reader salvation was an end to be pursued above all others; in his pocket he kept a small notebook crammed with pencilled passages from the books of Daniel and Revelation. Over-indulgence in alcohol, which he seemed to be aiding and abetting, would always constitute a barrier to the gates of heaven. So he was soon looking for a way of providing for his family which would prick his conscience less.

He came to hear about Tom Martin wanting to rid himself of the shop and post office at nearby Teston, and in no time had arranged with Roger Leigh, the landlord, to become the tenant of this property and have the more morally acceptable duties of postmaster and village shopkeeper. In these first years Alfred Reader and Tom Martin each minded their own business. One day at the end of October 1869 Edward Martin fell from his horse while returning from hunting with the Southdown hounds. He was taken to his house at Barcombe in Sussex, and two days later he was dead. He was only fifty-eight. Shortly afterwards, it seems, his son Tom Martin died too, or perhaps he just decided to retire and withdraw from business worries. Tom had no children, and in 1870 he bequeathed, or made a gift of, the Martin cricket ball works and all its goodwill to the three or four craftsmen who worked for him and Alfred Reader, in equal shares.

Alfred knew nothing about cricket ball making and left the men to get on with it, while he continued to dispense stamps and groceries from the front part of the establishment. But without a traveller to solicit orders from clubs and schools as Tom Martin had done, business began to decline. Soon it was in debt. The sleeping partner saw his inheritance in jeopardy, and suggested to his fellow shareholders they might consider assigning him their shares in return for his paying their debts. They willingly accepted, and in 1871 'T. Martin' became 'A. Reader'. In the same year, back at the university town which Edward Martin had vacated, Benjamin Harse, 'sole maker of the noted Oxford Ball' as he was to style himself, set up at 81 St Mary's Road.

The handing over at Teston did not put an end to Martin activity in London. The London Post Office Directory of 1877 carried this extended entry, of which the reader can make what he will:

> Martin, H. & Son; warehouse, 446 Strand; offices, 4 Adam Street, WC; wholesale cricket ball makers (established 1808). 1808 W. Martin, Tudeley & Hadlow, Kent; T. Martin, Teston, Kent; 1835 to 1873 Edward Martin, Kent County Player 1840 to 1850, afterwards Fuller, Pilch & Martin, Christchurch Ground, Oxford; H. Martin, Surrey Square, London; H. Martin & Son, London. The sales have exceeded 600,000 Matchballs, practice balls, youth's balls and trap balls.

What happened, and where, between 1835 and 1873, (linked with the name of Edward Martin who played for Kent between 1845 and 1851, went to Oxford in 1847 and died in 1869) only the writer of the entry can know. But he may have meant that whatever other activities took place in London and Oxford, cricket ball making by some member of

RECALLING attention to the best-selling lines and the most famous patterns in cricket balls, we especially emphasize the fact that our balls are used by the leading players at Lords, "The Oval," and on all famous County Cricket Grounds. Balls for use in the tropics, on matting pitches and bare grounds, are manufactured with specially dyed covers, guaranteed to retain their color.

Our experience in manufacturing cricket balls extends over a Century, and by concentrating on their production we are able to supply goods of exceptional quality and value.

THE
'Special Imperial Crown'
(Nulli Secundus)

This line is an excellent one to concentrate on. It is one of the most popular of our best makes which the trade repeatedly re-order.

PRICE LIST

Owing to the continued rise in price of leather, etc., the following prices will be advanced 5 ; this will be added at foot of invoice

Per doz.

No. 102 "Special Imperial Crown" (Nulli Secundus)		45/-
No. 103c Ditto Colonial (Covers dyed red throughout)	...	46/6
No. 104 "County Match" (Silk and Gut Sewn)		45/-
No. 105c Ditto Colonial (Covers dyed red throughout)	...	46/6
No. 106 "County" (Gut Sewn)	...	42/-
No. 107c Ditto Colonial (Covers dyed red throughout)	...	43/6
No. 108 "Invicta" (Special Match)		40/-
No. 109c Ditto Colonial (Covers dyed red throughout)	...	41/6

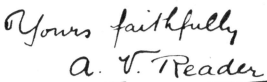

Yours faithfully
a. V. Reader

the Martin family continued in Kent over the thirty-eight years from the death or retirement of William Martin in 1835 to responsibility for the Teston business being firmly in the hands of Alfred Reader by 1873.

Be that as it may, Alfred Reader was not concerned with what H. Martin & Son were doing in London, and with evangelical fervour set about putting new life into the dying cricket ball works at Teston and spreading the news to those who sought an alternative to a Duke and Twort, that the answer to their prayers was a Reader. Defiantly he gave his factory a name that was the motto of the county of Kent, 'Invicta' – unconquered.

Only two of Alfred Reader's sons grew to manhood, Archibald Alfred and Joseph Villiers. (A daughter of his was still living in Harrogate in 1978.) Well before they were of an age to help their father, the running of the cricket ball business had become a full-time occupation for Alfred, and he bequeathed the village shop and post office to the manager. A. A. Reader and J. V. Reader, who was three years younger and all his life suffered from failing eyesight, both took their places on the benches at the Mid-Kent Invicta Works as soon as they had finished their schooling. The small account book which Alfred Reader kept in 1888 shows that he was making regular weekly payments to six wage earners: P. Page, W. Page, J. Hall, J. Wood, A. Reader, V. Reader. The scale of the operation at this time is indicated by a stock list which recorded a stock of fifteen qualities ranging from thirty-six dozen 'B. Match' balls at 36s a dozen (£64 16s) to Youth's at 5s a dozen, with a total value of £170 11s.

On occasion they were asked to turn out a product that was not a Reader ball but one that resembled a competitor's. In June 1891 they received a memo from Shaw & Shrewsbury of Nottingham:

> Referring to the sample Ball you sent some time ago, could you now supply us? It must be exactly on Duke's principle and resemble it in every way. We should require 300 to 400 dozens per year and must be of the best possible quality. We should prefer having them made in our own place and it can possibly be arranged. We shall be pleased to hear from you on the subject.

The strangeness of the request presumably accounts for its survival, though Alfred Reader's answer is not on record.

Benjamin Harse of Oxford offers Catgut-Sewn cricket balls in *Athletic News Cricket Annual*

By 1895 the number of craftsmen on the Reader payroll had grown to thirteen, one of whom was still J. Villiers Reader. The two brothers became fully acquainted with every process, but Archie became the leather expert superintending the preparation and dyeing of the hides, and Villiers concentrated on the manufacturing side. A notebook of 1895 shows that Reader customers include Martin's Oxford competitors Harse Brothers, Lillywhite & Frowd, 'Wotton [Winton ?] College, Winchester', and an export account Holdsworth, Macpherson & Co of Sydney, New South Wales.

The Oxford firm had obviously been weak on the promotional side, for from a letter which a friend of Alfred Reader called Walter wrote from Hastingden in Lancashire in April 1887, it seems they had failed to get their name across even after sixteen years.

> ... The clerk tells me they [E. J. Riley of Accrington] get nearly all their balls from a Mr Arch (I don't know if that is the correct spelling) of Oxford. He seems to think nobody's balls equal to his, but I cannot see how yours can be beaten in quality at any rate; of the price I am no judge.

Of course Harse were saddled with an unfortunate name from the point of view of promotion if they had to rely on too many salesmen with the inability to aspirate.

Alfred Reader made rapid progress – though of course he was building on a foundation of sixty-three years. But he was always willing to learn. Someone told him of a way of producing a 'bright scarlet' and he jotted it down among the names and addresses: 'Cochineal, alum & Carbonate of Potash'. He established a London office at 8 Wood Street Square, EC, which later moved to 47 Moor Lane, EC, and eventually appointed agents in Wellington and Capetown. He adopted two trade marks: one with the Kent Invicta crest; and another, 'The Centurial', incorporating three cricket balls beneath a crown and lion rampant, which was probably not devised till the centenary of 1908, unless it was meant to indicate that these were the cricket balls it was easy to hit a century with. Price lists and catalogues carried the message to all parts of Britain and The Empire. 'Balls for use in the tropics, on matting pitches and bare grounds, are manufactured with specially dyed covers, guaranteed to retain their colour.' Bright scarlet? 'Special attention is given to the manufacture of Balls for Colonial use ... These Balls are extensively used in India and the Colonies, and particularly in South Africa where Reader's reputation is unique.'

A crudely printed price list of the 1890s divided twenty-three types of ball into three qualities, A, B and C, without fancy brand names. Heading the list was the Four Seamed Presentation Match ball at 50s a dozen. 'Best Double Seamed, Catgut and Silk Sewn, County Match' came second at 45s a dozen. The seven A quality balls ranged from 50s to 30s a dozen; the seven B quality from 40s to 24s; and the nine C quality from 37s to 16s a dozen. These of course were the prices to the trade. 'We Do Not Compete With Our Customers' had been the policy from the start. 'We wish it to be distinctly understood that under no circumstances do we accept orders from Clubs or Schools.' Alfred Reader & Co were Wholesale Cricket Ball Makers to the Trade, and let there be no mistake.

A later, and more elegant, price list on yellow card bore a photographic likeness of the bearded founder with an endearing twinkle in his eye. Over a facsimile of his signature, he drew attention to the fact that his cricket balls were 'used by the leading players at Lord's [so the Dark monopoly had gone!] "The Oval", and on all famous County Cricket Grounds'. The qualities were given high sounding names. 'Special Imperial Crown' balls cost 45s a dozen, 'ditto Colonial (covers dyed red throughout)' 46s 6d. These were the most expensive on the list – wholesale prices again of course. Treble Seamed Regulation cost the trade 28s a dozen and Double 26s. But an overprinting in red warned that 'owing to the continued rise in the price of leather etc' prices would be advanced five per cent. A photograph of 'Barnes MCC, England's Famous Bowler' appeared on the front implying his recommendation without actually giving it.

In the metropolis in 1845 another cricket ground opened which demanded a local supply of the tools of the game just as had Thomas Lord's enterprise in St John's Wood. In 1844 the Montpelier Club which had been founded in 1796 leased the oval-shaped market garden in Kennington in south-east London from the Duchy of Cornwall for twenty-one years. From this club emerged the Surrey Cricket Club which the following year made The Oval its headquarters.

Five years before The Oval opened, when Matilda Dark was proprietor of the cricket bat workshop at Lord's, another lady cricket bat maker, Eleanor Page, set up a similar factory at 7 Orange Row, Kennington Road. In 1842 the firm became Mrs E. Page & Son. By the time the Surrey Cricket Club had started operations at The Oval the Page enterprise was well established. The club was anxious to keep everything that appertained to Surrey Cricket in the county, and in 1846 placed orders with the Pages for both cricket bats and cricket balls. To their chagrin the Pages had to admit that though they could sell the club Page bats made in Surrey, they could only supply someone else's cricket balls made in Kent. Within five years however they had remedied the situation by luring someone from Duke's workshop, which had just moved from Redleaf, to come and show them how to do it. On the back of Bat's *Cricketer's Manual* of 1851 they were proudly advertising that theirs was 'the only place in London where balls are made on the premises'.

Eleanor Page eventually dropped out and entrusted the business to her two sons William Thomas Page (1814–1876) and Edward James Page (1819–1879). In the last year of his life Edward Page took an advertisement in the first issue of the new *Cricket and Football Times* (2 May 1878):

> Edwd J. Page, 188 & 190 Kennington Park Road, SE
> E. J. Page's Cricket Balls are used in all the great matches
> at The Oval

He had become the Robert Dark of Kennington.

By the time Edward Page had died, the firm which continued in his name, was no longer able to substantiate the claim that it was the only place in London where cricket balls were made on the premises. By the 1880s J. T. Finney had set up as a cricket ball maker in Windmill Lane,

Cricket ball makers Thomas Twort and Richard Daft, and cricket bat makers C. Lillywhite and E. J. Page, vie for custom in the advertisement pages of the 1 June 1893 edition of *Cricket, A Weekly Record of the Game*

New Hampton and he was probably one of many who had jumped on the wagon since the opening of The Oval in 1845. There was for instance the firm run by W. E. Bussey and J. S. Pinder at Museum Works, Peckham. These two filed a patent in 1885 (no 122, 3 January) for improvements in manufacturing balls for cricket, football and other games. 'First, using wire, preferably copper, instead of hemp, cat-gut etc. in stitching the cover; and second, inserting a rubber sheet between the outer casing and the inside (technically known as the "quilt") of the ball.' This was known as 'cable' sewn.

In 1890 F. H. Ayres of 111 Aldersgate Street and G. F. Evans of 222 Railton Road, Herne Hill patented a method of dyeing cricket ball covers (no 4935 of 29 March). 'The leather cover, preferably rendered waterproof subsequently, is dyed by means of eosine in methylated spirit or alcohol to a much greater depth than usual, so that scratches and the like will not show a slight streak. The dye may be forced into the leather by pressure or induced to enter by employment of a vacuum.'

4 Spliced Bats and Cane Handles

Cricket bat craftsmen of the 19th century

The Duke of Dorset of Knole, to whom the systemisation of cricket owed so much, died in 1799 at the age of fifty-four. It was the passing not only of a century but of an era in cricket history. When the nineteenth century opened, the Marylebone Cricket Club had been established, with the Duke's aid, in the London borough of St Marylebone, for some thirteen years. The practice of the game was regulated by a system of laws corrected and improved by the decisions of that club and 'generally adopted by practitioners in all parts of the kingdom', as William Lambert wrote in *The Cricketers Guide* or A Concise Treatise of the Noble Game of Cricket as practised by the most eminent players, published in Lewes in 1816. The Hambledon Club, which had been the lawgiver for most of its life, is thought to have closed in 1796 (though there were still references to it in the 1800s).

Lambert claimed that a manual such as his had never before been attempted. In fact, Thomas Boxall of Ripley in Surrey had anticipated him with his *Rules and Instructions for Playing at the Game of Cricket* published by J. Blake of Maidstone in 1803. A copy of this came to light in a testator's box in a London bank in 1929. It reprinted the New Articles on the Game of Cricket as settled and revised at the Star and Garter, Pall Mall, 25 February 1774 by a Committee of Noblemen and Gentlemen of Kent and C. Boxall's book and *The Laws of Cricket* published by Reeve in 1755 were the first books on the game; but Baxters, the Lewes printers who persuaded Lambert, a noted player, to lend his name to their publication, considered the practice of cricket still sufficiently fluid in 1816 to justify a guide 'to reduce Cricket playing to a system and therefore render it liable to as little variation as possible'.

An important aspect of this systemisation was seeing that everyone played with roughly the same equipment. It was a question of fair play. To get runs by a bigger bat rather than superior skill was not playing the game. Lambert's Guide of 1816 quoted the latest Laws of Cricket as merely specifying that the ball should not weigh less than five-and-threequarters ounces, and the bat should not exceed four-and-a-quarter inches in the widest part. A footnote commented:

> There is no particular height for a bat, but it is adviseable not to have it higher than twenty-one inches in the pod and as much narrower and shorter as may be thought proper.

Aquila Clapshaw (1801–60) – a small portrait by an unknown artist in Lord's Museum – the fourth generation of a cricket bat making family which traces its origin to Aquila Clapshoe, born in 1714. The firm of Aquila Clapshaw & Son continued to make bats into the 1970s. The portrait was presented to Lord's in 1963 by Miss P. C. Hyslop, the subject's great granddaughter

Ideas on what was proper no doubt varied from one part of the country to another, and those who made cricket bats enjoyed considerable latitude in creating them in accordance with their own and their clients' preferences. A cricket bat could still be something very personal.

In his two-part review of John Nyren's *Young Cricketer's Tutor* in the *Gentleman's Magazine* of July and September 1833, Rev John Mitford wrote vividly of the bat of a master Surrey cricketer, William Beldham (1766–1862) which had been made personally for him by a master craftsman, alas unknown.

> He took the ball, as Burke did the House of Commons, between wind and water; not a moment too soon or late. Beldham still survives. He lives near Farnham; and in his Kitchen, black with age but, like himself, still untouched with worms, hangs the trophy of his victories; the delight of his youth, the exercise of his manhood, the glory of his age – his BAT. Reader! believe me when I tell you I trembled when I touched it; it seemed an act of profaneness, of violation. I pressed it to my lips, and returned it to its sanctuary.

There was a revision of the laws by the MCC in 1830, but three years later John Nyren was able to comment:

> The Bat – must not be more than four inches and a quarter in width at the broadest part. There are no restrictions as to the height of the bat; it may be as tall, short or narrow as the player chooses; twenty one or twenty two inches however will be found the most convenient height for it, independently of the handle.

In 1835 the MCC, which had moved to the present Lord's Cricket Ground in 1814, restricted the length of the bat to thirty-eight inches, but for some time there were still players who thought they could get away with variations of width. A match was played at Durham on 11 November 1844 between William Mather and William Williams. In his innings Mather had made fifteen runs when Williams objected (rather belatedly) to the width of his bat and claimed the fifteen runs should be cancelled. According to the report of the match in *Bell's*, Williams's own bat turned out to be an eighth of an inch wider than Mather's!

The solid wood, one-piece 'plain match' implement was the only kind of cricket bat well into the nineteenth century. Old craftsmen like Aquila Clapshoe, the Petts, John Small senior and John Small junior continued to make them, and new firms like Edward Ayres who started making cricket bats in Clerkenwell in 1810 as part of a general cabinet-making and wood-turning business, began with nothing else.

In the drawings of eight bats portrayed in books by W. G. Grace and Frederick Gale, no 5 is dated 1800. The blade runs straight into the handle, all from one piece of wood. No 6, said Grace, was 'marked on back with brass brads 1827 – belonged to John Bowyer and weighed about 2¾ lb'. This was also a one-piece bat. Who made these bats of 1800 and 1827 it is impossible to say. Christopher Thorn's name does not appear in Kent's Directory of London, Westminster and Southwark for the year 1800. It seems he had closed down by then; or he may have moved to the country. Pigot's Directory of London for 1826/27, unlike Kent's, is divided into trade classifications, but disappointingly there is no list beginning 'Cricket ...' between 'Cotton Wick Makers' and 'Crape and Bombazine Dressers'.

Gale talked about bats to John Bowyer at Mitcham in 1871 when the old player was eighty-one. He had played his first match sixty-six years before the conversation took place – 1805. The bats used by players then, he said, were 'much superior to those specimens of old bats which are occasionally now found in country villages; but though they are heavier and thicker than those now in use, the weight and balance were carefully considered'.

But Bowyer's bat of 1827, if typical of a 'best' bat used by a top player, was among the last of its kind. For, ten years later, there is evidence of a bat with a separately made blade and handle, not only in a drawing but in the bat itself. In the MCC museum at Lord's is a spliced bat and with it this inscription:

> This is one of Cobbett's bats of 1837, and it is presented to the MCC as a standing reproof to those who maintain that in the days of Fuller Pilch, E. G. Wenman, Marsden and Messrs C. G. Taylor, N. Felix and Alfred Mynn and others, men played with clubs.

There was no splice to the bat which thirty-eight-year-old Fuller Pilch is holding in this picture of 1841, but when he started making cricket bats with Edward Martin at the Christchurch Ground, Oxford, he probably made both types. An unspliced product of the Pilch and Martin partnership which once belonged to Alfred Mynn (1807–51) is in Lord's pavilion

It was a present from Frederick Gale in 1880. The incident which provoked the reproof has not been recorded but, though the players he mentions had certainly never used 'clubs', for much of their careers they would have used solid wood bats of the no 4 and no 5 type in W. G.'s illustrations.

Fuller Pilch was born in Norfolk in 1803 and when he first played for the county at Lord's as a lad of seventeen in 1820 he would certainly have used a 'plain match' bat. There is an unspliced bat of his in the collection in Lord's pavilion, and the bat he holds in the G. F. Watts portrait of him has no splice. But between 1830 and 1845 when he made ten centuries he probably experimented with both types, and by the time he was ending his cricketing career in the 1860s he was no doubt entirely won over to the 'new' form.

At the end of his life he was himself involved in cricket bat making, as has been seen, becoming associated with Edward Martin at the Christchurch Ground in Oxford. At Lord's there is a cricket bat which belonged to Alfred Mynn (1807–51) 'made by F. Pilch and E. Martin Oxford' – and it has no splice. 'Edward Martin' became 'Fuller Pilch & Martin'. A descendant of Fuller Pilch still runs a sports shop in Norwich.

James Cobbett's cricketing career, as his life, was short. He died in 1842 at the age of thirty-eight. In 1837 he played at Lord's as what was called a 'given man' for Hertfordshire against Cambridge University, and the bat of that date which Frederick Gale presented to Lord's was probably the one with which Cobbett scored 58 and 90 on that occasion. He would not only have used the bat but have made it. His home was at Frimley in Surrey, but his cricket bat workshops – if in fact he actually ran the business himself and did not merely lend his name to it – were in one of the streets round Lord's. Three spliced Cobbett bats are in the Gray-Nicolls collection at Robertsbridge: one of 1820 with 'J. Painter' stamped on each corner, another made in 1836 with 'Fred Lillywhite' in the corner, and an undated bat with a bone (?) insertion from the top of the handle to the end of the splice at right angles to the shoulder.

But the name of James Cobbett did not appear in the section headed 'Cricket-Bat and Stump Makers' which featured in Robson's London Commercial Directory of 1835. Only two names were given:

> Clapshaw, Ag [sic]   23 Peerless Row, City Road
> Dark, Ben   St John's Wood Road

Ben Dark was the eldest of the three Dark brothers.

The Clapshoe workshop which had set up in Turnham Green in 1780 was firmly established by the dawn of the nineteenth century; and in 1803 the family decided to call themselves Clapshaw. The second son of Aquila II, Charles Clapshaw, who was born in Froyle in 1776, was designated 'carpenter' in documents of 1813, but by the time he died in 1851 he was unmistakably 'cricket bat maker'. Charles's son by his first wife Sarah Seward, whom he married at Farnham in 1798 – Aquila III, born in Farnham in 1801 – served his apprenticeship as a turner, as he is described as late as 1822. But he is certainly the 'Clapshaw, Ag' who turns up in Robson's 1835 directory with an address in City Road.

The Turnham Green workshop does not seem to have been aban-

'Cobbett' bats abound, but few of them are likely to have been made by James Cobbett (seen here) whose short life ended in 1842 at the age of thirty-eight. He came from Frimley in Surrey, but his cricket bat workshops were near Lord's cricket ground

doned; the London accommodation was probably a retail outlet and warehouse – and a residence. Peerless Row still existed in 1979 – as Peerless Street, running into Old Street. Indeed Turnham Green seems to have been retained well into the nineteenth century, for the inscription on a bat in the pavilion of Southgate Cricket Club, a gift to mark the club's centenary 1855–1955, reads:

> This bat was made in 1854 by the firm of Aquila Clapshaw and Son, then of Turnham Green and since 1890 of Southgate. Presented by Bernard I. Taylor.

Aquila III was joined by his younger brother Charles who was born in Farnham in 1813. The two of them moved their London office in 1840 to New Street, City Road, and five years later to 2 Nelson Place, City Road, but this time without Charles who set up on his own at 3 West Place, Islington Green. The year 1850 found Aquila Clapshaw at 3 Upper Fountain Place, City Road, and Charles Clapshaw at 26 Queen's Row, Pentonville Road.

Aquila III's son, Samuel Clapshaw, was born in Peerless Row in 1837, the year of Queen Victoria's succession. Sam finished his apprenticeship

No hump on the back of this pre-Grace cricket bat made by one of the Clapshaw family now in Lord's Museum as a cricket bat maker in 1856, and after four years as a journeyman took over the business as a master cricket bat maker on the death of his father in 1860. His uncle Charles Clapshaw was still in competition. An Aquila Clapshaw bat dated 1860 is in the museum at Lord's, and it may be one of the bats which Prince Albert, husband of Queen Victoria, played with at the St John's Wood ground. The Prince Consort not only bought his cricket bats from Aquila Clapshaw & Son but gave the firm his royal warrant. Prince Albert died in 1861, so this would have been during the regime of Aquila III, whose picture, presented in 1963 by his great-granddaughter Miss P. C. Hyslop, also resides in Lord's Museum. Two of Sam's sisters married cricket bat makers: Sarah married John Crane in 1848, and Emma married George White in 1855.

A third member of the family set up in London in 1856 – Mark Clapshaw, with an address at 14 Lower Kennington Green. Sam was joined by his brother Albert who was born at the New Street house in 1842 (and died in Wakefield in 1885). In the 1860s and 1870s some dozen craftsmen were employed in the Aquila Clapshaw workshops in City Road. Each of them turned out ten to twelve cricket bats a day, some twenty-five going through the shop at any one time. Around 1870 Sam moved the business from City Road to Palace Road, New Southgate, and took into partnership Louis Salmon; and when Sam died in 1876 it was under the latter's aegis that Aquila Clapshaw & Salmon, as it became, continued to trade for another hundred years. The firm's products were awarded gold medals at the Melbourne Exhibitions of 1888 and 1889, and the Jamaica Exhibition of 1891. In February 1900 the company registered a trade mark featuring a figure of W. G. Grace. The three sons of Louis Salmon continued in the firm up to the 1940s.

The Clapshaws had plenty of competition in London. At Lord's there is a bat dated 1830 made by W. H. Caldecourt (1802–59), another player who, like James Cobbett, had cricket bats made in his name, or perhaps actually made them, in a workshop at 14 Townshend Road, St John's Wood. In the Post Office London Directory of 1840 'Page, Mrs E., 7 Orange Row, Kennington Road' was still in business, but two years later she had become 'Page, Mrs E. & Son'. A newcomer in 1842 was William Dibb of 83 Friar Street, Blackfriars Road. William Gladman came to 190 Bethnal Green Road in 1845 and two others set up near Lord's, Thomas Couchman at 3 Hill Street, Regent's Park Road, and Richard Allen at 27 North Street, Lisson Grove. Richard Allen styled himself (in advertisements) Cricket Bat and Stump Manufacturer 'nephew and successor to the late James Cobbett', though later what was described as 'Cobbett's Cricket Bat Factory' was operating from 56 Capland Street, Grove Road, Marylebone. In 1850 the Pages had become simply 'Page Brothers & Co' at 6 Kennington Row and 11 Kennington Oval – Eleanor had retired, having led the team since 1840. Newcomers in 1850 were widely spread; John Bartlett in Lambeth, Charles Bentley in Vauxhall, Edward Block in Southwark; John Hulme in Whitechapel, John Ross in Walworth, Alfred Clark in Marylebone, Frank Ogden in Leicester Square. John Lillywhite had come to Princes Terrace, Caledonian Road, and 'Lillywhite & Wisden' to 2 New Coventry Street and 7 Sidney Alley, Leicester Square.

THE CRICKET BAT MAKING CLAPSHAWS
Five Generations

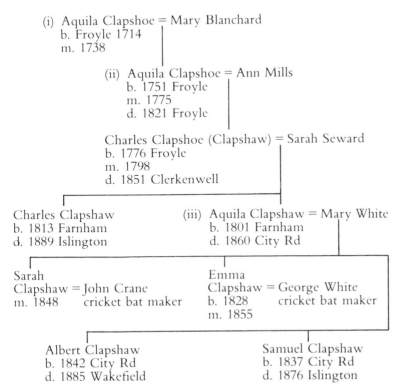

(i) Aquila Clapshoe = Mary Blanchard
  b. Froyle 1714
  m. 1738

   (ii) Aquila Clapshoe = Ann Mills
     b. 1751 Froyle
     m. 1775
     d. 1821 Froyle

   Charles Clapshoe (Clapshaw) = Sarah Seward
   b. 1776 Froyle
   m. 1798
   d. 1851 Clerkenwell

Charles Clapshaw   (iii) Aquila Clapshaw = Mary White
b. 1813 Farnham   b. 1801 Farnham
d. 1889 Islington   d. 1860 City Rd

Sarah   Emma
Clapshaw = John Crane Clapshaw = George White
m. 1848 cricket bat maker b. 1828 cricket bat maker
         m. 1855

  Albert Clapshaw   Samuel Clapshaw
  b. 1842 City Rd   b. 1837 City Rd
  d. 1885 Wakefield   d. 1876 Islington

It would be convenient to record that James Cobbett 'invented' the two-part, spliced cricket bat, but there is no evidence to show that he did. The idea was probably born of the occasions when cricket bat makers were asked to repair a solid bat whose handle had been knocked out by a particularly fast ball 'thrown' from the round arm of Alfred Mynn or William Lillywhite. With stinging hands the owner went round to the craftsman who had made his bat and showed him the handle with the jagged piece sticking out at the end and the blade from which the shaft had torn itself, leaving a corresponding vee in the neck. He asked him to put the two pieces together again which, with care and a pot of glue, he did. But as he did it for the umpteenth time it must have occurred to him that less accidents of this kind would happen if the bat started its life in two pieces and had a degree of 'give' to enable it to resist a hard knock in the critical place which spliced the bat in two.

That this was the sensible way of making cricket bats probably dawned sometime in the 1830s – at least between 1827 and 1837. Its superiority over the old solid method would quickly have become evident, though of course it would have required a higher degree of craftsmanship and cost more.

Cobbett's bat of 1837 in Lord's Museum – and the spliced bat by William Lambley dated 1846 in the pavilion – probably represent the *haute couture* of the bat-maker's art of the period; for the new look obviously did not replace the old style overnight or throughout the country. The new design caught on with players in county matches and at Lord's, The Oval, Trent Bridge, Trafford Park, but the old, cheaper 'plain match' bats continued to be made for lesser mortals and were used for many a year. Wisden's had 'plain match, not spliced' bats in their 1882 catalogue at 9s 6d. Plain match bats would have been sold by a firm like Cheek & Marsh at the sign of the Golden Perch, 32 Oxford Street in 1851 'at prices at least one third lower than usually charged'. Outside London prices were cheaper. Dark bats were being sold by Sadd of Cambridge in 1836 for 8s 6d – Ben Dark's bat making business at Lord's was taken over first by Mrs Matilda Dark, his mother ('Dark, Mrs M' replaces 'Dark, Ben' in the 1840 London Post Office Directory) and on her death by her son Frank.

These Dark bats of 1836–40 may have been spliced, and the first Duke bats of 1848 would certainly have been – though John Duke would have made both at Chiddingstone Causeway.

When he came from Redleaf to Chiddingstone Causeway (which everyone continued to call 'Penshurst') in 1841, Timothy Duke II found a craftsman had been making cricket bats in the adjoining village of Chiddingstone Hoath for thirty years or so. This was Luke Eade, born in 1785, the son of a Buxted (Sussex) farmer. With little to do on the farm in the agricultural depression which followed the end of the Napoleonic Wars, Luke Eade went to Mitcham to learn woodturning,

The Eade family at the Duke & Son works at Chiddingstone Causeway in the 1900s – young Charlie, Fred, Cecil and Old Albert. Third from the left in the top row is Henry 'Sailor' Eade

and then came to Chiddingstone Hoath where he set up as a maker of cottage furniture and cricket bats. Where his workshop was is not known, but witness to his activities is the circular, solid steel die-stamp with which he stamped the top of the handle of each bat he made with the mark 'L. EADE, Penshurst, Kent', still extant. That he was not just making cricket bats for local consumption is shown by the fact that he had a second stamp for the bats he made for the Marylebone Club.

Most people of this time kept a log of their large families on the flyleaf of their family bibles, but Luke Eade used his fine copy of Fox's *Book of Martyrs* for listing the arrival of his twelve children, all boys save one. He was married in 1814 and his first son was born in 1815, the last in 1833. Luke died, probably of cholera, when he was only fifty-seven, the year after Duke & Son moved to Chiddingstone Causeway (1842). He would have been making cricket bats to the end, but no 'L. Eade' bat has come down. He taught the craft to two of his sons, Frederick and Alfred, and they probably carried on the cricket bat workshop as an independent cottage industry for some years after their father's premature death.

Duke were not to make cricket bats on their own for another six years, but finding the Eade workshop on their doorstep they might well have 'bought in' a few Eade bats. The success they had in testing the market with them might well have encouraged them to enter cricket bat manufacture on their own account, using the Eade know-how as the nucleus of a Duke cricket bat tradition to match the reputation which they already had as pioneer manufacturers of cricket balls.

It looks however as if Frederick Eade for a time decided to learn something about cricket ball making, for a pencilled note by his son Henry Frederick 'Sailor' Eade states that he started working for Duke & Son *at Red Leaf* in 1844 and worked for them for thirty-six years, dying in the factory in 1874. 'Sailor' Eade may have been confused about Redleaf, or his reference to his father starting work there in 1844 may indicate that for a few years after the opening of the Chiddingstone Causeway works, cricket ball making continued at the old hut on the hill outside Penshurst opposite the house where the family were presumably still living (The Paddocks).

But Frederick Eade and Alfred 'Sixer' Eade, who died in 1915, were both essentially cricket bat makers. One of Sixer's sons, 'Brownie' Eade, was a cricket bat maker; another, Horace Eade, was a cricket ball maker – and both were with Duke. Three of Brownie's sons were in the trade: Bill Eade who died in the 1930s was a cricket ball maker with Duke; George Eade who died in the 1960s was a cricket bat maker with Wisden; Charlie Eade who also died in the 1960s was a cricket bat maker with Gradidge.

Apart from Sailor Eade, another son of Frederick's, Albert Eade was a cricket bat maker for Duke, and his son, also Albert Eade, was with the firm as a cricket ball maker. Two of Sailor's sons were cricket bat makers, Fred who had no children, and Cecil Eade who was born in 1885.

In Sailor Eade's day, he and his brother and cousins derived income from activities other than cricket ball and cricket bat making. He was a tenant-farmer, as was his brother Albert who ran Haycraft Farm at

Bough Beech. Other members of the Eade fraternity ran public houses – The Bat and Ball at Leigh whose name betrays the publican's other line of business, The Flying Dutchman at Southborough, The White Rock at Underriver. The cricket ball and bat makers were able to organise their lives in this way because of the informal way in which their masters, the Dukes, ran the factory. It was all piece-work and there were no regular hours. So long as the work got done some time within the fifteen hours or so in which the factory was open, no one worried. Sailor Eade and his fellow craftsmen might start the day at five in the morning, and then maybe they would 'get the bug' and go off hunting or shooting. The Duke family were very keen huntsmen, and they and the craftsmen/farmers/publicans who worked for them would down tools in the middle of the day, have an afternoon hunting, and then return to the factory to put in an hour or two in the evening, bringing their oil and lamps with them to illumine the intricate processes of binding the handles, fitting the splices, and finishing the blades.

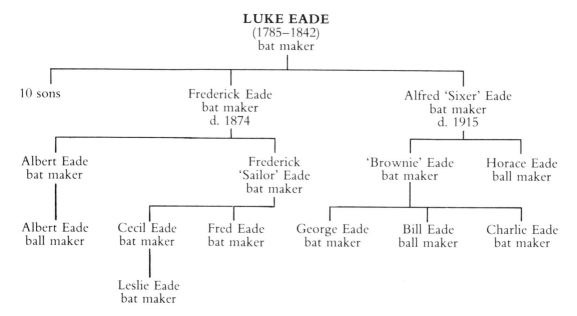

LUKE EADE
(1785–1842)
bat maker

10 sons — Frederick Eade, bat maker, d. 1874 — Alfred 'Sixer' Eade, bat maker, d. 1915

Albert Eade, bat maker — Frederick 'Sailor' Eade, bat maker — 'Brownie' Eade, bat maker — Horace Eade, ball maker

Albert Eade, ball maker — Cecil Eade, bat maker — Fred Eade, bat maker — George Eade, bat maker — Bill Eade, ball maker — Charlie Eade, bat maker

Leslie Eade, bat maker

The fourteen members of five generations of Eades look like the above.

Leslie Eade, who is the family archivist and possessor of his great-great-grandfather's Fox's Book of Martyrs, found a Duke cricket bat of late nineteenth-century vintage in Oxford in 1968. The handle has a wax binding, and the royal arms and the Prince of Wales's arms are on either shoulder of the bat. It has a solid piece of cane running at right angles to the blade down the centre of the handle, with wood on either side. There is no 'brand name' other than 'Duke & Son' on this bat, though later Duke bats were called 'Royal', 'Willow King', 'Premier' and 'Excelsior'.

Up to the 1830s flexibility of design turned mostly on weight. If the

Leslie Eade, the great-great-grandson of Luke Eade (1785–1842) the cricket bat maker of Chiddingstone Heath whose activities attracted the attention of Timothy Duke when he moved the family cricket ball operation from Penshurst to Chiddingstone Causeway in 1841. Duke & Son began selling 'L. Eade' cricket bats as well as their own cricket balls, and were soon making bats on the lines they learnt from Luke Eade. Leslie holds a rare example of a Duke cricket bat which he owns. Leslie's father, grandfather, and great-grandfather were all cricket bat makers, and he finishes Gray-Nicolls bats in a workshop set aside for him at Chiddingstone Causeway

word 'club' was meant to indicate something heavy and unwieldy, those whom Gale was reproving had a case. James Pycroft wrote of Edward Budd, who played his first match at Lord's in 1802: 'Being a man of great strength and quickness with fine wrist play, five feet ten inches in height and twelve stone in weight, no wonder he was a hard hitter, especially in days when bats were heavy. Mr Budd's bat weighed three pounds, but there were heavier bats than his. Mr Ward used one that weighed four pounds. When I was at Oxford (1832–6) two pounds ten was a common weight.'

Eric Parker reckoned that the bat held by the fifteen-year-old Lewis Cage in the 1768 picture of 'The Cricket Boy' by Francis Cotes RA owned by Lord Brocket must have weighed four pounds too.

Some players had a special bat made to cope with a particular bowler. R. Grimston had two bats, one his regular and the other for when he knew he would have to face Alfred Mynn. This weighed three pounds, much heavier than his regular bat, and was two inches higher in the shoulder and two inches shorter in the handle. Such juggling with the length was allowed so long as overall it did not exceed the legal thirty-eight inches.

Rev R. S. Holmes who wrote a weekly column in the magazine *Cricket* called 'Cricket Notches', told of John Wisden & Co giving him a bat in 1892 which he thought must be about thirty-five-years-old. If his guess is accurate, it would seem that by the 1850s the trend had swung right away from heavy bats. The blade was dark red, he said: 'that may be from age or stain, I know not; but there is no wood in it, it looks too frail for practical cricket. A young lad who saw it said he thought it would smash first time it was used.'

Odd & Son made cricket bats in Croydon for many years and their flexible handle was a leader in its field. Few of their bats survive; this one is in the small Winchester College collection in Hunter Tent

By 'no wood' Holmes meant no heartwood but mostly sap. It weighed, he said, scarcely two pounds. 'But at that time driving was little practised, most runs were scored behind the wicket. The half volley was respectfully played back to the bowler instead of being slogged to the boundary.'

The bat of Tom Adams who played for Kent between 1834 and 1858 had an irregular shape, but this was not given it by any cricket bat maker. 'I recollect,' wrote William South Norton who first played for the same county in 1849, 'he had a bat which he must, from the look of it, have used for about twenty years and oiled every day. It was a dark mahogany colour and from constantly receiving the ball near the end, it had actually become curved, something like a spoon, and he accommodated his style as I thought thereto, favouring more than ever his scooping to the on and leg.' Perhaps others had treated their bats as Tom Adams had done and credulous members of Lord's had taken them for 'clubs'.

But throughout these latter-day fluctuations in shape and weight whether by design or ill-treatment, the raw material from which cricket bats were made remained the same – willow, symbol of happy days on the cricket field.

> While sportsmen, brush and bugle laud, as emblems of the
> chase,
> And poets sing the trophies that baronial mansions grace;
> Sure notes as joyous can be struck from out the willow wood
> When carved to shapes that token peace and foster brotherhood.
> Then let us speed by word and deed wherever we may go,
> A mighty spirit in the land, now moving to and fro.

> 'The Cricket Bat An Emblem Of Peace', sung to the air of
> *The Days We Went Gipsying.*

It is difficult to trace precisely when makers first selected willow from all the other possibles, such as the alder and ash used in the Stonyhurst cricket bats. But it is probably safe to say that willow was the wood of which were made most one-piece cricket bats used by professionals, and county and university amateurs, between 1740 and 1840. Before the eighteenth century any hard wood had been used, particularly by those who took their cricketing less seriously. It was so even into the middle of the nineteenth century. As late as 1860 would-be craftsmen searching for likely timber at Goudhurst in Kent were confronted with the warning:

Take notice all
> That from this thicket
> You may cut stumps for your cricket.
> But never let me catch you at
> Cutting down a tree for a bat.

But willow became a favourite because it was not only extremely resilient and tough, but light. It was naturally soft, and here lay the secret of its strength. Hardness was given it mechanically. It came in two colours, red and white. Wide grained white willow was softer and thus less durable than the close grained red, favoured by W. G. Grace, C. B. Fry, G. L. Jessop, T. Hayward, Wilfred Rhodes and others for its superior driving power. Red willow was said to have made possible the 'mammoth hits' of J. N. Crawford. The bat Wisden gave Holmes was evidently red. But by the end of the nineteenth century the fashion had shifted almost entirely to white. Ranjitsinhji preferred 'light wood'.

The popularity of white wood was a fashion which had no foundation in fact. From the salesman's point of view a white bat probably 'looked' better in a sports shop window. But certainly as late as 1920 the timber experts, asked for a dispassionate view, specified the leading cricket bat willows as a hybrid which appeared near Chelmsford and Saffron Walden, and one found at Waterbeach in Cambridgeshire in 1814, known as the Red-twigged Willow of Pontey. How the wood 'looked' was distinct from its ability to hit a cricket ball. What mattered was whether the tannin stains disintegrated or strengthened the fibres of the willow. In the knowledge that red bats played better than white, timber merchants accounted for bat makers' preference for the latter by assuming their attitude to be that of the cutler who told a complaining customer that his razors were not made to cut but to sell.

There were seventeen recognised British species of willow (salix), divided into sallows, osiers and willows. Because they grew so quickly willows were planted to hold the banks of watercourses together. They did not always grow to any great height. A salix alba might reach eight foot, a salix herbacea only a few inches. For many years on the wall of the office of Benjamin Warsop & Sons Ltd, cricket bat makers of Grove Gardens, St John's Wood (which closed in 1973), was a photograph of a giant willow tree grown at Boreham in Essex, one hundred and one foot high; it had been felled and was lying on the ground behind its proud fellers. It was five foot nine inches in diameter and weighed eleven tons. It had been planted in 1835 and was taken down on 19 April 1888 by B. Warsop & Sons 'for the sole purpose of making bats'. It was 'as sound as a bell'. Warsop made one thousand, one hundred and seventy-nine cricket bats from it.

In the nineteenth century at any rate the salix alba was the only type considered capable of yielding timber suitable for 'best' cricket bats – and only those grown moreover in East Anglia. And only very best bats could come from very fast growers. Types other than the salix alba were not thought to have the fibrous tenacity for bat making.

In those days a cricket bat could be said to start its life as a 'set', the shoot cut from either a maiden or pollard willow tree – the latter being one which had had its top lopped off, the former one which had been allowed to live its life undefiled. The set, which would grow into a tree suitable for the blade of a best bat, had to be some two inches round and six to ten feet tall – and very straight. It had to be of the 'close bark' order as opposed to open bark.

Not everyone went about willow culture the same way, but the general plan seemed to be to plant sets in rows twelve feet apart along the banks of a stream or the sides of a ditch. It was no use growing them on fenland, though sets were often begun in a meadow and transplanted to the bank of a stream after a couple of years. Soon the diameter of the trunk began to swell at a rate of about half an inch or an inch a year. The side facing the sun grew more quickly, sometimes twice as quickly as

the shady side. It was a delicate sapling sensitive to its surroundings. Horizontal cracks could appear in the bark which would shrink from too hot a sun or too extreme a frost. It was no use removing the bark to prevent the trunk being gnawed by cattle, as without bark the sap could not nourish the tree and the trunk would decay. Cow hide and willow were destined to meet head on at a later stage, but a premature engagement at this point could mean an expensive miscarriage.

This giant willow felled for Benjamin Warsop at Boreham, Essex, in 1888 made 1,179 bats. The tree was one hundred and one feet long, weighed eleven tons and was fifty-three years old, being planted in 1835. It was three times the age of a normal cricket bat willow, but proved to be 'sound as a bell'

The bark had to remain and the cattle had to be kept at bay. But a twig which began to grow from the bark had to be removed instantly, for if it stayed the trunk would close round its base. When the tree was felled some twenty years or so later with a circumference of forty-five inches, this base would have swollen into a knot. Such a blemish on the blade of a bat was thought by many to shorten the life of a bat. This was not in fact the case, but the legend spread by the know-alls had its effect on sales. A similar mark could be made by rain water trickling into a hole made by an insect, or through cracks caused by the tree swaying unduly in the wind, and taking with it some of the tannin from the bark. The rising and falling sap spread the stain slightly up and down, leaving faint lines like the wings of a butterfly. The process continuing year by year stained each succeeding ring to a greater or lesser degree, till finally the full design resembled a whole moth or butterfly. Such stains became known as 'butterfly markings'. The stain was very marked on first splitting the trunk, but soon became bleached by the sun.

Insects were not the only hole borers. The farmers who came to shoot duck and hares by the river carelessly sprayed the weeping willows with lead shot. This would perforate the bark and remain unnoticed in the interior until the tree was felled. Through the holes made by the pellets came the rain, and round them formed the butterfly stains. In a letter to *The Field* in July 1921 A. L. Ford related how E. J. Page the old Kennington Road bat maker who died in 1879 was fond of selecting old wood stained in this way. 'Once somewhere in the 1870–80 period I was in his place . . . and he showed me some of the wood with the shot in it. The young tree with its white wood is not stained because the wet has not had time to work into the end of the shot hole.'

Similarly George Bussey of Peckham, a competitor of Page with his London-made 'Demon Driver' cricket bats, considered butterfly markings added to the surface strength of the part of the blade where the blemish was found. 'The finest blades are produced from timber having this "stainy" mark', he wrote in *The Bat of the Victorian Era*, 'inferior quality timber rarely possesses it'.

In a blatant piece of editorial publicity for Ayres bats, A. Craig, the nineteenth-century Cricket and Football Rhymster, wrote of someone with a relative who obviously agreed with Bussey. 'Another gentleman who hails from Tooting treasures a Bat that belonged to a long-deceased uncle. It is one of those curiosities lined with water marks, and has a grand looking blade. I believe he would rather be deprived of his gold repeater than lose it.'

A willow tree was seldom chopped down before its girth measured forty-five inches – and the taller the better. George Bussey's ideal was a seventy-five-year-old monster seventy-foot high, fifteen-and-a-half foot in circumference and weighing seven tons. But since a willow grew fast, its life was short. Natural decay set in early. Many oaks lived to a hundred, but few willows could do so without developing a large hollow in their midst.

In his early days Bussey stomped round East Anglia backing his judgement on what trees seemed to him ripe for the job. He admitted it was something of a gamble. Landowners would not let him fell a tree, look inside and then decide whether to buy. It was a pig in a poke. 'You see the outside of the trees certainly, then you make your bargain and the next thing is to put down your cash.'

Only after he had acquired it, was he allowed to examine the tree and know the worst. 'If the timber turns out sound, well and good, but if it doesn't (there's the rub) well, we must smile and put up with it.' He hoped cricketers would think of this when purchasing their bats; the sound trees had to pay for the unsound ones.

Willow trees were felled in winter when the sap was down. If they were chopped when the sap was up it would dry the trunk and deteriorate the timber. The felling operation began with cutting about one-third through from the side towards which the tree leant, and then cutting from the opposite side. The trick was to cut it as low down as possible, removing the surrounding earth to do this, and to lop off the branches.

The trunk was then cross cut on the site, into two-and-a-half foot lengths, beginning from the butt end. 'By this,' explained Bussey, 'we do not mean that a man simply marks off uniform lengths of thirty inches. Much consideration and judgement are necessary, requiring a man of experience and capability who will be guided by many little outward signs to which the uninitiated would be indifferent. An error of judgement may convert dozens of guinea bats into as many half-guineas.' It was the same for the butcher who did not know where to go for the sirloin, where for the rump steak. Now the tree was dead the bark could be removed to allow the moisture to evaporate freely, decreasing the weight and preventing discoloration.

The technical revolution of the 1830s in making the bat in two parts and fitting them together had brought no alteration to the design of either of them. The first spliced bat was just the old solid bat taken apart and put together again, the solid handle vee and the blade's 'female' socket precisely carved for an exact fit, and the two firmly wedged together and securely glued. The bat looked exactly the same except for the tell-tale splice. Personal modifications were still made as before, to the *blade*, for reasons connected with better striking power, better protecting the body, better defending the wicket. But in 1840 or thereabouts attention switched from the blade to the *handle*.

Provision of more 'give' by making the bat in two parts was an improvement, but the solid handle still stung the hands whenever a ball struck the blade other than well in the centre. The obvious remedy was to give the handle some kind of spring. G. B. Buckley (*Historical Gleanings*, unpublished MS in Lord's MCC Library) tells of a spring-handled bat selling for 10s 6d in 1840 with a bar of steel in the middle of the handle. 'The first bat to have a handle other than wood.'

But a more suitable, and presumably lighter, spring was whalebone, which was being used so successfully for the same purpose in ladies' stays. In the 1840s cricket bat makers started inserting a single strip of whalebone into cricket bat handles. No 7 bat in W. G. Grace's drawings is one he possessed in 1891 but probably dated from much earlier, and this clearly shows a single whalebone strip down the splice. In 1851 E. & W. Page, the cricket bat makers of Kennington Road, were advertising 'Superior whalebone-handled Bats which for strength and durability cannot be surpassed' and they will have been one of many. Soon three strips of whalebone were being inserted.

Up to the 1850s run-of-the-mill bats were mostly all willow, either one hunk of wood carved into the shape of a bat, or a willow blade spliced into a willow or ash handle, at first solid and then made springy and resilient with whalebone strips. But in 1853 a craftsman-cricketer called Thomas Nixon conceived the idea of making the handle springy, not by inserting springs in a naturally unbending handle, but constructing the handle of a wood which was itself springy. He chose cane.

Thomas Nixon was born in Nottingham on 4 June 1815 and became a lace-maker by trade. He was a 'spare built man' hardly five foot ten inches tall, but had the reputation of being a fine round armed bowler. In 1842 he played his first game at Lord's for Slow Bowlers against Fast Bowlers, and in 1851 he was engaged as a professional at Lord's. He was active there for the next six years. It was in this period that his inventive mind devised the new type of handle with which his name is ever linked. 'By machinery (made by himself also),' wrote Haygarth in *Cricket Scores and Biographies* Vol 3, 'he is enabled to produce cane handles and to handle bats with the same material.' Cane handles for cricket bats were not his first 'invention'; in 1841 he was responsible for introducing cork knee pads.

In 1856 Thomas Nixon moved to Oxford where for five years he was landlord of the Old White Horse Inn and Cricket Ground. In 1861 he accepted a permanent appointment at Chelford in Cheshire where he established a cricket ground. His inventive powers were by no means spent, for in 1862 he contrived a bowling machine he called the 'Balista'. He took out a patent no 1026, dated 10 April 1862, with John Lillywhite for this 'improved bowling apparatus for cricket balls'.

An advertisement in *The Times* of 2 May 1878. The Trimmings mentioned at the top also made cricket bats

In this year the number of cricket bat makers in London, encouraged no doubt by the reception given to Nixon's cane handle invention and the boost it gave to the trade, swelled to twenty. White & Helyer came to Lambeth, Joseph Feltham to Barbican, Charles Armstrong to Oxford Street, Thomas Mayo to Stoke Newington.

Using a wood from the East Indies in place of one from East Anglia naturally put the price up. The first to be used were either malaccas or rattans. Malacca was the rich brown wood from the stem of a palm (*calamus scipionum*) grown at Malacca in the Malay Peninsula and made into swagger walking canes with silver knobs carried by the toffs. Rattan was another species of the calamus from Malay, and was generally prefered to the other because it was stronger for its weight and as a rule more uniform in its quality. For 'all-cane handles' the round rods of cane were cut into handle lengths and flattened on two sides.

Three, four or five canes were glued side by side to form a flat 'slip' about two-and-a-half inches wide. The top and bottom of the slips which showed the rounded surface of the canes were flattened, and four of them glued together to form a solid shaft of cane from which the handle was then modelled. There were no laws governing the shape or size of handles, and the cricket bat maker was free to make it as he liked and in whatever material he chose. But the new fad was the status symbol of every aspiring batsman – and bat maker. In 1860 Edward Page proudly proclaimed himself 'cricket bat, ball, stump . . . maker, by special appointment to the Surrey County Club and under the immediate patronage of the gentlemen of the Marylebone Club and manufacturer of the superior cane handle bat warranted not to break'.

Once the cane handle principle had been established many hastened to devise modifications and introduce their own 'improvements', such as layering the canes with india-rubber. George Bussey thought this made for too much elasticity – 'after a little use the handle becomes more flexible than is desirable, if not altogether too *flimsy*' – and for his 'Demon Driver' he sandwiched between the two slips of cane a combination of rubber and canvas.

> Few bat makers have had any experience of india-rubber and that is doubtless the cause of their having overlooked the important fact that no adhesive solution having water for its solvent will effectually unite with india-rubber, therefore, glue cannot properly attach india-rubber to Cane. Partly to overcome this the somewhat clumsy expedient of using pegs and dowels is sometimes adopted.

His method was to join two strips of a textile fabric to the rubber strip, one on each side, by means of an adhesive of which the principal component was rubber itself. The rubber strip protected by the canvas on the outside was then stuck to the cane with another kind of adhesive which held equally well to either, so there was no fear of the handle dividing in the centre. To prevent the rubber strip stretching and poking out of the top of the handle whereby 'the utility of the handle is perceptibly diminished and in consequence the driving energy of the bat curtailed', he put a piece of leather about two inches long at the top of the handle to abut on the rubber. 'This semi-rigid substance produces just what is wanted, it permits the India-rubber doing all there is required of it, while causing the handle to regain its normal condition promptly and without that sluggish action that is noticeable in many bats.'

Kumar Shri Ranjitsinjhi, the ace Indian batsman of the time, had distinct views about handles (although they may have been those of C. B. Fry who some say was the real author of *The Jubilee Book of Cricket*).

> In the choice of a handle attention should be paid to its elasticity; for if the handle gives a bit when the blade strikes the ball, the jar resulting from the impact is considerably diminished. Stiff-handled bats sometimes sting horribly. Those with good blades and fairly elastic handles make the feeling of striking the ball perfectly delicious.

And that is what Cricket was all about.

But, he warned, 'a handle should not be too springy or it is liable to break and strain after it has been used once or twice. A weak, springy handle is a mistake. A handle should bend like the butt-end of a good fly-rod and not like an aspen stick.'

Part of the delicious feeling of striking a ball perfectly was the *sound*, and the whalebone handle bat and Tom Nixon's cane handle bat was followed in 1868 by the 'repercussive' bat – a word that means resounding or reverberating and, applied to a cricket bat, can only be meant to indicate its capacity to make a satisfying smack when driven against the ball. As a dictionary word it was not a brand name belonging to one maker only, but was adopted by many of them to mark, presumably, a harmonious combination of blade and handle that struck the right note in the ear and a sufficiently delicious sensation in the hand. J. D. Bartlett who had a manufactory at 71 Waterloo Road, by London's Waterloo Station, was one of such who advertised 'Bartlett's Celebrated Repercussive Bats'. E. J. Page & Co of Kennington Park Road promoted their 'Combination Flexible Non-Jarring Bat' – 'the jar or sting is entirely obviated and the hardest bat can be made without feeling any unpleasant sensation'.

By 1868 cricket had begun to be transformed by the approach to batting by W. G. Grace. As the author of the *Jubilee Book of Cricket* put it:

> He revolutionised batting; he turned it from an accomplishment into a science ... It was bad cricket to hit a straight ball; as for pulling a slow long-hop, it was regarded as immoral. What W. G. did was to unite in his mighty self all the good points of all the good players, and to make utility the criterion of style. He founded the modern theory of batting by making forward and back play of equal importance, relying neither on the one nor on the other but on both. Any cricketer who thinks for a moment can see the enormous change W. G. introduced into the game. I hold him to be, not only the finest player born or unborn, but the maker of modern batting. He turned the old one-stringed instrument into a many-chorded lyre.

To enable it to play the role given it by the Grace Revolution and give it strength to drive the ball continuously to the boundary, the cricket bat developed a supporting hump of wood at the back of the blade. Hitting the ball to the extremity of the field became so frequent an occurrence that in 1866 the laws were altered to give four runs automatically to a striker who hit the ball to the edge of the ground. The change in bat design between the flat bat of 1827, and the bat with the bulge behind the part of the blade with which the ball should be correctly hit, is clearly shown in the profiles of bats nos 6 and 9 in W. G.'s drawings.

In the wake of the new impetus which Grace gave to cricket in the 1860s, several new cricket bat makers entered the London scene, like Peacock & Graham who set up in White Post Lane, Hackney Wick in 1867, Henry Day in Westminster, Thomas Eaton off City Road, John Grimwood in Old Ford, William Mortlake at Waterloo Station (presumably underneath the arches) and John Peters in the Strand. But naturally the most popular area was near Lord's, the ground to which everyone flocked to watch the doctor putting his skill into action. Among them were John Fensom at 33 St John's Wood Terrace and

Lambert & Hammond at 68 St John's Wood Road. Nothing is known of these besides their names and addresses, but the history of another firm which settled here at this time is better known, for it continued the craft of cricket bat making without a break in St John's Wood until 1973.

The photograph of the giant willow on the wall of the office of Benjamin Warsop & Sons has already been referred to. Benjamin Warsop opened up as a cricket bat maker at 36 and 38 Charles Street (now Charlbert Street), St John's Wood in 1870. He had come there from Nottingham. The sons in the title were four in number, Alfred, Arthur, Frank and Walter, and they all helped their father to make the bats to which he gave the name 'Conqueror'. Ben was of course a player too, and an old photograph at St John's Wood showed him in front of Lord's with Inspector Cox (a police officer) and C. Absolon, two noted players of the day.

Benjamin Warsop with his four sons: Alfred, Arthur, Frank and Walter, each holding a tool of the cricket bat making trade

In the Post Office Directory of 1877 Ben Warsop at 36 Charles Street, Portland Town, N., was one of thirty-eight cricket bat and ball makers *and outfitters* – of course the inclusion of this last title makes the list deceptively large and, from that year on, of little value for this record, for few firms indicated whether they were retailers, wholesalers or manufacturers. An exception in 1877 was Feltham & Co, with offices at 52 Little Britain and a manufactory at 64 Aldersgate, who stated they were 'makers of cane handled bats and balls'.

Though Warsop can only have operated on a comparatively small scale, one of his bats won a First Order of Merit at the Centennial International Exhibition at Melbourne in 1888. An order book of the

1890s shows that in twenty years he was supplying large and regular quantities of cricket bats to Slazenger, Wisden, the Junior Army & Navy Stores and similar firms, as well as clubs, schools and a host of individuals. An order for 'Slazengers, London' dated 29 February 1892 indicates a range of six bats from the most expensive 'Patent' at 13s to the cheapest 'no 6 Common' at 3s 6d.

3 doz Patents	£23	8
3 doz Superior	£18	
3 doz 2nd Quality	£13	10
3 doz 3rd Quality	£10	16
3 doz no 6 Sup	£ 9	18
3 doz no 6 Common	£ 6	6
	£81	18

In May 1892 Wisden paid £377 for a big order that included thirty-four dozen Superior bats, seven dozen youths' no 6 at 6s each, two dozen short men's at 10s each and two dozen boy's no 4 at 4s 6d each. In the same year Warsop was making bats for other bat makers like F. H. Ayres, Lillywhite & Frowd and E. J. Page. He also supplied the latter with sundries like cane handles, blades and balls of twine. In 1897 he had an order from Messrs Twort & Son for a dozen Superiors at 10s each. To Gunn & Moore in 1893 he sold:

17 doz all canes at 6s 6d	£66	6
2 doz Best ditto at 9s 6d	£11	8
3 Patents at 12s	£ 1	16

He seems to have had a connection with the public schools; in the 1890s he was getting orders from 'Mr Page, Eton', 'Mr Todd, Oundle' and 'B. Lee, Winchester'. A Warsop bat used by Sir Arthur Shrewsbury in 1885 was to be seen in a case at the St John's Wood premises in 1973. With it Shrewsbury scored 224 not out for Nottinghamshire against Middlesex at Lord's. Gray-Nicolls have a Warsop bat of 1890 at Robertsbridge with which someone scored 3,069 runs.

In 1893 Ben received an order from the Master himself:

W. G. Grace Esq, 18 May 1893

2 Patents	£2	2
1 Patent	£1	1

Presumably this was the retail price of a 'Conqueror'.

Wisden's £470 order for 10 October 1893 included

5 doz Patent hlds	£39	
2 doz lovely Harrows at 8s 6d	£10	4

'Harrow' was a term indicating a size between men's and youths', and was still in use in the 1970s.

Wisden of course were placing orders for bats with several makers. One of them was Richard Allen who had taken over the Cobbett business. Hard hitting in the style of W. G. Grace meant that bats had to be more than unstinging and unjarring. In 1883 Wisden were at pains to claim that the Cobbett's cane and other handled bats, 'manufactured expressly in accordance with our wishes of the best procurable wood' were 'almost unbreakable'. 'The handle has not too much spring, being

The Patent Triangular Bat made by J. Browning of Bristol in 1887. It weighed two pound two ounces and cost 10s. It is now in Lord's Museum

prevented by the introduction of wood (a sort purchased expressly) which is worked into the centre of the handle. All bats are well nourished with oil, splendidly balanced, plenty of wood and light cane handles ... Bats made any size (under that allowed by law). Young beginners and gentlemen with weak wrists are particularly recommended to play with light bats.'

Wrists had to be used for swinging the bat now, not just holding it. Over-arm had been legalised by the MCC for twenty years, and a firm grip and a strong action were required to deal with the 'demon' bowling of Fred Spofforth and his imitators.

A Wisden/Cobbett bat of 1882 'with selected cane handle' cost 21s; 'best treble cane bat' 17s 6d; 'single cane bat' 14s; ash handle 11s; youths' cane handle, 15s 6d; youths' plain spliced, 5s 6d. These were retail prices; if Warsop's wholesale prices are anything to go by, Wisden's mark up must have been considerable. They undertook repairs as well. If a fast one shattered the blade from its handle, they would put a new blade to it for 12s 6d.

In 1888 Wisden became sole agents for Crawford's Patent 'Exceller' Bat which had an all-cane handle with india-rubber inserted crossways down to the shoulder of the blade. It differed from all others, it was claimed, in pliancy and driving power. A 'selected' bat cost 21s and a second quality sold at 17s 6d. These bats were made by a player/manufacturer, R. T. Crawford. A 1901 'Exceller' signed by W. G. Grace is in the pavilion at Lord's. Another cricket bat maker of the same name, H. C. Crawford of Plumstead, Kent, may have been of the same family. In 1884 he was one of many who filed patent specifications for an improved cricket bat handle (no 8246 of 26 May). 'Vertical cuts are made through the handle from top to the bottom and strips of india-rubber about the same in width as the diameter of the handle are placed therein so that each strip is wedged between the inner sides of opposite segments of the handle as shown at a. The handle is then bound in the ordinary manner.'

Strangest 'improvement' produced at this time perhaps was Browning's Patent Triangular Bat, of which there is an 1887 example at Lord's weighing two pounds four ounces and costing 10s. This was the year J. Browning of Alexandra House, Fishponds, near Bristol, patented this novel design (no 1484 of 31 January) which consisted of 'constructing bats with blades triangular in cross section as shown in the figure, reproduced here, a receptacle A in the blade being filled with linseed oil or other preservative substance'. Design variations were limited for anything as basically simple as a cricket bat, but obviously there were bold innovators ready to explore every avenue. Wisden took it seriously enough to become agents for Browning's bat at any rate. Another freak bat of the period was made by Cobbett's and is in the Gray-Nicolls collection. It has an ash frame and a cork playing surface reinforced with cat gut.

A new type of handle was patented in the same year by R. F. J. C. Allen of 29 Grove Road, St John's Wood, who may have been the Richard Allen (or his son) who in 1845 claimed to be the nephew and successor of James Cobbett. But 'Cobbett' bats were now being made by all sorts of people. There is a 'Cobbett' bat – the name is stamped on

One of the many 'Cobbett' bats in circulation at the end of the nineteenth century, but probably unique – with an ash frame using racket-making techniques and with playing surfaces on either side, each made of cork reinforced with catgut. One of the small collection at Gray-Nicolls, Robertsbridge

each shoulder – made by Lillywhite & Wisden of 1858 in the pavilion of The Oval, along with another similarly stamped bat made by Frederick Lillywhite & Ward presented to T. Burbidge by the Surrey CCC in August 1864. But in 1893 Cobbett's Cricket Bat Factory of 56 Capland Street, Grove Road, were warning 'on account of some persons stamping Cobbett's name on common and inferior made goods, none are genuine unless they bear Cobbett's registered trade mark'.

James Henry Dark, Frank's father, the proprietor of Lord's, had died in 1871 and his brother Robert two years later, but bat making continued. In 1891 H. S. Dark filed a specification for yet another handle (no 7842 of 6 May). The inner core, built up of lengths of cane or bamboo cemented together, was surrounded by cork strips which were then shaped to the form of the handle. A wooden button or cap was cemented to the top, 'and the handle may be covered with a wrapping of cord if desired'. The general idea of covering a central core of cane rods with cork had first been patented by H. S. Dark in 1886 (no 13,912 of 29 October).

While the Dark Dynasty continued at Lord's, the Page brothers had similarly maintained their association with The Oval. But by the 1870s Edward and William had gone their separate ways. Edward remained in Kennington. In 1874, five years before he died, he was using in his advertisements as a testimonial a letter from Dr E. M. Grace to Pulling, the Gloucestershire umpire, dated 'Thornbury, 11 Sept, 1874

> Dear Pulling,
>   I find there is still one bat due to me. Will you kindly get E. J. Page to make one for me half an inch longer than usual in the handle and 2 lb 3 oz in weight, and plenty of wood; tell him the last I had of his made over 6,000 runs and he is sure then to make me a good one. If he makes it now I can oil it all the winter.
>   *Edward Mills Grace, Secretary Gloucs CCC'*

There is an undated bat with 'E. J. Page' stamped vertically on the splice, which is sticking out of the blade, in the glass case of nine bats below Chitty's in the pavilion of The Oval.

William Page had become proprietor of Tufnell Park Cricket Grounds. In an advertisement he had placed in *The Cricket and Athletic News* of 2 June 1874 he ran the line 'First established in Middlesex 1811' but what that refers to has proved impossible to trace.

Tufnell Park Cricket Grounds, Tufnell Park Road, Upper Holloway
Under the immediate patronage of HRH the Prince of Wales
W. T. PAGE & CO, Cricket Bat, Ball & Stump Manufacturers
(by appointment to the Middlesex County Club, etc)
Please note address: Tufnell Arms Hotel, Tufnell Park Road.
First established in Middlesex 1811

William Page died in 1876.

As useless as a cracked blade was a misshapen handle, and a way of preventing this was devised by one of the new out-of-London cricket bat makers, the carpenter/cricketer L. J. Nicolls of Robertsbridge in Sussex. 'Patentee and Manufacturer of the Automatic Bat Handle', he

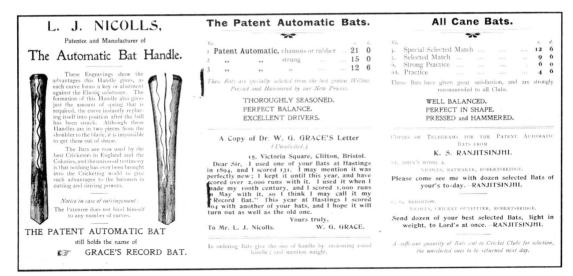

introduced his innovation in 1889, having filed his specification (no 14,250) on 4 October 1888. The method was to interlock the two sides of the cane handle with curves instead of having two flat surfaces meeting face to face. How it was 'automatic' is not clear, but it was a good selling line. The picture in his advertisement showed how it went. Carving the curves must have taken some skill and put the price up. 'Each curve forms a key or abutment against the elastic substance,' he stated in his advertisement. 'Impossible to get handles out of shape though in two pieces from shoulder to blade.' The patent specification gave details of construction.

To what extent did an 'automatic' bat handle work by itself? This drawing explains what L. J. Nicolls was claiming for it when he introduced it in 1889. W. G. Grace scored 2,000 runs with one and called it 'my record bat'. He bought a second Automatic

> Consists in inserting gutta percha therein. The handle is made as usual but before it is bound up and either before or after it is attached to the blade, an undulating saw cut is made longitudinally down the centre thereof, so as to be in line with the width of the blade. Into this cut the solid gutta percha is inserted.

Hard-hitting Dr Grace bought himself a Nicolls 'Automatic' bat and scored more than two thousand runs with it. In fact he was using it when he made his hundredth century. He called it 'my record bat' and bought himself another. A photograph of him wielding his record Nicolls bat hangs in the front bar of The George Inn at Robertsbridge.

Incidentally the doctor never played in a new bat himself. According to A. Craig, 'first of all he would let a boy who had not the power to hit hard play with it. By this means the article gradually acquired its face'. And in due course the bat was ready for the Master to handle and make centuries with.

Like other players L. J. Nicolls began making cricket bats for himself. These became so admired by his friends that they asked him to make copies for themselves. A bat he made for his brother A. Nicolls in 1856 is still at Robertsbridge. The demand for his handiwork became so large that in 1876 he decided to devote himself entirely to cricket bat making and to spend all day every day in his small, white boarded workshop (which still stands) below The George on the same side of the street. In

L. J. Nicoll's workshop in the High Street of Robertsbridge, East Sussex, near the George Inn. It extends some way to the back

1978 it was occupied by A. W. Gore & Co, licensed property agents, and for many years before that by a hairdresser.

He obtained his wood from local willow plantations. Stuart Surridge, who made cricket bats in Clapham Park, said the largest willow tree he had ever seen was grown at Robertsbridge – it was twenty-one feet in circumference and more than a thousand cricket bats were made from it.

Clapham Park was thoroughly rural in those days and Surridge's house and workshop stood in an acre and a half of grounds. 'His bat making is carried on with a very picturesque setting,' stated a report in *The Sportsman*, 'as there are no less than 130 fruit trees in the garden and 60 recently planted willows.' When the writer of this piece visited Surridge's works he found 'the well-known "Razor" Smith, the Surrey professor, hard at work with a "Beetle", a heavy wooden mallet. The swinging of this instrument requires considerable strength and is perhaps as fine exercise as one could have. Smith, who for seven years did practically no manual labour in the winter, finds this hard work beneficial, and has most satisfactory results so far as fitness is concerned. Last season it no doubt helped him to the top of the English bowling figures.'

'The young Princes Albert and Edward Prince of Wales may rest satisfied that the bats he [Surridge] has supplied them with were fashioned in the most congenial surroundings of any manufactory.'

Stuart Surridge began his cricket bat making business in 1893 in the part of south London known as The Borough, after having served an apprenticeship with James Lillywhite. After he had axed his willows at

Clapham Park and put them through a planing and a spindle machine and left them to mature, he sent them to his Borough workshop for modelling and finishing.

Apart from the royal brothers, Surridge counted among his customers the cream of the aristocratic amateurs of this Golden Age of cricket, Lord Hawke, Lord Dalmeny and the rest, and 'many cases of his famous bats have found their way to the Rajah of Patiala and the Jam Sahib of Nawanagar, the well-known "Ranji"'.

A rival of Surridge's for royal patronage could have been John Thompson, 'Cooper and Furnishing Turner to Her Majesty' of 8 Peascod Street, Windsor, who at least by 1851 was also a cricket bat maker. But perhaps he had fallen by the way before he was able to share in the rich harvest of the Golden Age, a fate unlikely to have been shared by the unknown Henry Pettifer who made cricket bats some time between 1853 and 1911, and certainly not by the very well-known Harry Gradidge who founded his famous cricket bat company in 1870.

British cricket bat makers revelled in the situation which gave them a world monopoly of a craft which 'the Dominions' had not yet acquired. With an increasing demand for English cricket bats coming from Australia, New Zealand, India and South Africa, cricket bat manufacture for home and overseas markets became an industry in the fullest sense of the word. Exporters like Surridge tended to congregate in the capital where the transport facilities were.

Surridge's workshop in The Borough was close to the factory of the man who had taught him the craft, James Lillywhite of James Lillywhite, Frowd & Co who had been at Newington Causeway since 1863. Here they stored and seasoned well-oiled cricket bats in a fifty-foot long warehouse, and in winter kept them at a high temperature to bring them to first-class condition for the following season 'and fit them for export to the hottest climates'.

The Lillywhite boys are a confusing bunch and they need sorting out. Was the James Lillywhite, manufacturer, 3 Queen's Circus, Cheltenham, who was advertising in James Lillywhite's *Cricketers Annual* of the 1870s the James Lillywhite (1825–82) who was the cricket coach to the public school in that town, and the eldest son of the famous Sussex cricketer William 'Non Pareil' Lillywhite? And did he have Stuart Surridge as his apprentice? This James's brother Fred (1829–66) had, as noted, gone into partnership with John Wisden in 1855 in the London 'depot' and when this was dissolved in 1858, according to Alison Adburgham, he set up a cricket bat making business with his brother John (1826–74), William's second son, who was also a public school cricket coach, at Rugby and Harrow. This was the firm trading as John Lillywhite from 10 Seymour Street, Euston Square, London, who exhibited 'articles connected with Cricket' in the International Exhibition held in London in 1862. In the same year John Lillywhite filed a patent for a bowling apparatus in conjunction with Thomas Nixon the inventor of the cane handle.

Surridge's master may on the other hand have been James Lillywhite, junior, cousin of the other James. This James was a member of Willsher's team which visited North America in 1868 and in 1877 managed the first 'Test' match, captaining the England side against

Australia. Again according to Alison Adburgham, James Lillywhite junior had a business, separate from the enterprise at Cheltenham and Seymour Street, which was absorbed into the firm of James Lillywhite senior in 1885.

Which of the two was the partner in James Lillywhite, Frowd & Co.? The odds are it was James Lillywhite senior, for his firm at Cheltenham was soon also designated 'Lillywhite, Frowd'. The Frowd was G. W. Frowd who was followed by his son W. G. Frowd, a member of the Forest Hill cricket club in south-east London, born in Dulwich in 1831.

James Lillywhite, Frowd & Co flourished at Newington Causeway. According to their advertisement in John Lillywhite's *Cricketer's Companion* of 1865 they were making not only cricket bats but stumps and balls. The balls may have been bought in, but certainly not the stumps. In 1885 G. W. Frowd took out a patent with P. Surridge for a new type of cricket stump. Soon after the death of James Lillywhite senior the Frowds acquired the property on either side of no 4 Newington Causeway where they began, eventually stretching from no 2 to no 18. G. W. Frowd died in 1903 by which time his son Walter George had taken over. A few years earlier they had opened a cricket ball factory beside the Medway in Tonbridge.

A competitor of Surridge in Aldersgate Street, F. H. Ayres successor to the Edward Ayres who had first set up in Clerkenwell in 1810, highlighted Britain's central role in world cricket and world cricket bat manufacture by calling his products 'Ayres Improved "International" Bats'. An Ayres bat of 1909 is at Lord's.

The empty space marks the site of Riverside Works. G. W. Frowd had been making cricket bats with James Lillywhite at Newington Causeway and Cheltenham since the 1850s. Shortly before he died in 1903 he opened a Lillywhite Frowd cricket ball factory, which he called Riverside Works, beside Beardwell's Bakery overlooking the Medway in the centre of Tonbridge. The building was demolished some time after 1951

Ayres had his own ideas on handles and patented his version of one for cricket bats 'and similar striking appliances' in 1894 (no 11,632 of 15 June) 'formed of rods, preferably of cane, portions of which usually near the centre are cut away and the recesses filled with sheet india-rubber covered with canvas. Other strips of cane are then glued to the rods and the handle finished in the usual manner.' The drawing with the abridged specification showed a cross section of a finished handle with two central rods composed of cane, a portion of which had been cut away and replaced by rubber.

Others who like Surridge and Ayres made cricket bats in the City were Davenport at 20 Eldon Street, established in 1882, Robert Henderson & Sons who set up in the City Road in 1891 (they had a place in Berners Street too) and John Bryan who opened a small factory at 38 Charterhouse Square off Aldersgate Street in 1875 where he and his son Frank made 'President' spring handle bats and factored 'Grasshopper' cricket balls made in Tonbridge. In 1896 Frank Bryan patented a new kind of blade. 'The striking faces are covered or protected wholly or in part with cane. The figure shows a section of a bat blade with cane strips let into recesses so as to be flush with the face.' (No 661 of 10 January.)

Early in the new century Frank Bryan moved his cricket bat workshop to Long Lane Bermondsey, and shortly afterwards opened a small works to make batting gloves in Worcester, the centre of England's glove industry. Soon a larger factory was built in Worcester and in the 1950s the Bermondsey operation closed down and all Frank Bryan activities were centred on Worcester; but cricket bat making had already ceased many years back. Frank Bryan Ltd still operates as a sports outfitter in Bromyard Road, Worcester.

The Kent connection was being maintained through Amos Pett, a descendant of Thomas Pett, still operating in Sevenoaks, though no longer making cricket bats, merely repairing them and loking after them; though one of his customers seemed to have doubts about his capability to do even that. In 1899 when he was 70, Amos Pett received a letter,

> Sir – Yesterday I received a bat of mine. I now learn that you sent it up to Ashgrove because you thought it *might* belong to me. Last autumn I sent my bats to you to be looked after for the winter, and to be repaired, the above mentioned bat being amongst them. I shall think twice before I ever leave my bats with you again. – Yours faithfully, M.K.H.

Amos and his father Geoffrey never aspired to be cricket bat makers or minders in the tradition of their famous ancestor. They bought willow it was true, but for basket making not bat making. However to cricket in general, and to the Sevenoaks Vine Club in particular, he devoted the whole of his spare time. In 1978 there was a bat in the Vine pavilion with a silver shield on it which read: 'Presented to Mr Amos Pett with the thanks of the Sevenoaks Vine Cricket Club Committee for his great exertions in promoting the improvements on the Vine, 1881.' His son retired in 1928. Over his shop was the sign 'Henry Pett. Household Repairs, Blinds etc., Garden Seats, Cricket bats'. It was as well to spread the risks.

But the tours of the rival All-England Elevens and the formation of county clubs had spread the popularity of the game far beyond the southern counties where the game was born, and cricketers like R. G. Barlow who first played for Lancashire in 1871 and set up a cricket bat manufactory in Victoria Station Approach, Manchester, brought the craft to the north. Frank Sugg of Lord Street, Liverpool, who also played for Lancashire, having first played for Derbyshire, turned out 'Clinker' bats for 7s 6d and a 'Boundarie' model at 21s. Walter Lambert left his employment as a cabinet maker in Nelson, Lancashire, in 1877 to become a cricket bat maker on his own account. He was a keen cricketer and played for Nelson in the Lancashire League. His son and grandson carried on the business and 'Walter Lambert' bats have been used by Test players Wilfrid Rhodes, Learie Constantine and Clyde Walcott. After ninety-six years Walter Lambert & Sons are run by Walter Lambert III mainly as timber importers but they still make a certain number of cricket bats every year.

H. J. Gray, the champion rackets player of England in 1863, began making rackets for this game in his home town of Cambridge in 1855. This led to the formation of H. J. Gray & Sons and the manufacture of cricket bats – and indeed of golf clubs, squash, tennis and badminton rackets. Henry Gray was strategically placed for Suffolk willow, and 'Grays of Cambridge' soon became famous for their 'Playfair Driver' and 'Half Guinea' cricket bats well beyond the confines of the university. Their factory in Benson Street was called Playfair Works. The drawing of their 'Playfair Driver,' showing the way the cane handle was built up of separate canes, how it looked before and after turning, and how slips of india-rubber were inserted, was the only illustration of a bat in the making used by Ranjitsinjhi in *The Jubilee Book of Cricket*. Ranji had a Playfair Driver in 1893 according to Gray's records, but in his chapter on Batting (1897) he mentions only three makes, Wisden's, Odd's and Nicolls's – though he spells the latter 'Nichol's'. Perhaps he thought the full page illustration was a sufficient plug.

He said nothing of Richard Daft's bats, for he probably never tried one, but of his batting Ranji was emphatic. He was 'the most graceful and stylish batsman that ever adorned the cricket field'. But Daft not only played for Notts to the close of the 1880 season – he was born in 1835 – and wrote a classic on the game *Kings of Cricket*, he also made cricket bats. In the Cricket Guide of the 8 January 1880 issue of *Cricket and Football Times* he appeared in the list of 'Bat and Ball Manufacturers' as 'Daft, R. 1, Lister Gate, Nottingham', but he had probably been making them for some time before then; though his advertisement in *Bell's Life in London* of 30 May 1874 was only for a 'stock of articles connected with the game'. Around this time however he took into his Nottingham cricket bat workshop a fourteen-year-old lad called William Gunn. The boy showed promise both at the bench and the wicket, and when Notts gave him a trial as one of the colts of England for their match against the MCC, it was the beginning of a great cricketing career which continued until his retirement in 1904. Neville Cardus linked the tall and elegant William Gunn with Arthur Shrewsbury – the 'Hobbs and Sutcliffe' of their epoch. In 1885 Gunn persuaded T. J. Moore to join him in opening a sports dealers shop in Carrington Street, Nottingham, and Gunn & Moore were in business.

Five years later a young man called William Sherwin, son of a great Notts wicket keeper Mordecai Sherwin, opened up a bat making workshop a few doors down from Gunn & Moore – they were then on the opposite side of the street to their present premises. William Sherwin had served an apprenticeship with a well-known bat maker and become a consummate craftsman. He began in a small way, fashioning blades from clefts he bought from outside, and received many orders from Gunn & Moore for re-blading and repairs. When eventually they joined forces the famous 'Gunn & Moore' cricket bat had arrived.

Like Bill Sherwin, Harry Hayley, a popular cricketer of his day, also learnt the craft from one of the old cricket bat makers – none other than Aquila Clapshaw. Hayley played as a professional for Yorkshire and was engaged by the Leeds Cricket Club. In 1882 he opened a sports shop in his home town of Wakefield – at 74 Westgate. Shortly afterwards he acquired additional premises in Market Street beside the Corn Exchange as a cricket bat workshop. How many craftsmen he employed making cricket bats is not known, but the name of one of them is on record – Gosnay. As late as 1892 'H. Hayley, 74 Westgate, Wakefield' was advertising Hayley's Double Spring Handled Match Bat at 16s 6d in *The Athletic News Cricket Annual*, so it looks as if he was soliciting business from a wider market than the local clubs and had the capacity to supply it. He eventually moved his sports shop to the Corn Exchange building.

Henry J. Gray (left) was only nineteen and rackets coach at St Johns College, Cambridge, when in 1855 he opened the racket workshop which became H. J. Gray & Sons. He was Champion Racket Player of England in 1863, 1864 and 1865, and was also a fine cricketer. He retired in 1896 and died in 1915. In 1940 his firm amalgamated with L. J. Nicolls, the Robertsbridge cricket bat manufacturer, to form Gray-Nicolls.

His great-grandson, Bill Gray (right), joined the company in 1950, and in 1979 was chairman of Grays of Cambridge (International) Ltd.

One day in 1893 Harry Hayley had a visit from a fellow Wakefield man, cricketer/journalist/cleric Robert Stratten Holmes who wrote the weekly Cricket Notches article in *Cricket*, already quoted. Holmes understood from Hayley that the best willow came from Norfolk but that Yorkshire and other counties also yielded the wood, though it was of an inferior quality. The trees Hayley commandeered were sawn cross ways, allowance being made for cracking. Then the lengths were cleft with wedges into pieces large enough for a cricket bat blade. It was in this form that Hayley took delivery of them. At his Westgate workshop he roughly shaped each cleft with a hatchet or an axe, and then stacked them in the open air to get seasoned 'for a year or so'. Holmes remarks in his account of his visit that before Lord's was extended by the inclusion of Henderson's Nursery there used to stand such a pile of shaped clefts at the South East Corner – presumably made and put there by Robert or Frank Dark.

After this open-air seasoning, Hayley brought the rough blades inside and stowed them away under cover for another year or so, after which time he brought them out and hammered the face and edge of each one to enable it to resist the impact of the ball. He further hardened the wood by passing it through a press which reduced it by some eighth of an inch in bulk. 'Then comes the shaping of it. All done by hand and eye. The draw knife first; then the plane; whilst for the shoulder a spoke shave is used. A groove was made first for the handle.'

In 1893 every bat had a cane handle. Where, asked R. S. Holmes, was the old whalebone splice of yesteryear? The cane Hayley used was bamboo – twelve, sixteen or twenty pieces glued together and wedged into a frame to make them hold. 'Then the lower part – for the spliced blade – is most carefully tapered. And a very delicate and difficult business this is; for there is nothing to keep the handle firm in its place but perfectly accurate measurement and glue. Not a nail or peg or screw of any kind.' If the handle was too small for the groove in the blade, it would not hold; if it was too large, the strain on the blade would make it split down the face as soon as the bat was used.

'Just think of that, all batsmen, and specially when you examine an old favourite bat. Why is the handle as firm as a rock? Answer: Good workmanship in the making of it. And let me remind you that you never can compensate the best workmanship, either in bat making or anything else.'

Hayley finished off the blade with a hand file and glass paper of various textures, the piles of sawdust from the soft willow wood filling his floor. With a well-used steel he put the final touch on the pod.

He turned the handle on a lathe, first with a gouge and then with a broad chisel. He took it off and filed and smoothed it with glass paper. He wound well-waxed string on to it with the lathe. When he had done this for all but the last three inches, he inserted another looped piece of string by hand, with a loop long enough to show when the stringing was completed which caught up the stray end of the main string. The loop was then pulled out from its position three inches down the handle and the end drawn under the bound string so that it was hidden out of sight and made secure. Hayley rubbed linseed oil into the blade to fill the pores of the wood and harden the face and put a surface on it. He also put it for a final hardening through the press. The whole process had taken 'three or four hours'.

'It's all very well for batsmen to brag about their skill,' was the reverend's last comment, 'but it would never come to light unless it were supplemented by the genius of the mechanic.'

He was surprised to find how heavy (but well balanced) Hayley's bats were. He conceded that heavy bats were needed in 1893. He thought there would be a market for three pound bats. 'To make them light for cutting might not a piece of lead be inserted on the flat disc which forms the handle top?' If the idea was worth considering any bat maker was at liberty to make use of it and patent it, as J. N. Crawford had patented the diagonal insertion of strips of india-rubber down the length of the handle when other makers inserted india-rubber in vertical lines.

Cricket bats, wicket and outsize cricket balls surmount the shop front of John Wisden & Co's London showrooms in Cranbourn Street. Cricket bats line the top shelf of the window display, though the lettering on the glass spells out every sport but cricket

Harry Hayley Ltd still flourishes under Mr Bush's management, though Harry's shop and cricket bat works were demolished in the 1960s along with the Corn Exchange and most of Market Street to make way for a new office block. They are now in The Springe.

In London George Bussey was going through similar procedures as Hayley in Wakefield, but on a very much larger scale. By the 1890s he found he could no longer acquire the quantity of willow he required by personally choosing trees from landowners in East Anglia and having the timber sent down to his London works. So he made a mass purchase of all the 'really A1 timber' he could discover, and erected timber mills in the heart of the best willow growing district on two acres which he secured at Elmswell in Suffolk. 'We have a holding,' he claimed in 1897, 'of the finest timber without parallel in the history of the cricket trade, exceeding 1,000 tons.' At Elmswell he planted willow saplings too, so that in time his saw mills would be surrounded by a forest of *salix*.

At these mills he organised the cleaving of the clefts. Splitting willow for cricket blades required large experience and good judgement, he said. 'Much valuable timber has been spoilt by inexperienced men.' It was not merely a question of splitting round timber into pieces of a certain size, there were a number of details of an ever-varying nature which required consideration, and the sacrifice of an enormous amount of timber was entailed.

A two pound blade was taken out of twenty-four pounds of timber in the trunk. Half of this loss came in the conversion of the trunk into clefts. For every cleft another had to be wasted. The butt end was always better than the upper parts in all timber, but never more so than in willow. Bussey saw a willow trunk in terms of the comparative retail prices of the cricket bats that would come out of it. From the first length at the bottom would come a 25s bat; from the third a 12s bat; from the fifth a 7s 6d bat; from the sixth one costing five bob. Above that were 'boys' bats'.

But he could not always rely on *all* first lengths turning out 25s bats. Many would not produce a single 'best' bat from the whole trunk. 'It is the highest class tree that produces timber fit for the best, and then only in the first length or two. Many trees will not give any bats of higher quality than 5s or 7s 6d. An experienced judge can tell with a remarkable degree of accuracy from which length a particular blade has been taken, without resorting to any scientific or mechanical method of testing.' But as a precaution he had had a machine designed to test blades. The existence or absence of grain, incidentally, he said was no indication of quality.

Chopping the blades was done at Elmswell. 'This process requires an amount of skill that takes years to acquire.' It was not only an alteration of form, the chopper had to study the peculiarities of each cleft which frequently required considerable manipulation to bring the right face to the front and the best edge on the right side.

There was a misconception about a blade being all sap and no 'heart'. As a rule the heart of the timber was better than the sap portion, but not with willow. Bussey had as much as possible of the heart removed but not all of it, and what was left remained on the upper edge. This chopping reduced the cleft by a further eight pounds. By this stage

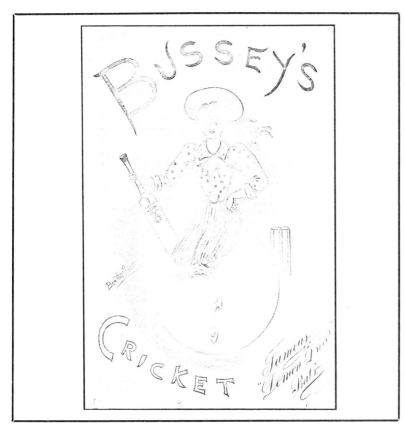

The trade mark of C. G. Bussey, London cricket bat maker on a large scale in the 1890s – his speciality the 'Demon Driver' – taken from his booklet *A Popular Treatise entitled the Bat of the Victorian Era*, published in 1897

enough seasoned timber to make five cricket bats had been discarded in the effort to make one.

His men at Elmswell daubed these rough blades with size and whiting to prevent them splitting, and stacked them in piles so the air could circulate. They were left in the open for twelve months. 'Our experience has so convinced us of the advantage of thoroughly seasoned timber that in order to inaugurate a system whereby no unseasoned bats should leave our factory, we declined orders for best bats during one season.' Six months seasoning in his view was not enough.

When the year was up, the seasoned rough blades were taken to Bussey's factory in London, where the fashioning into a finished cricket bat followed much the same lines as at Wakefield. The first activity was called drawing out. A craftsman took one of the pieces and marked on it with a template what wood was to be removed to give it the shape of a bat. He then proceeded to pare away the wood with a double-handled, chisel-shaped tool known as a draw knife. 'This is rather a laborious process, and in consequence the heavy task is apportioned amongst the workers of the Bat Shop. It does not fall to the lot of one or two men, but to all in their turn.'

The blade, looking very much more like the Demon Driver it was to become, then underwent a very severe process. Some blades did not survive it. It was passed into what Bussey called 'a self-acting machine, specially designed and constructed by ourselves, which performs the twofold function of hardening the surface and testing the strength of the grain.' This was a press which compressed the wood. The blade which survived a test of this magnitude earned its rating as a 'best' best.

Bussey had another 'specially constructed apparatus' for cutting 'with mathematical accuracy' the V-shaped opening at the top of the blade into which the handle would be spliced. This done, to give a perfect face the surfaces of the opening were carefully pared with a chisel by a skilled workman.

The making of a cane handle for a Demon Driver has already been described. One end was shaped to correspond with the V gap in the blade. The surfaces both of this and the surfaces of the V were fitted with extreme accuracy before finally being united with 'the finest glue procurable'.

> When we say the 'finest' we mean it, price does not enter into the question. Have you ever considered the tremendous strain the splice has to stand when the enthusiastic batsman, doing what we believe he calls 'getting the handle into condition', places the handle on a block or ledge raised a few inches from the ground, with the end of the blade on the ground itself, and then performs with his whole weight on the junction as if the bat were a spring board?

After handle and blade had been wedded, the handle was turned, though not shaped. The finishing process, which put the stamp of the individual craftsman on the end product can best be described in Bussey's own lyrical words.

> The bat is now passed to the most skilled workman, viz. – the 'finisher', in whose hands the blade acquires the graceful outline and comely form, coupled with the delicately designed proportions of a perfect and finished cricket bat. The good finisher is necessarily an experienced and competent workman, with a real affection for his craft. Machinery, however ingenious, cannot 'finish' a bat; it requires human skill combined with intelligence. Bats cannot be made in moulds, nor shaped in exactly similar form. As we have previously explained, good Willow is the reverse of plentiful, and the maker cannot afford to throw on one side blocks of first-class timber because perchance they may have disfigurement.
>
> The good finisher shows what an artist he is by removing eye-sores while preserving the comeliness of the blade, and this he does without damage to the serviceability of the bat. At times, in getting rid of these disfigurements, the blade must necessarily assume a somewhat modified form, so, if you should notice it, do not at once exclaim, 'The man that made this does not know how to make a bat.' He may have been a bad workman but, on the contrary, he may also have been a most skilful one. He cannot afford to throw away the material; if he did so the prices of best cricket bats would be still further advanced; and as cricketers object to a blemish, his only course is to make the most of his skill and remove disfigurement with as little injury to the outline of the blade as possible. For our own part we should prefer, if cricketers would only permit it, to pay less regard to the appearance of a 'gall' or other mark that does not affect the playing qualities of a bat.

George Bussey wanted to make razors that sold *and* cut.

The finisher completed his handiwork with a spoke shave. He then passed the bat to the paperer who with glass paper and bone rubbed away at the surface until he produced a shine.

Bussey's trade mark, as can be seen from the reproduction on page 125, was a fair young batswoman in straw hat and bloomers, her hair flowing in the breeze, her right hand clutching a Demon Driver, perched on an outsize cricket ball in front of a wicket. This was not only an eye-catching piece of commercial artistry; makers like Bussey turned out cricket bats of a special weight and design not only for boys but also for women. Cricket had been popular with women in its early days; there are reports of regular women's matches throughout the eighteenth century and into the beginning of the nineteenth. Contemporary pictures remind us of the gay abandon with which the ladies disported themselves. One of the last matches of this classical period of women's cricket was depicted by Rowlandson in 1811 showing eleven Hampshire women playing eleven Surrey women. But when young Princess Victoria ascended the throne in 1837, the climate of opinion of what was proper and what was improper for women to do in public changed, and women's cricket went into a decline. Badminton, croquet, riding to hounds, roller skating Yes; cricket No. But by the 1880s the Queen could not have cared less, and women took to cricket again. In 1890 the Original English Lady Cricketers' Club was organised by the English Cricket and Athletic Association 'to prove the suitability of the National Game as a pastime for the Fair Sex in preference to Lawn Tennis and other less scientific Games'.

Two teams known as the Red and the Blue Elevens were trained by professionals G. G. Hearne, Maurice Read and others. The Reds and the Blues, reminiscent of the rival teams who contested in the Colosseum of Ancient Rome, gave a series of exhibition matches throughout Britain, each team being accompanied by a chaperone. This was such a rapturous success that the girls were only prevented from following it up with a tour of Australia by the unanimous veto of every parent. They were equipped and dressed by Lillywhites, the sports shop which the cricketing brothers had established in London in 1863.

The official outfit was described as being 'calf-length dresses, with sashes, sailor collars and cricket caps' and the costume of Bussey's Girl was obviously inspired by this. A Mrs Ada Ballin, contemporary advocate of 'Rational Dress' for women, hoped that lady cricketers would don a generous pad between their dress-body and their underclothes at the wicket, but there was no sign of Miss Bussey falling for that one. Women's cricket has never looked back since those days, and Lillywhites are still suppliers to the Women's Cricket Association.

5 After the Golden Age

Bat and ball craftsmen of the 20th century

A measure of the boom in cricket ball making was the formation in 1897 of a trade union, the Amalgamated Society of Cricket Ball Makers with a registered office at the Mitre Hotel in Hadlow Road, Tonbridge (later at the Station Tavern, in the High Street). The secretary was Frederick Boorman who lived in St Mary's Road, and there also seems to have been an anonymous Organising Secretary.

By the end of 1907 there were one hundred and eighty-six members, a falling off from the previous year. Fifty-six members had been struck off for being more than thirteen weeks in arrears with their subscriptions, and several members had been discharged from their jobs through slackness of work. By 31 December they were still on the unemployed list. The Golden Age was evidently beginning to lose some of its glitter – for the ball makers, at any rate, if not for the bat makers.

The president was W. T. Humphrey and the treasurer H. M. Heath, with three retiring committee members W. Burr, H. Card, and H. Martin, and nine others due to retire in March, June and September: W. J. Biddle, E. Bristow, G. Eade, G. Challen, A. Rabbitt, F. Wells, J. Bonwick, W. Ives and F. Killick. William Ives was the brother of Thomas Ives II and Frank Wells was foreman at Duke; both were also trustees.

Hopes for fuller employment among members were raised by W. G. Frowd, who some time before G.W.'s death in 1903 opened the Lillywhite Frowd cricket ball factory in Tonbridge. This was a two-storey works on the north bank of the river Medway some hundred yards from the iron bridge downstream from the castle. In 1979 its site was marked by the empty space beside the National Westminster Bank. A half-derelict building (still standing), with 'Beardwell's Bakery' painted on the outside wall, formed the other half of this little row of buildings and is identical to the Lillywhite Frowd workshop which once stood beside it. At this first Riverside Works some twenty cricket ball craftsmen were employed. The windows were near enough to the river for the quilters and seamers to hang fishing rods from them in the hope that every now and again a bell would summon them to land an object large enough to fry for supper. Bert Dyer, who in 1974 was working for Tworts, was foreman.

The annual report of the ASCBM for 1907 said their expenditure had been heavier than in the previous year, but in spite of that they had added £83 to their capital. Permission had been obtained to bank up to £1,000 in the Post Office Savings Bank, though they only had £340 in there at the time. Prospects of aggrandisement must have looked rosy. The 'Members Share Account' showed two hundred and sixty-one shares with a total value of £765 2s 4d, with the average share being between £4 and £6. They had £500 stacked away in Consols.

A traditional whip-round of threepence a member on the death of a member's wife had raised £2 8s 3d for J. Woodhams (whose name as a cricket ball maker in Southborough has already been noted). The payment of expenses for delegates coming to the annual general meeting from Oxford, Penshurst, and Teston had cost £1 9s 4d. Oxford members were probably still being employed by Benjamin Harse, or Harse Brothers as they had become, with their workshop at 30 Pembroke Street, St Aldgate's, Oxford. Victimisation Pay to a member for eight weeks amounted to £10. A grant of 10s was made from their meagre funds to the Transvaal Miners Association for some fraternal reason, and a similar one to Ruskin College, Oxford. Three members who had left the trade had been paid out – S. Hitchcock, A. H. Dyer, C. Orrom. Grants ranging from 7s 6d to 10s had been made to eight members. A Distress Fund raised by each member giving a penny a quarter stood at £5 2s 10d. In 1908 this was raised to a penny a month as the fund was too small to give any practical assistance to anybody. The secretary and organising secretary each visited Teston (Reader) 'but we have lost nearly all our Members there'. They had also been to their Putney section, mainly to find out who was the employer there. It was probably

According to this annual report of the Amalgamated Society of Cricket Ball Makers several members were discharged through slackness of work during 1907 (scarcity of orders or lax workmanship?). Many were still on the unemployed list at the time of the AGM on 8 February 1908, leaving a membership of 186

Amalgamated Society of Cricket Ball Makers.

Annual Report and Balance Sheet for Year ending Dec. 31, 1907.

The ANNUAL MEETING will be held on MONDAY, FEB. 3rd, 1908, at the Station Tavern, Tonbridge, to commence at 8 p.m. sharp.

Officers retiring, but are eligible for re-election—

President: W. T. HUMPHREY	Trustees:	Auditors:	Committee: W. BURR
Secretary: F. BOORMAN	W. IVES	F. BELCHER	H. MARTIN
Treasurer: H. M. HEATH	F. WELLS	C. E. COCKERELL	H. CARD

Committee:

Retire March—	Retire June—	Retire September—
W. J. BIDDLE	G. CHALLEN	J. BONWICK
E. BRISTOW	A. RABBITT	W. IVES
G. EADE	F. WELLS	F. KILLICK

Spalding. Between 1908 and 1913 the Society was affiliated to the Labour Party, but never sent a delegate to their annual conference. There were two hundred and sixteen members in 1908; the figure fell to one hundred and sixty-five in 1911 but rose again to one hundred and seventy in 1913. The society continued to operate until 1946.

With the attempts to organise labour in the cricket ball industry went efforts to improve the product. In 1912 one of Henry Luff's sons, Ernest Constantine Wisden Luff, patented a cricket ball whose middle circumferential seams were sewn 'with a thread composed of steel, phospher bronze or other wire lapped with wax' (no 19,505). Two years later he and his brother incorporated Wisden as a limited company.

Cricket bat and ball making achieved the status of a growth industry only to be stopped in its tracks by the Great War which broke out in 1914. Craftsmen of eligible age either joined the forces or a factory making more warlike products than the weapons of the national pastime. First-class cricket adjourned 'for the duration' and the industry's main customer became the NAAFI. The Golden Age had been eclipsed. The Golden Age had been eclipsed.

W. H. Duke, John Duke's son, died in 1913 at the early age of fifty-seven, and in 1920 Duke & Son were acquired by John Wisden & Co whose cricket balls had been made by them for forty years or more.

'Our Sporting Offer' – in Duke & Son's catalogue of 1909

DUKE AND SON, 23

MARCH, 1909.

To Cricketers Everywhere !

OUR SPORTING OFFER.

In order to promote the cause of Cricket and to increase the interest in Club Matches, we have decided during the Season of 1909 to present, **FREE OF ALL COST,** a large number of

OUR WELL-KNOWN

CRICKET BATS

Upon certain Simple Conditions, viz. : To any member of a Cricket Club using any one of the following **Duke & Son's Bats,** purchased during Season 1909, viz., The "Century," The "Australian Match," The "Clarence," The "Victory," The "Reliance," The "Special Club," The "Best Practice," or Youth's "College Driver," Sizes No. 4, 5 and 6, or Youth's "Junior Match," Sizes No. 4, 5 and 6, and scoring **Fifty Runs** with the same in a Single Innings in an **Afternoon** Match, we will **Present Him** with a Bat of the same quality as a Prize.

The Conditions to obtain a PRIZE in a **Whole** Day Match will be that the number of Runs required to be obtained in a Single Innings will be **Eighty,** as there is a better chance of having Two Innings in a Day than during a Half-day Match, and that the Bat used was purchased in 1909.

To prove that a Bat has been Won all that will be required by us is an authentic copy of the Score Sheet of the Match, signed by the two Captains, or the two Umpires, together with their Addresses, and, if possible, a copy of the Local Newspaper reporting the Score, stating these particulars and that the Bat used was purchased in 1909. When satisfied that the Runs were honestly made during the progress of an Eleven-a-side Match the

PRIZE BAT WILL BE FORWARDED IMMEDIATELY, CARRIAGE PAID.

We hope this Unique Offer will be appreciated by Cricketers, and that their assistance will be tendered in every way to make it widely known.   DUKE & SON.

— **RULES.** —

1.—Only one Bat can be won by the same individual.
2.—Only one Bat can be won by the use of one particular Bat, i.e., one Bat can only win one Prize.
3.—The name of the Bat with which the runs were scored to be stated.
4.—The Name and Address of Firm from whom the Bat was purchased and Date.

5.—The Bat used must be the **personal property** of the player claiming the Prize, but in the case of Schools, or if the Winner used a Club Bat, proof must be given that the Club or School possess at least Three of our Bats, and that they were purchased in 1909.

PENSHURST, KENT ENGLAND.

CASE OF CRICKET GOODS AS SHEWN AT THE AUSTRALIAN EXHIBITIONS
AND AWARDED HIGHEST HONOURS WITH MEDALS
SYDNEY, MELBOURNE AND ADELAIDE.

Duke & Son, Chiddingstone Causeway, in its heyday as manufacturers of a wide range of sports equipment, including cricket bats and balls, before being acquired by John Wisden & Co in 1920

Duke had now been making bats as well for eighty years, and in 1921 the Duke–Wisden combination produced a bat inspired by the Australian tour of that year associated with the Australian left-handed batsman Warren Bardsley. Duke's 'Warren Bardsley' bats were a brand which continued into the 1950s. Wisden sold their West Ham factory in 1925 and built themselves the Fitzgerald Works in Mortlake to take its place.

Harry Duke, a popular figure in Penshurst and a keen player well remembered by many in the village in 1974 (like Harry Towner of Rectory Cottage who had played cricket with him as a boy fifty years before) ran the Chiddingstone Causeway operation with the help of his brother John, under Wisden. When he died at the Ivy House in 1923 his cousin Arthur Duke took over. But he, too, was to die the following year – the last of the Dukes.

But it was not the last of Duke – thanks to the deep roots of the Duke tradition and the craftsmen who never let it die, and to the fortuitous appearance the year before the Wisden merger of an accountant with a head for administration able to take over the reins.

Harold Tipper, a Londoner, born in the City in 1895, had been articled to Ellermans the shipping firm for four years before war came in 1914. He joined the army and was badly gassed in France, so when he was demobilised in 1919 his doctor advised him not to return to his desk in Leadenhall Street but seek a job in the country where there was no smoke and fog to attack his lungs. On holiday in Kent he visited Penshurst, heard of the activity at Chiddingstone Causeway and applied for a job as an accountant. He was twenty-four. When, within four years of his joining, the three members of the family hierarchy who ran the firm died in quick succession – it was a partnership in which they held all the shares together with A. H. Constable, Arthur's cousin – Harold Tipper became responsible for the whole of what by 1924 had become the Duke side of Wisden. There were some hundred craftsmen

THE INDUSTRIAL COURT.

(664.) CRICKET BALL MAKERS—TONBRIDGE AND DISTRICT.

(*Claim for a reduction of wages.*)

Parties :

Cricket Ball Manufacturers' Association

and

Amalgamated Society of Cricket Ball Makers.

Terms of Reference.—An application dated 26th May by the Association for a reduction in percentage increases of $22\frac{1}{2}$ per cent. as from 4th June and a further 15 per cent. as from 3rd September, 1921.

---

1. The matter was referred under the Industrial Courts Act, 1919, by the Minister of Labour to the Industrial Court for settlement.

2. Representatives of the parties were heard in London on 27th June, 1921.

3. The workpeople concerned are about 240 men employed by a number of associated firms in and around Tonbridge. Practically all the men concerned are pieceworkers, paid an agreed rate per dozen balls for the particular process on which they are engaged.

4. In April, 1919, the parties arrived at an agreement as to piece-rates. In February, 1920, the agreed rates were increased by 25 per cent. and in October of that year they were increased by a further $12\frac{1}{2}$ per cent., so that the present rates are the rates agreed to in April, 1919, with the addition of $37\frac{1}{2}$ per cent. The total advances made since the outbreak of war have resulted in an increase in wages of approximately 200 per cent.

employed at the peak period; marquees were put up in the fields behind the Quilt Shop to house those for whom there was no room in the small buildings.

They had no hesitation in using their industrial muscle to secure high wages. In April 1919, through the Amalgamated Society, they won a good agreement with the employers on piece rates. It was reckoned that practically all the two hundred and forty cricket ball makers in and around Tonbridge at that time were piece workers. Two increases followed within eighteen months – twenty-five per cent in February 1920 and another twelve-and-a-half per cent in October. Total increases made since the outbreak of war in 1914 amounted to two hundred per cent. In 1921, compelled to reduce selling prices to meet the competition from India and Australia, members of the Cricket Ball Manufacturers' Association, formed pre-War, asked the Industrial Court for permission to reduce wages – a cancellation of the thirty-seven-and-a-half per cent increase and a return to the 1919 rate. The application was opposed by the Amalgamated Society who claimed that the 1919 Agreement

The official reply of the Industrial Court to the request of the employers' Cricket Ball Manufacturers' Association in 1921 to reduce wages which was opposed by the craftsmen's trade union, the Amalgamated Society of Cricket Ball Makers. The thirty-seven-and-a-half per cent increase since 1919 was reduced to twelve-and-a-half per cent

5. The employers propose to return to the rates of April, 1919, by withdrawing the percentage addition of 37½ in part from 4th June, and in full from 3rd September, 1921.

6. The employers state that in order to meet the competition of makers in India and in Australia they will be compelled to reduce their selling prices. They contend that the fall in the cost of living, as shown by the official index number, justifies a return to the rates agreed in April, 1919.

7. On behalf of the workpeople it is submitted that, under the terms of the agreement of April, 1919, seven months' notice, terminating on 1st February, must be given by either side of any alteration in rates of wages, and further that, apart from the question of due notice, no real necessity exists for the proposed reductions.

8. So far as the question of notice is concerned, it appears that the provisions of the agreement were not strictly adhered to when the percentage additions made in February and October, 1920, were negotiated.

9. The Court, having carefully considered the evidence submitted and the contentions of the parties, are of opinion and so decide that the addition of 37½ per cent. which is being paid upon the rates laid down in the agreement of April, 1919, shall be reduced to 22½ per cent. from 27th June, 1921, and to 12½ per cent. from 3rd September, 1921; that is to say, from 27th June, 1921, the rates paid shall be those of the agreement, with the addition of 22½ per cent. and from 3rd September, 1921, the rates paid shall be those of the agreement, with the addition of 12½ per cent.

WILLIAM W. MACKENZIE.

J. McKIE BRYCE.

D. C. CUMMINGS.

R. J. HUMPHREYS,

Assistant Secretary,

5, Old Palace Yard, London, S.W.1.

28th June 1921.

required seven months' notice, and that in any case the reduction was unnecessary. But, ruled the Court, the provisions of the agreement were not strictly adhered to when the increases were negotiated in February and October 1920, and from 3 September 1921 piece-rates would be the 1919 rate plus only twelve-and-a-half per cent.

Ernest Ward found the shops at the Tonbridge cricket ball factories in 1927, 'mainly at Quarry Hill', were so closely guarded to preserve the secret of how balls were made that not even apprentices were allowed in the workroom to see the final assembly of the parts.

> The seven shillings cost of a cricket ball in Farington's time was relatively higher than the seven shillings or so of our pre-war price. But since the war [1914–18] labour and material have sent up the cost for retailers to the thirteen shillings now [1927] charged by Wisden. The workers in the ball factories are a fine race of men. All did their bit in the war. Most of them, as a species of holiday, are the 'gate' men on the Kent county grounds. It was a system established by the late Tom Pawley who was above all a Tonbridge man. Meantime the main secret in cricket ball manufacture is splendidly kept by Duke and Wisden.

It was said that a quilt maker had to swear on oath before a magistrate not to take a job with a competitor and divulge the techniques he had learnt.

This was a stand taken by all employers in the area, and to formalise it and other matters of common interest, in 1923 they re-formed the Cricket Ball Manufacturers' Association as the English Cricket Ball Manufacturers' Association. The first meeting of the new association at the Angel Hotel, Tonbridge, on 20 September 1923 was attended by representatives of Duke & Son, Wisden & Co, T. Ives & Son, Hitchcock, the KCC (the Kent Cricket and Football Manufacturing Company, of which Duke were proprietors), and Alfred Reader & Co. A sub-committee was formed to revise the old rules and Mr Gradidge and Mr Twort were accepted as members. Five days later at a meeting attended by A. H. Constable, H. Gradidge, T. Ives, H. Ives, H. Duke, C. Smith, A. Smith, E. H. Hitchcock, T. W. Twort, E. Twort, H. Tipper (whose younger brother John joined the staff in 1923) and G. Gooch, J. V. Reader was elected secretary. He was Alfred Reader's younger son who had himself become the father of a son, Donald, in 1910.

These are mostly familiar names. Tom Ives and his son Harry attended the meetings, and in 1921 Harry's son Thomas Richard Ives, representing the third generation, joined the firm aged sixteen. Ned Hitchcock had married in 1900 when he was twenty-one, and when war came in 1914 he joined the Army Service Corps. He ended up as a Fire Master at Marseilles which he found so exhilarating that only the bribe of the house which his father bought for him in Goldsmid Road brought him back to wife, home and cricket ball making. Edwin Twort and his brother Thomas William Twort were in charge at Southborough; Edwin's son Thomas Twort III had been born in 1904. Charles Smith represented Wisden's Baltic Road works. Harry Gradidge was the Woolwich cricket bat maker for whom a number of Tonbridge firms had been making cricket balls for many years. However, like Wisden, he decided it would be more economical to form a

Minutes of the first meeting (in Tonbridge) of The English Cricket Ball Manufacturers' Association formed in 1923 after the dissolution of the first employers' grouping, The Cricket Ball Manufacturers' Association

Representatives of Messrs Deebe & Sons, Wisden & Co, J. Ives & Son
Hitchcock, K.C.C & Alfred Reader & Co being present at a meeting
held at the Angel Hotel Tonbridge on Sept 20th 1923, all the
members having expressed their willness to become members
of the English Ch. Cricket Ball Manufacturers Association 1923
Mr Gooch was asked to place before the meeting the result of the
Sub Committee formed to revise the old rules & his having been done
& the revised rules having been unanimously adopted
Mr Gooch proposed seconded by Mr J. Ives that Messrs
Gradidge & Twort be accepted members of the New Association
this was carried unanimously.

It was resolved to call a meeting for Sept 25th to elect officers
& fix prices for Season 1923-4   A H Constable
                                        Jan 8th 1924

Present at a meeting held at Angel Hotel Tonbridge on Sept 25 1923
Messrs A. H. Constable, H. Gradidge, J & H. Ives. H. Duke, Tepper, Gooch, C Smith
A. Smith, E H. Hitchcock, J. W & E. Twort & J. V. Reader
Mr Constable welcomed the two new members Mr H Gradidge &
Messrs Twort & Sons & then the members proceeded to elect the Officers
for ensuing twelve-months. Mr A. H. Constable Chairman
Mr J. Ives Vice Chairman, Messrs H. Duke & J. Ives Trustees
Mr J. V. Reader Secretary Messrs Constable & H. Ives Auditors
all being unanimously elected to the several offices.
                                        A H Constable

A. READER & Co., Teston, near Maidstone, Kent, Eng.

Concerning Cricket Balls

IN the manufacture of our Balls we select the finest hides procurable. These are dressed by our own special process, which ensures perfect rigidity. The leather is dyed with a brilliant fast colour, giving an excellent and permanent finish.

¶ We make a speciality of Quilts (or Cores). These are built up entirely by hand with best quality cork and worsted.

¶ All Balls are guaranteed accurate in size and weight, conforming with Law 4, perfect in shape, possess sufficient resiliency to obviate stinging the hands, and capable of withstanding the hardest wear and extreme climatic conditions.

¶ Special attention is given to the manufacture of Balls for Overseas use. The covers are dyed red right through with a special fast dye, which is guaranteed to retain its original colour when subjected to the hard wear on dry wickets, matting pitches, and bare grounds.

Alfred Reader & Co's pre-Great War advice 'Concerning Cricket Balls'

cricket ball unit of his own. A. Gradidge & Sons are given in the Tonbridge directory of 1932 (though surprisingly not earlier) as having an upper room at 149a High Street. It was here they had a small cricket ball workshop.

Alfred Reader had carried on cricket ball making in the workshop and two wooden huts in the garden behind the village shop at Teston throughout the 1914–18 war with the aid of his two sons Archie and Villiers. He was now personally stamping the name and trade mark on each ball and giving it a final inspection and polish before it left the factory. They were making hockey balls as well, the same as cricket balls except that they were not dyed red but given a final coat of white enamel. A price list dated 1 September 1914, but obviously sent to the printers before the fatal 4 August on which the conflict began, warned 'It must be understood that in the event of Strikes, War or other unforeseen contingencies that delivery of orders or contracts already in hand cannot be guaranteed.' Trade prices were much as they had been at the end of the century: 'Special Crown' (guaranteed fully hand-made quilts) with ninety to ninety-five stitches at 51s a dozen, Second Treble Sewn Match with eighty-five stitches at 45s a dozen, Best Match Treble Sewn with eighty stitches at 42s, Treble Seamed Halves (Men's) with sixty stitches at 30s a dozen.

A Note stated: 'From this date the qualities and prices of all Cricket Balls quoted in this list have been standardised by the Cricket Ball

Manufacturers' Association. All Balls will be impressed with a Letter, as above, A, B, C, D and E which will denote their quality and the number of Stitches the Balls should have.' Another note said the prices were subject to alteration without notice, and in 1920 they soared. 'Special Imperial Crown' balls 'as used at Lord's' were 144s a dozen to the trade; the Treble Seamed Halves which had been 30s were now 96s. An introductory letter to retailers explained the increases:

March 1st, 1920

Dear Sirs,

The Cricket Ball Manufacturers' Association having granted a 25% increase on wages to their workmen, and taking into consideration a 14% advance in price of leather and 20% advance on Worsted, and also heavy increases in prices of all other materials used in the manufacture of cricket and hockey balls, we are obliged to notify the Sports Trade that prices . . . will be increased on and from 15th March 1920.

By the end of the decade prices had fallen again. The A quality 'Special Imperial Crown' were 108s a dozen, and the E quality Treble Seamed Halves back to 60s in 1926. In their wholesale price list for this year Reader were anxious to point out 'All Cricket Balls specified in this list are made by thoroughly experienced ENGLISH WORKMEN AT OUR OWN FACTORY.'

A writer in *Sports Trader* describing activities at Teston at this time gave the average length of service of those who were with Reader before the war as twenty-eight-and-a-half years. 'After the war much new blood, all sons of fathers already in the firm, was introduced, but the average length of service is still as high as $17\frac{1}{2}$ years and the percentage of ex-Service men is still about 50 per cent. Everything is done to make the conditions under which the men work as attractive as possible

Villiers Reader applies the 'Go-No-Go' gauge to a product of the Teston factory to test its correct circumference. The wording stamped on the gauge shows it is approved by the MCC

and singing and the playing of gramophones is encouraged. "Our output has actually increased since we stopped working on Saturdays," said Mr J. V. Reader, "except the principals, of course" he added with a smile.'

Villiers Reader was the driving spirit behind the new English Cricket Ball Manufacturers' Association. Their principal object was presumably price fixing and an attempt to provide the trade with a uniform standard of qualities. At their first meeting they agreed for instance that a 'Red Halves' ball other than the one scheduled could be made, so long as it did not have more than fifty stitches.

Their main worry, however, was the competition from the manufacturing 'commune' in the old skating rink in Tonbridge set up by cricket ball craftsmen themselves. Some of these put in an hour or two early in the morning or late at night or at weekends, when they were not working at their regular place of employment; others worked there full-time. They elected one of their number as chairman and shared the profits. Some have said it was partly subsidised by Gamages, the London store, who kept them going with orders for these cut-price pirate products. This commune was a menace which demanded immediate investigation, and at a Special Meeting called for 1 October they agreed that on the following Friday 'as near as 5 o'clock as possible' they would all ask each man in their employ to say whether or not he belonged to the Workmen's Guild, as it was called. Tom Ives thought any man who did not give a negative answer should be given a week's notice to quit work not later than 8 October, and everyone agreed with him. When they met again two hours after the agreed time for taking the census, they learnt to their dismay that of the one hundred and eighty-eight men questioned, seventy-eight said they were members of the Guild.

> After some discussion Mr T. Ives proposed, and Mr Gradidge seconded, that known members of the Guild be notified they cannot serve two masters, and would be given the option of withdrawing from the Guild and remaining in the employment of their respective firms; if on the contrary such men who persist in supporting the Guild must consider themselves under notice of terminating their present employment week ending October 12th 1923, each firm to notify their employees on Monday October 8th.

The minutes do not show whether this resolution was passed, and indeed make no further reference to the Guild which was eventually forced to its knees and the skating rink workshop taken over, it is said, by Lillywhite Frowd, who already had their Riverside Works beside the Medway, though today its proprietors have no knowledge of this.

An employee working for two masters however was less of a crime in the eyes of the association than an employer undercutting. Harry Gradidge wrote and complained that Wisden had supplied balls direct to the MCC at a price lower than agreed by the association. Wisden's George Gooch confirmed that they had indeed sold balls at 108s a dozen to the Marylebone Club, but if that price was against the undertaking of members they had acted innocently and had had no intention of going against the rules. He pledged Wisden not to act contrary to the rules in future. They then proceeded to agree that prices and terms for 1925

Only the hats, caps and boots of these craftsmen in the Duke & Son cricket ball factory at Chiddingstone Causeway betray the fact that the picture was taken in 1925

would remain the same as 1924, but retailers in the Midlands and north of England felt that they were not being treated properly and they decided to hold a conference with the association in London to sort out the best collective buying procedures. The accent was on collective. There was a semblance of closing the ranks at any rate, but the deceptively calm surface was soon to be broken. At the meeting of 1 January 1925 a letter was read from George Gooch, who did not attend, tendering the resignation of the entire Wisden/Duke combine. Looking back on it after fifty years Harold Tipper thought it had something to do with Wisden's objection to the other firms making cricket balls for bat makers and dealers at lower prices than the same balls stamped with the manufacturers' name. His recollection was that Duke/Wisden broke from the association when the others refused to stop this practice, and that Wisden, in an effort to beat them at their own game, set up a ball factory, separate from the Chiddingstone Causeway unit, in Tonbridge to make non-'Duke' balls stamped with their customers' names. This, he said, was the Kent Cricket & Football Manufacturing Company with a workshop employing some thirty men beside the Medway opposite Tonbridge Castle. They may have given the Kent Cricket Co this role in 1925, but in fact it had been going at least since 1899 when it appeared in the Tonbridge Directory of that year with 'Duke & Son, proprietors' after the entry in brackets.

From the minutes of the association however the cause seems to have been resentment at not being allowed freedom of action on prices. They were not too happy either at being accused of rocking the boat of which, after all, as the biggest producer in the area, they were the helmsman. 'It was resolved that should the associated firms of Messrs Wisden cut prices, notwithstanding their expressed resolve not to do so, that any Member should take their own line of action after first verifying the fact and in every case report the circumstances and their subsequent action to the association.' After only two years the association had split into two camps. Harry Gradidge who had provoked the secession became the association's chairman.

In 1926 the MCC were considering altering the law relating to the size of the cricket ball for the first time since 1838 when they fixed the circumference at between nine and nine-and-a-quarter inches. News that the Advisory Committee which had been set up by the club to make recommendations favoured reducing the circumference, caused consternation among association members, the Wisden/Duke group and every cricket ball maker in the kingdom. The association called a Special Meeting on 12 January 1926 to debate the implications of the proposed new Law 4, and while they knew that members would play their part in enforcing it, 'it was a matter of some concern regarding the stock of balls that were undersized i.e. of the wrong size, and would mean a great loss if those balls could not be cleared.' Tom Ives and Villiers Reader were deputed to seek an interview with Mr Lacey the secretary of the MCC to put the makers' case, and at least get official sanction for clubs other than county clubs to use the old ball until stocks were exhausted. Villiers Reader telephoned Lacey there and then, and fixed an appointment for the following afternoon.

Inevitably the MCC's Advisory Committee appointed a Special Sub-committee which had instructions to 'provide for a ball in size as near as possible to that which was in use prior to 1926'. The association were invited to give their views, as were Wisden, who decided in this case to bury the hatchet and to call for a combined meeting at Cranbourn Street to draft a recommendation which would represent the whole of the industry. This was that a ball not less than eight and seven-eighths inches in circumference and not more than nine and one-eighth inches, with the same weight as at present, was the right size. If there was to be a new Law 4, they considered that it should not come into force till 1927 to allow present stocks to be cleared. On 8 January 1927 they were drafting a circular to the trade suggesting a proportion of two-thirds of the larger ball to one-third of the smaller ball to fill orders. Cyril Luff, manager at Gradidge's, suggested pooling all the large balls from the various firms and putting them into one place, and agreeing a price per dozen. All orders for the outsize ball would be met from the common stock, no particular make being recognised. And what about offering the oversize cricket balls to the Colonial Market at a reduced price?

In the end the new ball did not become law until 1927, and the MCC settled for a circumference between eight and thirteen-sixteenths and nine inches. It was hoped that introduction of a smaller ball and higher stumps would end the negative batting and negative bowling which had been the bane of the post-war game, part of the general paralysis which had been a feature of first-class cricket ever since it had been resumed in 1919. 'English cricket in the 1920s,' wrote Neville Cardus, 'was, like the country as a whole, psychologically, even spiritually, ill; character and skill in cricket were becoming standardised, with everything else in the land.' Standardised downwards, that is.

To reduce the size of the ball was a technical ploy which did not

DUKE & SON'S
"SPECIAL COUNTY" Cricket Ball

Specially Made for County and First Class Cricket. Something Entirely New.

SINGLE
BALLS

Per Doz.

½ and ¼
dozen
at same
rate.

Postage
extra.

each.

Postage
extra.

Interior, Showing Construction.

A PLEASURE TO BOWL WITH.   A PLEASURE TO BAT WITH.   A PLEASURE TO FIELD WITH.

NO MORE BRUISED FIELDSMEN'S OR WICKET-KEEPERS' HANDS.   NO MORE BROKEN BATS.

*The Most Perfect Cricket Balls ever made. County and First Class Cricketers will use
no others, on account of their Great Superiority over any other Cricket Balls.*

THEY ARE DELIGHTFUL TO PLAY WITH.

Used at Lord's, Oval, Melbourne, Sydney, Johannesburg, Cape Town, University, County and Colonial Grounds.

'Not nearly so hard', 'do not hurt the hands' – selling lines for Duke cricket balls in 1909 to counter competition from imported products which were said to bruise fielder's hands and break bats

involve a lowering of standards, but by gad, those damn Aussies flooding the country with *machine*-stitched products was another matter – especially as the machine-stitched balls were forcing English hand-stitched balls out of other 'colonial' markets like the West Indies and Ceylon.

But it was no joke for the traditional hand-stitchers of Kent, as Pat Lee who began his working life as a fourteen-year-old boy at Wisden in 1911 well remembered sixty-two years later. In 1926 about a third of the entire work force was laid off as a result of it. In 1973 in the second year of his retirement after sixty years as a cricket ball maker – he took over from Frank Martin as foreman in 1938 and stayed on for thirty-three years – Pat Lee, born at nearby Charcott in 1897, was one of sixty craftsmen when first he went to work as an apprentice at Chiddingstone Causeway. His father was head keeper to Mr Hills at Redleaf House, Penshurst, which all seemed to fit the tradition. He received a shilling as his first week's wage, but once a tradesman he got a certain amount per dozen balls.

The whole cricket ball making operation took place in the two buildings which faced each other on either side of the road round which Chiddingstone Causeway village clustered. In the two-storey building, still standing and occupied, they did the seaming and stitching, closing and turning, polishing and stamping. The cottage behind it was used for washing and drying the leather. In the cottage on the opposite side of the road, demolished in 1949, known as the quilt shop they did the 'secret' work of making the cores of cork and thread. No one who was not a quilter could enter. William, Harry and Timothy Duke were taking part then. Their office was in a corner of the top floor of the main building, the rest of which was occupied by stitchers. William Duke liked to take a hand as a workman polishing cricket balls with rags and elbow grease (no 'polish' then). The foreman was Frank Wells who lived in the village and, unprompted, Pat Lee thought was a relation of the Dukes.

Pat began work at five in the morning, and in those pre-1914 days would take himself off to the fields with a colleague on a bright summer afternoon – 'I know where there's a pear tree in bloom' – and return in the evening to do his quota of piece work by the light of his lamp, for which he had to bring his own oil, like the framework knitters of Hawick and craftsmen everywhere.

> On the top storey where I worked you could tell by the different hammerings from the floor below who had come back for a stint at the bench, as I had, after a day's hunting or fishing – the three beats in a row of the closers, the steady continuous beating of the turners. We'd stay till seven or eight. Sometimes Mr Harry would look in – his home was at Horse Shoes just up the road. The other two lived in Tonbridge – quite a way in a chaise. They had cars later, but the first man to have a motor in Chiddingstone Causeway was the vicar. That was in 1909. We came out on strike once. Our union, the Amalgamated Society, came to the village with a brass band and marched up and down the road outside our windows calling on us to come out. The boys, who were on 15s a week, were out for six weeks and spent their time playing pitch ha'penny. There was a second strike in 1914 but we had to return without getting the rise we asked for. I joined the Territorial Army in the war, and at 18 was in India and Afghanistan. Things were different when I returned in 1920, but we still 'rounded the quarters' with a knife, cutting round the edge of a pattern placed over a piece of leather like a razor, and the turners still sewed three stitches through them to hold them in position. They glue them now; saves money. We made some 90 dozen best balls a week in the mid-twenties, and exported most of them to Australia. Till 1930. Overnight, as it were, the business disappeared. The Australians had found a way of machine-stitching cricket balls; and not only did they not want the hand-stitched balls which we made, but they sent over their very much cheaper brand and swept half our market from under our feet. There was wholesale sacking.

A further trouble was that the cheaper Australian produce almost entirely excluded British cricket balls from the export market. Duke were, in fact, compelled to dismiss a large number of their employees as a result of the Australian Government's tariff imposed on cricket balls in 1930 – and so were Wisden in Tonbridge. When in addition Duke cut wages by ten per cent in view of the slackness of trade – exports had been reduced by fifty per cent – the two hundred man work force at Chiddingstone Causeway went on strike.

Reader exported none of their much smaller output to Australia – they had some twenty-five craftsmen employed at this time – so the Teston operation was very much less affected by the removal of the Australian market for English hand-stitched balls than the Duke/Wisden works at Chiddingstone Causeway and Baltic Road, Tonbridge. Donald Reader joined the family firm in 1926, and the following year they acquired the 'Gradidge' cricket ball works in Tonbridge of which Cyril Luff was manager, a relative of the Henry Luff who became proprietor of Wisden on the death of the Little Wonder in 1884 and who died in 1910. Reader took over the stock of oversize 'Gradidge' balls which was proving such an embarrassment to them following the MCC's new law.

The bat making side of Gradidge, which had started in Artillery Place, Woolwich in 1870 and become famous for its 'Len Hutton' bats, went (in 1930) to the sports goods manufacturing firm which Albert and Ralph Slazenger opened in Manchester in 1881, and moved to the famous Laurence Pountney Hill works, off Cannon Street, London, in 1883. This was Slazenger's first entry into the cricket bat making field, and was followed up a few years later by the acquisition of William Sykes & Co who made 'Don Bradman' cricket bats, footballs and other sports goods on a big scale at Horbury in Yorkshire. Twenty-three-year-old William Sykes started the firm when he bought a Horbury saddlery for £19 in 1880. Sykes were not themselves cricket bat makers but entered the field by buying the old London firm of F. H. Ayres of which much has already been written. So 'at a stroke', as it were, Slazenger became instant cricket bat makers by assuming responsibility for the two old-established houses of Ayres and Gradidge, and then slowly transferred a name which hitherto had been associated with the game of tennis to the equally ancient game of cricket.

Whether or not it was due to the smaller ball, cricket had now come out of its doldrums with the sparkling displays of Bradman and Hammond, and those who served the game by providing equipment found the demand once more on the increase.

Reader stepped up their own production facilities when a number of experienced craftsmen suddenly came on the market in Oxford. Reader, who were known to have had this association with cricket ball making in Oxford, were appealed to, but they were as reluctant to set up in the university town as the men were to leave their homes and move to Kent. They had the need to increase output however, so they came to a compromise by arranging for some half a dozen or so of these cricket ball makers, one of whom was significantly named Martin, to stitch cricket balls at home – balls which had been seamed at Teston and were sent to them in boxes through the post. When they had done the stitching they packed them up in their boxes and posted them back to Teston. It was the outworkers' system which Ives practised from Preston Road, Tonbridge – at one time they too had a stitcher at Oxford, probably also an ex-Harse craftsman.

In the light of this expansion the village shop annexe which constituted the main Reader factory, with the two wooden huts on either side, became too cramped, and in 1927 they bought a couple of acres on the other side of the road and built themselves a new works. They moved in the following year, abandoning the old place which had served Tom Martin and Alfred Reader so well for sixty or seventy years. The latter still stands together with the second of the two huts put up alongside in 1895 and the village shop and post office to which it is attached, now run by L. and G. Phillips. A visitor who was shown round the new cricket ball factory in 1928 was told they were making fifty dozen cricket balls a week there, thirty thousand a year. He noted that on the day of his visit they were dispatching orders to New Zealand, South Africa and British

Billy Biddle, a vastly experienced quilt winder, making a weight test to ensure he has wound in enough worsted at the Alfred Reader cricket ball works at Teston in Kent in 1930

Columbia. They were still dyeing the leather for 'colonial' balls red all through, in order to stand up to hard, bare pitches as they had been doing in the 1880s. There had been the affair of Reader's Blue Ball which they had tried unsuccessfully to urge on the MCC for women's games. There is one of them to be seen in the pavilion at Lord's.

The Australian threat was followed in 1930 by the Indian menace – and right in the middle of the world-wide economic crisis, when the English cricket ball makers were attempting to reduce the high wages which they were forced to pay immediately after the end of the Great War. In 1930 the English Cricket Ball Manufacturers' Association reckoned the rate of living had dropped fifty-six per cent since 1914, and the cricket ball industry had yet to have its first drop in wages, though it had had to lower selling prices to meet outside competition. And now there was this additional rivalry.

'Following a discussion of the menace of the Indian made ball,' ran the minute of the association's meeting of 23 June 1931, 'the Chairman proposed that the Society write to the Council of the Sports Trade Association pointing out that Indian made balls should bear the name of the country of origin.' The Board of Trade was written to, and means sought of bringing the menace to the attention of the British Public by means of a poster. Edwin Twort attended a Board of Trade enquiry, but for some reason or other was not allowed to state the case for clearly marking Indian cricket balls 'Made in India'. 'The secretary was instructed to write to Rex Bentall, President of Tonbridge Chamber of Commerce and to Lt Col H. Spender Clay PC, CMG, MC, MP calling their attention to the state of the English Cricket Ball Industry through Indian competition and asking that they do their best to get a duty put on all imported balls.' The Colonel asked for a memorandum from the association setting out in what way the import of cricket balls made in India by cheap labour had been prejudicial to English cricket ball makers, which he could present to the Chancellor of the Exchequer. In 1932 the Government issued an Order in Council stipulating that foreign sports goods had to bear an indication of origin, but association members were uncertain what 'indication of origin' meant and who was to be responsible for carrying out the branding. However it was a step in the right direction, and the association were justifiably pleased with one immediate result of their representations.

But a situation they found less easy to handle arose in 1933 from the development in the Duke/Wisden camp of what was known as Tipper's Patent.

This was applied for (no 403/32 of 6 January 1932; specification no 385,436) in the name of Harold Tipper of Chiddingstone Causeway and John Wisden & Co Ltd of Fitzgerald Works, Mortlake, and had as its object 'to provide in an economical way the outer surface of the ball with means whereby a good finger grip on the ball can be obtained'. So why the consternation?

Harry Martin and his son put a final polish on Reader cricket balls at the Teston works in the 1930s

An ordinary ball, stated the specification, had six circular series of stitches on its face, the two covers being sewn together (seamed) by three series of stitchings. This made for a ball with a very firmly secured cover, but the cost of auxiliary stitchings which was considerable was not always justified, as it had been found that for ordinary purposes a single seam was sufficient. 'According to this invention we provide a ball in which the cover sections are provided, laterally of the seam, with one or more rows of stitching, exposed at the surface of the ball, but not connecting the sections in addition to stitching by which sections are seamed.' Since this stitching did not serve to seam together the covers, it could conveniently be applied before the covers were placed on the core (the quilt) and sewn together and made in a wavy line or in a series of short lines at an angle to the seam.

The crunch came at the end. Normal cross stitching could only be done by hand, but 'dummy' stitching which did not connect the covers could be done by a sewing machine. It would lock the lining or inner reinforcement to the cover and prevent it from slipping. Machine stitching, they claimed, represented 'a considerable saving in expense … while as good or even better finger grip is provided'.

The Tworts, Ives, Hitchcocks and Readers determined to oppose the patent with every means at their disposal and share the costs. The aid of a Mr Webber of the London Football Company was enlisted, and on examining the specification declared that the idea had been previously used about forty years before by Rowe of Woolwich.

> Mr Ives read a statement from a Mr Stroud which stated that he was at work at Rowe's at the time machine-stitched balls were made there, and Mr Webber stated he had a Mr Stotts in his employ who also was there and seamed the covers after the stitching had been machined. It was also recalled that a machine-stitched ball has been exhibited by Dukes during the latter months of 1931, Mr Ives having had one shown him by a customer, a fact which would tend to make invalid any application for a patent if it was applied for after said exhibition. It was also thought that the proof of prior making would effectively dispose of a right to a patent … Mr Webber said he had machine stitched cricket balls several years ago but discontinued as he did not consider them to be an effective, useful or saleable article.

Webber was instructed to buy a stitching machine used by a Mr Fearey of Messrs Gorden, Edwards & Neville who had once worked it for dummy stitching, and Ives was given all necessary powers to lodge a challenge against Tipper's Patent, and an 'honorarium' of ten guineas to mark the association's appreciation of all the work he had put in. But within a year the matter had disappeared from the minutes. Wisden and Duke successfully launched their machine-stitched 'Royal Corinthian' with which they were able to recover much of the ground lost by the Australian bombshell of 1926, and most of their competitors had recourse to a method which soon became an acceptable and routine part of the English cricket ball making scene. In 1936 ECBMA members were working out an agreed price for the tenders for machine-stitched balls they had received from the London County Council – a minimum of 38s a dozen for men's size and 35s for youth's, less five per cent for cash. A year later the commotion had died down to the extent of admitting the patentee who had caused the rumpus, Harry Tipper, into their deliberations in order to give Wisden's assent to machine-stitched prices. It was also mentioned that Duke and Wisden might shortly be giving their workmen a week's holiday *with pay*. But even an Association that included Duke and Wisden was not representative of the whole of the cricket ball industry in Tonbridge; firms like the Harlequin Ball & Sports Co and the Games Ball Co were still going it alone.

Machine stitching was the most important but not the only deviation from the traditional, best quality, hand-stitched cricket ball with the solid cork quilt, promulgated in the 1920s. G. W. Beldam and C. A. Beldam who were experimenting at this time with all kinds of sports equipment, patented a cricket ball 'of superimposed hemispherical shells surrounding a spherical core formed of cork cuttings or powder. Shells are drawn together and held by bindings or worsted. Cork is moulded under heat and pressure and may be mixed with an agglomerating material such as rubber latex, either vulcanised or unvulcanised (no 226,675 of 1923).' T. and H. Ives of Ives & Sons Ltd patented a cricket ball with 'sinuous or undulatory' edges 'stitched together circumferentially of the ball' (no 317,227 of 1928). Beldam's 'squabs' became a permanent feature of cricket ball making, but Ives' edges were never widely adopted.

Tom Ives died in 1936 and at their meeting of 5 May members of the English Cricket Ball Manufacturers' Association stood in silent remembrance of a chairman who had played a leading part in the industry's affairs for so long. The same honour was accorded Ned Hitchcock of Hildenborough who died suddenly the following year. The Hitchcock business was acquired by a Colonel Arkwright who immediately upset his fellow members of the association by awarding a unilateral rise in wages without consulting them. It was not the kind of gesture they appreciated in the least bit, and indeed in 1938 they rejected outright a request from the Amalgamated Society of Cricket Ball Makers to restore the 1930 wage cut.

On Ned Hitchcock's unexpected death, another Mr Smith – no doubt a relation of Charlie's – who was an accountant and was lodging with the widow of Ned's brother, managed the firm of Hitchcock until Arkwright took over. The Colonel was a colourful figure without, as far as can be judged, any previous connection with cricket ball making before his dramatic entry on the Hildenborough scene in 1937. Ronald Creed, who at sixty-five was still working at Twort as a stitcher in 1973, remembered the impact which this flamboyant Old Etonian, ex-Indian Army character had on the Hitchcock craftsmen of the time, of which he was one. The Colonel let it be known that he was a descendant of the Sir Richard Arkwright, sometime travelling barber and eventually knight and high sheriff of his county, who in 1769 had invented a machine for spinning by rollers worked by water power, one of the pillars of the Industrial Revolution. Inheritance of the spirit and energy of so famous an ancestor would doubtless have enabled him to bring similar benefits to the cricket ball making industry. He had an estate in Sussex from which he would motor over every day to supervise, with the aid of a male secretary, his new-found hobby, and on some days filled his tourer with his actress friends to whom he delighted to show off his latest fad – 'my dear, would you believe it, *cricket balls!*'

He played a bit of cricket – Eton Ramblers and all that – and indulged in the usual patrician pastimes of salmon and trout fishing, shooting and golf. He had plenty of money and was not greatly concerned with making more. The five per cent rise he gave Ron Creed and his fellow craftsmen was from a genuine feeling that they were underpaid and to hell with what other employers could afford. And to hell with the ECBMA for that matter! He produced biscuits and tea in the afternoons which Neddy Hitchcock had never thought of doing, and the dank workrooms lost something of their austerity as they filled with the aroma of Turkish cigarettes.

Ron Creed spent three years at pre-Arkwright Hitchcock as a boy – he went to the Ball Shop, as they called it, at fourteen and returned to it for long periods afterwards. When production was in full swing, there were some eighteen men employed there. Like others, Ron Creed worked at most of the cricket ball factories in the area. At one time in the 1930s he, his father Frank Creed, and his father's two brothers Sidney Creed and Walter Creed, were all working at the Wisden works in Baltic Road. His grandmother was a Twort, and his grandfather, again like many others, was part-time cricket ball maker and part-time publican; he ran the Royal Oak at Southborough.

The Colonel's new broom failed at Hildenborough where Ned's more plodding, businesslike methods, building on his father's achievement, had made Hitchcock so successful. In any event, another war diverted the military gentleman's attention to activities more proper to his calling. Soon there was nothing at Hildenborough which his pride would allow him to show his girlfriends. It gradually ran down until finally, after eighty years, it ground to a halt. The Ball Shop stood empty for a while; it was used off and on by others for making cardboard boxes and the like.

In 1941 the new cricket bat company formed in that year from the merging of Grays of Cambridge and L. J. Nicolls of Robertsbridge as Gray-Nicolls Ltd, decided to diversify into cricket balls. After a short period of manufacture at Robertsbridge with Bert Dyer as manager, the most experienced man in the business (still at Twort part-time in 1974), they acquired the empty ex-Hitchcock factory at Hildenborough which once again was filled with seamers and stitchers, closers, turners and quilt makers for making 'Gray-Nicolls' cricket balls – but no afternoon tea and no lovely visitors from the glamorous world of the theatre. Three Gray-Nicolls cricket balls stamped 'The National, Dyed Red Throughout' can be seen mounted pawnbroker-fashion beside the front bar of The George Inn at Robertsbridge.

Reader were not bound by the association's decision to reject the trade union's request, for, as noted, the Amalgamated Society had managed to make little headway with the Teston men, and in 1919 the latter had formed the Teston Independent Society of Cricket Ball Makers, which was registered as a friendly society in 1921. It was the smallest union in the country and as such became the butt of music hall comedians and television comics for years to come. But in a close community of craftsmen such as at Teston, industrial relations were

This is how strips of leather were washed in colour tubs at the Alfred Reader cricket ball works at Teston near Maidstone in the 1920s

necessarily less formal and more personal. Son followed father with regular precision at Reader, just as the Shoebridges, Drapers and Orroms did at Ives. One of the earliest Reader craftsmen, William Page, died in 1936 aged seventy. He had learnt hand-stitching at Southborough and came to Teston with his brother Peter, a turner, in 1888. William's son Fred had come to start his fifty-six years as a closer and turner in 1900 (he died in 1957 aged seventy-one), and Fred's son Alan joined the craft in 1929.

Archie Reader had no children of his own, so he adopted an orphan who, when she grew up, married a man called Adams. As Archie Reader's 'adopted grandson' their son was part of the Reader family. Leslie Adams was set to learn the business from the bottom upwards in 1932, and by the time war broke out in 1939 he had mastered every aspect of it except seaming, just as Donald Reader, Villiers's son, had had every process at his finger's tip except stitching by the time he was

Leslie Adams weighing and fitting for size, surrounded by quilts, at the Alfred Reader cricket ball factory at Teston – a photograph taken in 1935

diverted to help with marketing. When Archie died he left his half share in the business to be divided between Leslie Adams and his brother Villiers. In 1935 Donald Reader married the youngest daughter of Jack Hubble, the Kent cricketer and sports retailer, and his son John was born the following year.

New firms joined the old ones, but the men they employed were of course 'the old firm' of traditional craftsmen of the Tonbridge area, which was the reason why the newcomers came there. Stuart Surridge of London came to Tonbridge in 1938 and took one of the houses in the centre of the elegant Salford Terrace in Quarry Hill Road which had belonged to a Dr Watts (old Tom Ives's physician incidentally), and converted it into a cricket ball factory. It was still there in 1979 beside St Stephen's Church on the Tunbridge Wells side of the railway line, as was the whole terrace with its name engraved beneath its central arch but with its fine frontage spoilt by the row of shops at street level. No 19 which became Surridge's cricket ball works, is now White's.

To Tonbridge too came Lillywhite Frowd & Co, owned by Frowds Limited who started making cricket balls in Bradford Street, and maybe later took over the Workmen's Guild experiment, as noted, after lack of management and financial skills had brought the experiment to a halt.

The optimism which prompted such expansion at a time when Britain had at last pulled out of the economic crisis, was sustained by the reminder of the antiquity of the cricket ball making craft which came from the find made by George Edwards, Penshurst builder and chief bellringer, in the grounds of The Mount, dower house of Penshurst Place and next door to The Paddocks where the Dukes had carried on the craft up to 1841. The story was related in 1974 by Edward 'Ginger' Meade, the Penshurst organist who, after thirty-five years at Wisden/ Duke, spent each summer sitting in a white coat at a gate of Penshurst Place controlling the visitors. According to Ginger, George Edwards was doing repairs one day at The Mount in the 1930s and came across an old ball mallet in the undergrowth which must have been dropped by one of Timothy Duke's men a hundred years or more before as he wended his way home down the hill to the village from Redleaf. It was a symbolic link with the past, and an omen for the future of a craft which would surely survive the ambitions of a Fuhrer whatever New Order he might be planning for the 'decadent' cricket loving English and their far-flung Empire. But when peace was threatened in 1938, it was obvious that the wares of the cricket bat and cricket ball makers would take a low place on the shopping list of a nation preparing for total war. The Empire's in-fighting had already dealt the Mother Country's cricket ball industry a hurtful blow, and now the Third Reich delivered the *coup de grâce*. In 1938 Wisden went into voluntary liquidation. They had collared the market with their stitchless tennis balls, but when the patent ran out competitors like Slazenger made them too and Wisden lost ground. Management consultants were brought in to revitalise the organisation, and much of the reserve capital was spent in implementing their recommendations – but to no avail. A receiver and manager was appointed who kept things going at Chiddingstone Causeway and Tonbridge with Harold Tipper as best he could. When war broke out, within twelve months large numbers of staff were called up and the Baltic Road building was requisitioned as a Civil Defence Centre. Wisden became a shadow of its former self but, with the aid of an Admiralty contract for balloon stabilisers, managed not only to keep its head above water but to recover much of the lost capital.

For this second interruption to his working life, Fred Sayers, now fifty – he had had a stint at Thomas Ives's works in Preston Road, Tonbridge in the 1920s and then returned to Baltic Road – it was a matter of leaving his bench once again, this time to join the War Reserve Police in a full-time capacity.

At their meeting of 18 September 1939, the English Cricket Ball Manufacturers' Association 'expressed apprehension as to the future of the industry owing to the outbreak of war' and then proceeded to fix prices for the next season – 119s a dozen for Grade A 90-stitch balls to the trade, or 18s each retail. Semi-machine stitched balls were 59s a dozen wholesale, or 9s each retail. The Board of Trade tried to encourage concentration of effort, but the association wrote to point out that member firms were in country districts in small factories and since no machinery was used the space required was quite small. 'The average age of men now employed was high, as all the younger operatives had either been called up or had joined in some civil defence force. Those still employed were expert only in this particular industry, having been so engaged from a very early age and would prove very unsuitable in any other industry, particularly where machinery was in use. Concentration was not practical except that in certain work (hand stitching) a centre could be arranged from which the work could be issued and collected when finished. The Industry were now engaged solely on providing for the services and schools.' There was no concentration and the union asked for higher wages, which sent the cost of the Grade A 95-stitch ball up to 130s a dozen in 1941. But the following year the cricket ball makers were faced with shutdown from a proposal of the Government to prohibit any sports goods being made from cork. A licensing system obviated complete closure and when the first new member, W. G. Frowd, was admitted to the association for some years, in 1944, the price of the Grade A ball had gone up to 150s a dozen, or 22s 9d each including Purchase Tax. But it was Mr Frowd's first and last meeting, for that 5 January 1944 chairman Harold Tipper, T. R. Twort III, Tom Ives, Donald Reader and J. V. Reader decided not, on second thoughts, to dissolve the association but to suspend it *sine die*. It became affiliated to the Federation of British Manufacturers of Sports and Games which had been founded in 1918. A price fixing association in any event was no longer of any practical value. With labour as short as it was, the individual firms could sell all the 'utility' cricket balls they could make without the slightest difficulty.

With Penshurst in the front line of the Battle of Britain and the flying bomb attacks, the Duke factories were lucky to escape damage, but at a quarter to eleven on the night of 13 November 1944 a German V2 rocket destroyed the wooden Twort cricket ball works at Southborough, luckily taking with it none of its human occupants but blasting away the cob nut bush, walnut tree and grapevine which Tom Twort had planted so lovingly that spring of 1861. The firm moved to temporary workshops in Edward Street.

Edwin Twort had retired in the middle of the war through ill health, and handed over to his son Thomas Richard Twort, born in 1904, who had started to learn the craft as a boy of fourteen and became a partner at twenty-one – Thomas Twort III – the fourth generation of the family to be involved in cricket ball making counting William, father of Thomas Twort I. A new factory was built on the old site and they had moved back to Park Road by the time Edwin Twort died in 1947.

The policy of giving independence to India and the colonial territories involved helping these countries to develop their own industries, and this meant encouragement of indigenous cricket ball manufacture of the type that had begun in Australia and India between the wars. It was not for the British Government to impose import duties on their cricket balls or give an 'unfair' subsidy to Britain's cricket ball makers. This however was the first step of those who came to power in the new self-governing countries.

This was hard on the British cricket ball industry, and many of the craftsmen, in a spirit of 'if you can't beat 'em join 'em', accepted posts overseas to teach the traditional English crafts to those who sought to compete with the employers they had just left, not only for the custom of the clubs and schools of Britain but the markets of the world. And who can blame them? Demobilisation was the moment for redirecting lives which had been diverted into the side stream of war, and many chose it to break with the past and start again. The cricket ball firms of Tonbridge–Teston–Southborough had been denuded of craftsmen for six years, and in 1946 they never expected to return to the level of production of 1938. For not only was there the competition from the Commonwealth producers but from the new way of life in which cricket no longer played the part it had. The market which Britain now had to share had become very much smaller. There were now too many other, rather jollier week-end diversions in which the whole family, and *girls*, could join. Father's solemn, lone rituals at the cricket club no longer seemed to fit the more relaxed, less respectful community of post-war Britain. And those who did play were coming to *like* the 'other' type of cricket ball. Australian cricket balls were first used in first-class matches on the MCC tour of Australia in 1946, and the English Cricket Ball Manufacturers' Association's worst fears of ten years before were being realised. The eighty per cent of the world cricket ball market which then had been theirs was fast slipping from their grasp, never to return. How could their prices be competitive when sixty-five per cent of the cost of making a 'best' cricket ball was in the wages, and the 'skilled' labour employed for the same job in Australia and India was so cheap?

Typical of the best English craftsmen who had stuck to the job was Charles Springate who had joined Reader in 1897, served in the Royal Artillery between 1914 and 1918, and in 1947, at the end of another war, was still putting in a forty-five-hour week as a seamer at the age of seventy – and ninety-five stitches was the rule then. Seaming twelve dozen balls a week was his stint, and he was by no means the oldest employee at Teston nor was his fifty years service the longest.

After the Baltic Road cricket ball factory off Quarry Hill, Tonbridge, had served as a Civil Defence Centre, it was occupied by the RAF. But the Wisden which had it back at the end of the war was no longer in the hands of the Receiver; it had been bought in 1944 by the Co-operative Wholesale Society of Manchester who reopened it as the 'Wisden' cricket ball works. In 1949 they demolished the old quilt shop on the south side of the Chiddingstone Causeway road and on the site built a very much larger new factory. The 'Quarry Hill' works at Baltic Road continued to operate until 1961, when Chiddingstone Causeway became the centre of the whole Wisden undertaking.

When Wisden celebrated the centenary of the opening of their Mortlake Works in 1850, Percy Wells was one of the craftsmen to help them. He had been making quilts for Duke in the same shop for fifty years and, as John Hadfield tells in the booklet produced for the occasion, Percy's father had sat there for fifty years before *him*. Percy Wells died, but his craftsmanship lived on in Pat Lee who in 1973 remembered the old quilt winder as one of his first teachers. Another of the Duke stalwarts at

Chiddingstone Causeway in 1950, the Wisden centenary year, was Joe Whibley who came to the shop in which he was then still hand stitching best cricket balls, in 1888 – sixty-two years before.

Surridge managed to carry on throughout the war, and when Fred Sayers was released from his duties as a War Reserve Policeman he joined them as one of four stitchers on the top floor of the Salford Terrace house, which had a shed in the garden to house the three quilt makers. Bill Ingrams was manager, and altogether there were some twenty-six men making 'Surridge' cricket balls.

When Southborough Urban District Council decided to apply for a coat of arms to mark the coronation of Queen Elizabeth II, they gave the heading of the shield a cricket ball flanked by two bricks to symbolise the town's main industries. The arms were granted in 1953, the year Twort celebrated *their* centenary. Old-timers like Henry Farmer the cover maker, Charlie Tingley the quilt maker, Joseph Woodrow who had been at Park Road for forty years, and Albert Risley who had stitched cricket balls there for seventy, told the newspapers of a craft they had loved and practised, and how little it had changed. The head of the firm, Thomas Twort III, himself an artist, told listeners on BBC Radio Newsreel how a hand-made cricket ball was a work of art. 'We have to work to a fraction of an ounce,' he said. 'There's no question of turning out as many balls in as short a time as possible. In fact one man won't make more than twelve balls in a week. The cricket ball not only has to be strong. It has to be soft enough to be knocked for any number of sixes, without bursting or losing shape, and it has to please both the batsman and the bowler.'

The following year the speaker brought out what was described as 'the first innovation in cricket ball design for 400 years'. The thickness of leather of T. R. Twort's new cricket ball at the seams was no greater than elsewhere – the antithesis of the Stonyhurst ball which balanced on its thick protruding seam as it hurtled along the hard pitch. He patented the 'Perko' Perfected Uniform Thickness Cover (double-lined) in 1954 (no 3788/54, specification no 761,892). It had three rows of ninety stitches, and the secret lay in its two sets of linings. 'Perko' balls cost 6 to 8s a dozen more than ordinary cricket balls.

After fifteen years of a declining market the Tonbridge cricket ball makers decided to apply the Board of Trade's wartime remedy of concentration. In 1961 the cricket ball departments of Surridge and Ives in Tonbridge and Gray-Nicolls in Hildenborough closed, and they amalgamated with CWS-owned Duke/Wisden as Tonbridge Sports Industries. TSI confined their cricket ball making activities to the old Duke factory at Chiddingstone Causeway which produced one range of cricket balls but marked 'Duke', 'Wisden', 'Surridge' and 'Gray-Nicolls', each firm marketing its own brand. Harold Tipper retired after forty-two years and Tonbridge-born Bill Mepham joined the office at Chiddingstone Causeway to look after the accounts.

The cricket bat manufacturing activities of Stuart Surridge at Witham, Essex, of Thomas Ives at Preston Road, Tonbridge, Gray-Nicolls at Robertsbridge and Duke/Wisden at Chiddingstone Causeway each continued to operate independently of each other, and of TSI. Thomas Twort, now sole proprietor of the one hundred and eight-

The coat of arms of Southborough Town Council with the cricket ball making industry, which at one time was so extensive in the area, represented by a cricket ball between two bricks beneath the helmet. The first cricket ball maker was Leonard Woodhams, and an R. W. Woodhams of Lady's Gift Road was still practising the craft at Southborough in the 1970s. The last Southborough cricket ball workshop closed in January 1978

year-old family firm, which only made balls, declined to join the consortium and carried on under his own banner for five years. By 1966 however the competition had become too fierce and he sold out to TSI, taking a seat on their board.

Only Alfred Reader & Co remained outside. Villiers Reader had retired in 1951 and Donald's son John Reader (another JVR) began ten months of hand stitching in 1953 before national service in the Royal Air Force Regiment. He returned to the Teston works in 1956 to complete his apprenticeship until 1962 and was able to acquire a practical knowledge of every process. John Reader will still stitch you a club match ball in thirty-five minutes flat. Indeed when another Australian import, the 'Kookaburra' ball, led to a total strike in 1962 he and Leslie Adams and his father, Donald, sat down at the benches, and in a month they had made eighty dozen balls between them.

In his 1966 thesis *The Cricket Bat and Ball Industries of Britain* Malcolm Goodman said he thought the formation of Tonbridge Sports Industries Ltd achieved real economies. The four firms who got together in 1961 had, he said, up to then 'organised their output on such primitive lines that they could fairly be called "quasi-cottage industry workshops"'. In 1959/60, he reckoned, 150,000 cricket balls were produced, of which TSI companies made 85,000. In 1965 TSI made 44,600 and Twort (taken over the following year) 12,000, and Reader 56,740. So roughly TSI and Reader had half the market each. 'Cricket ball making is a craft and the production process has changed little since the dawn of the nineteenth century. Balls are largely hand-made, only a little preparation work being done by machines.'

Reader were making plastic cricket balls in 1963. TSI made one with a polyurethane finish which was more durable, but the MCC would not recognise laminate treatment. Total production went down from 153,795 balls in 1956 to 100,625 in 1963 and up again to 113,339 in 1965. Australia had a twenty per cent tariff on English cricket balls and a heavy export subsidy on their own makes. They had captured the lucrative South African market.

In 1967 TSI claimed they had made 90,000 cricket balls. Their general manager Beverley Ives, son of Tom Ives II, said there had been more changes in the previous four years than in a couple of centuries. But there was still one to come. The men's trades union, the National Union of Furniture Trades Operatives, which had taken over from the Amalgamated Society, accepted the introduction of women for certain processes in return for a three-and-a-half per cent wage rise for their members.

And there was still further concentration in the offing. For in 1970 Grays of Cambridge bought from the Co-operative Wholesale Society the whole of John Wisden & Company, then mainly wholesale but which, a few years earlier, had manufactured a full range of sports goods including tennis racquets and tennis balls at Chiddingstone Causeway, where Bill Mepham had become manager. George Medlock, director of CWS and chairman of TSI/Wisden, took possession of the Wisden Museum of one hundred and sixty-nine historic cricket bats which had been removed to Chiddingstone Causeway from Wisden's shop in Great Newport Street, London, and put them in safe keeping.

Gray-Nicolls, both as cricket ball and cricket bat makers, were of course already part of Grays of Cambridge, who thus became the majority shareholders of the TSI cricket ball manufacturing group consisting of Duke/Wisden and Twort, and a cricket bat manufacturing group consisting of Duke/Wisden and Gray-Nicolls. Of the Kent manufacturers Thomas Ives stood outside the bat group; Alfred Reader outside the ball group.

After 1971 the market for English leather cricket balls, which had been declining ever since the end of the war, took an upward turn; Reader made 52,000 English leather cricket balls in 1971 and 74,000 – 65% of the total market of 115,000 – in 1973.

Neville Cardus saw the Golden Age of batsmanship extending from 1890 to 1914. 'Years of sowing were now reaped; the technique was ready for cultured use.' The cricket bat and cricket ball makers who had started up at the end of the nineteenth century found that in living through to the twentieth they were undoubtedly – to coin a phrase – onto a good wicket. Many of them sought to consolidate their position and make provision for an expanding market. It was a growth industry which, it seemed, nothing could stop.

In 1900, for instance, B. Warsop & Sons, which for the previous thirty years had been run as a family partnership, was incorporated as a private limited company (27 September). They also moved from Charles Street to another part of St John's Wood – Park Road, to the south of Lord's. The subscribers purchased the business from the partners as a going concern for £5,164.

The subscribers were Benjamin Warsop of West Hampstead 'manufacturer'; Alfred Warsop of Regents Park, 'manufacturer', with whom the company later became involved in a law suit; Walter Warsop of Kilburn 'cricket bat maker' who subsequently went off and set up on his

A device similar to that outside Wisden's London showroom marks the front of the little cricket bat factory off Regents Park at 127a Park Road of B. Warsop & Sons where bats were made up to 1973

The back of Warsop's fac-
tory beside the railway line
(still standing in 1979)

own at Danbury in Essex to make 'Walter Warsop' bats; and Henry
Luff, the head of Wisden of Cranbourn Street, who also had five
hundred shares. These four were directors. Arthur Warsop of 36 Charlbert Street, St John's Wood, the former Charles Street premises of
1870–1900, described as 'cricket bat maker', was a subscriber but not a
director. It looks as if he might have been carrying on independent
manufacture. A Thomas Henry Warsop of Willesden, also described as
'cricket bat maker', was likewise a subscriber but not a director; but
Francis Henry Warsop was a director without being a subscriber. The
capital of B. Warsop & Sons Ltd was £10,000.

Though the address was 127a Park Road the new premises were at the
end of a short but broad alley off Park Road, now known as Grove
Gardens, which backed onto the Regent's Canal alongside the railway
line. A drawing of how the works must have looked in these first days
of operation with an avenue of trees constitutes the company's
letterhead, which was still being used up to 1973. The kind of bat which
was being made there in that first year could be seen from the 1900
Warsop bat, used by W. Storer of Derbyshire, which stood in a glass

The first floor workshop of B. Warsop & Sons at the turn of the century

case in the office up to 1973. Storer made 2,540 runs with it.

Benjamin was joined in 1900 by a craftsman who had learnt the trade from Venables of Lee Green, Blackheath, Stuart Surridge and George Bussey, and was to stay with the firm for more than half a century. This was George Hunt, a keen cricketer, whose home was in Catford. He died in 1969, aged ninety-one.

Incorporation as a limited company warranted a new 'Bought Journal' with a leather cover specially printed with columns headed Wood, Cane, Glue & String (with Brown Paper added in ink), Leather and Rubber, Stationery and Printing, Advertising. In that first year they paid Jacobs, Young & Co £9 10s for cane; Saunders & Son £1 1s 5d for glue and string; Webb & Co £2 2s for leather and rubber; Pyle, Rawlins and Kindon £2 2s 6d for canvas; Samuel Skinner £6 16s 6d for cane; and Slazenger & Sons £16 12s 3d for leather and rubber. They bought wood from themselves: from Walter Warsop (£22 2s 1d), Benjamin Warsop (£46 13s 6d), and Alfred Warsop (£7 10s). For the half-year ending 30 March 1901 they had bought in raw materials and other goods to the value of £527 6s 2d, which included £317 worth of wood, and £68 worth of cane. Their first year sales amounted to £1,673.

The journal of 1907 shows that after six years they were in the big league, supplying Harrods Stores Ltd, for instance, with six ordinary

Conqueror bats at 13s, three no 5 at 8s, three no 6 at 8s 6d, and the Rio Cricket and Athletic Association of Brazil with cricket bats worth over £30. In October 1910 a parcel of five cricket bats and six cricket balls of value £4 ('to be paid at destination') was being sent at the request of Philip Need of Lord's Cricket Ground to The President of the S & I Corps Cricket Club, Nowshera, India – and this order must have been one of many.

Securing enough willow to keep pace with the increasing orders became a major problem. A more businesslike approach was necessary if production was not to be held up. In 1909 a separate Timber Account was started and a drive made to find new growers.

Feb 20, 1909	To cash (3 trees)	£9	
	At Hertford, splitting, felling, fares, etc.	£4	
	Mr Alan K. Gibson		19s
	Cartage	£1	

These produced 340 men's bats and 50 boys'.

Feb 15, 1909	To cash (3 trees)	£55	
	Felling & Fares etc.	£11	10s
	Cartage	£3	12s 6d
	Splitting etc.	£4	

These came from a London County Council estate at Hampstead and were made into six hundred and fifty men's bats and twenty-four boys'.

How the sizes of trees varied can be judged by the single willow tree purchased from George Child in September 1909 for £4 which cost another £4 15s for splitting, felling, fares and cartage and was made up into ninety-five men's and six boys' bats; and the three trees obtained

George Hunt (left) joined Benjamin Warsop at St Johns Wood, London, in 1900 having learnt the bat makers' trade from Stuart Surridge and George Bussey. Here he is passing on the art of pod shaving to yet another generation of bat makers, the youngest craftsman in his team at Park Road

A page from B. Warsop's Bought Journal of 1901

from Thomas Pople in October for £7 with only £1 6s 9d for felling, splitting and cartage, which only made sixty men's and six boys' bats.

If a tree was blown down the cost of felling was of course avoided. 'My Council have accepted your offer of eighteen pounds (£18) for the two willows blown down and eight others standing at our Sewage Farm, Mays Lane,' wrote W. F. Wilkins, Surveyor of the Barnet Urban District Council, to Warsop in March 1909. This was obviously going to be a continuing operation, as in the same letter the surveyor asked Warsop to give him a price for the supply of fifty sets of the best willow from twelve to fourteen feet in length for planting at the sewage farm. This was in fact done, and Norman Hunt, George's son, who joined Warsop in 1930 remembers the large numbers of willows obtained from Barnet UDC in the 1930s.

Another ten willows from the Barnet Council's sewage farm went to Warsop the following year for £24. 'My council,' wrote the clerk, 'trust that you will be good enough to leave the tops for their own use as stakes for the other trees.'

Occasionally someone who had a willow in his garden which he was anxious to remove was glad to be relieved of the bother of having to fell it and take it away. Councillor J. T. Chapman, of the Mitre Hotel, High Barnet, and treasurer of the local Licensed Victuallers Association, told Warsop through his solicitors that the tree in his garden was believed to be worth £5 but he would take £4 'provided you fell it and carry it away, clearing up all branches &c and making good any damage you may cause in the felling and carrying away'.

The news that Warsop were looking for willow trees for cricket bat making spread around.

84 Mile End Road, London, E.
October 20, 1909

Dear Sirs,

We have a willow tree at Finchley within six feet of a good road comprising somewhere about 150 ft of timber. We shall be glad to hear whether you can do with it and the price per foot it is worth to you.

Yours truly,

H. E. Trafford & Carter, Auctioneers

1a Grove Park Road, South Tottenham, London, N.
Nov 9th 1909

Dear Sirs,

On my way walking from Lords cricket ground last summer, I passed your place and took note of the address. I have a somewhat large quantity of willow trees in Cambridgeshire which I intend to fall [sic] shortly. I fully believe they are suitable for your business. Of course they can be cut up into any lengths and split, or delivered whole, or as you like.

Are you a buyer, and if so will you arrange with me to go and see them. I shall be pleased to accompany you. If you are not a buyer perhaps you may know someone who will buy, and if not, can you give me the address of any trade journal wherein I can advertise them, so that they are likely to come before the notice of cricket bat makers likely to buy.

Yours truly,

W. Goulton

In a letter three days later he said there were forty or fifty useful trees. 'I have not measured them but think they will girt from say 4 ft to 6 ft, or 15″ to 18″ diameter, or perhaps more.' It must have been a very time-consuming occupation, taking a train from Liverpool Street, driving to the site, walking round the fields, getting home again.

But in 1909 Warsop got offers for willow from farther abroad than South Tottenham. In November they had a letter from Holland.

Dear Sirs,

As I have this season again a lot of very fine willows for the manufacture of cricket bats, I should be very pleased to be favoured with your kind inquiries. The willows are 42″ to 46″ in circumference, and I can offer them at £1 16s each f.o.b. Rotterdam. I can guarantee you, they are all of the very best quality and it would please me very much, if it is in your way, you come over to me, for inspecting them, while they are standing in the earth.

Yours faithfully,

D. J. Van Efferen

Warsop seem to have had a willow scout called Twitty Laurence on the look out for likely trees, and in December 1911 he told Fred Game of East Barnet to let Warsop know he had a white willow and a red willow for sale, comprising four tons of wood. They were down and ready for sale. 'Please let me know if you can do with them and oblige.' So red willow was still being used in 1911.

Mr Malcolm of Tostock Place, Suffolk was uncertain whether it would pay him to get rid of his willows and before doing so wanted to find out the market price of the trees in November 1913. Could Mr Warsop write and tell him about the value of willows, the best sort for

D. J. VAN EFFEREN,
ROTTERDAM.

TELEFOON No. 4861.

Telegram-Adres:
VAN EFFEREN - ROTTERDAM.

Rotterdam, Date Postmark 1909.

Gashouderstraat 29.

Dear Sirs,

As I have this season again a lot of very fine willows, for the manufacture of Cricket Bats, I should very be pleased to be favoured with your kind inquiries

The willows are 42" to 46" in circumference, and I can offer them at £ 1,16,- each f.o.b Rotterdam.

I can guarantee you, they are all of the very best quality and it would please me very much, if it is in your way, you come over to me, for inspecting them, while they are standing in the earth

Trusting to be favoured with your valued inquiries.

I have the honour to remain Dear Sirs with recommendation

Yours faithfully
no D.J. van Efferen

English cricket bats from Dutch willow – a letter received by Benjamin Warsop from Rotterdam in 1909

cricket bats, well grown trees measuring from 3 foot 7 inches to 4 foot 1 inch circumference four feet from the ground? But before Warsop had time to reply, he had sold them – and wondered whether he had asked enough.

The approach of John Francis of Bury St Edmunds was more direct and businesslike – obviously a regular supplier. He wrote to say he was having twenty willows felled in November 1913, open and close bark. He would have the wood brought to Bury in halves and quarters. He would give Warsop the first offer, say five hundred to nine hundred cleft lots, of all white and fairly wide grain.

> Sometime since I had the pleasure of meeting you, but my son told me he saw you last year looking wonderfully fit which I was glad to hear. Wood ought to be ready to hew in about a fortnight.

Fred Pelly, who worked in a shipping office in Lime Street, was anxious to have the willow tree cut down in the garden of his house at Buckhurst Hill, Essex, that winter of 1914 but had first to obtain the permission of his landlord, the rector, the Rev Dr Woodward DD, which the sporting parson was willing to give on a certain condition and for a high price. Mr Pelly's gardener would do the necessary, he wrote, no need to worry Mr Pelly himself.

> I agree to sell the tree nearest the greenhouse in the rectory grounds for eight pounds (£8–0–0); you on your part to plant one green set in its place and protect it. I should be glad to have a bat made from the wood.

The bat from the willow in the rectory garden doubtless drove a ball as hard as the rector drove a bargain. It may still be around somewhere among the brollies, shooting sticks and fishing rods in the umbrella stand in the hall.

Warsop would make an agreement to cut trees within a two-week period, paying so much in advance and the rest on felling. In January 1914 John Jordan of Ingrebourne House, Hornchurch, Essex, wrote to

The figure beside this ten-year-old willow is thought to be Mr Stockdale himself. Nowadays willows are not felled until they are between twelve and sixteen years old. They are always cut as low as possible – hence the earth removed from around the roots

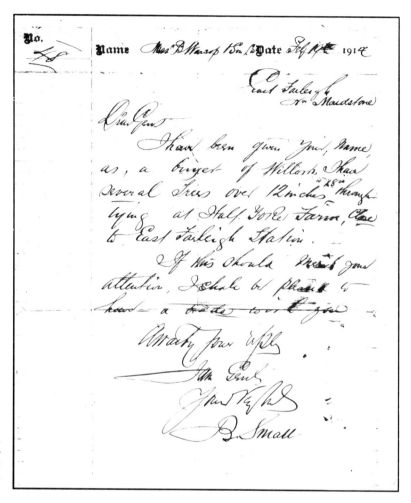

Benjamin Warsop has an offer of willow from someone with a name famous among English cricket ball and bat makers, B. Small

remind them that they agreed to cut down the fourteen willows at Upminster before the second week in January and the time was now up. 'I shall be glad if you would send on cheque for balance, £27; also I want the trees down as we are wanting the plants from them now to plant.'

He had forgotten about these because it seems by now he had as many as he wanted. For in pencil on the letter dated 19 February 1914 which he received from a man with the propitious name of B. Small of East Farleigh, Maidstone, offering several trees at Half Yoke Farm, Benjamin wrote 'Full up'.

At the outbreak of war he was fortunate to have a full stock, as he probably had to buy comparatively few over the four years that followed. When he started buying again on a full scale in 1919 the prices were up. In December 1919 he bought twenty-eight willow trees from a Mr C. A. Stallibrass of Hungerford for £100 with £38 for carriage and felling. Stallibrass's assessment was that the 857 clefts Warsop got out of the trees would make 645 at 4s and 212 at 3s. But when he examined the wood Warsop took a different view. He wrote back to Stallibrass that there was a lot of wood sent that was absolutely no good. This has greatly added to the expenses. However we want to be fair and meet you in the matter, and suggest we put the 72 doubtful men's with the 645, making

717 at 4s	£143 8s.
140 boys' at 1s	£7
	£150 8s.

He proposed sending him a cheque for £15 10s together with the £8 10s Stallibrass had already paid out on their behalf, amounting to £24. Stallibrass had expected £30. 'I am very disappointed,' he wrote reluctantly accepting the deal, 'as it gave me a lot of work.'

Up the road, inside Lord's Cricket Ground itself, Warsop's main competitor Dark had a warehouse under the Mound Stand for which they paid a nominal rent of a shilling a year. It is not clear when they stopped making cricket bats at Lord's. There is a bat ascribed to M. Dark & Sons at Lord's – Matilda – which is dated 1905, so it appears they were making them till then at least, though Matilda of course had left the scene long before then. But shortly after Henry Luff died in 1910,

An offer of willow to Benjamin Warsop, December 1911, referring in the postscript to Twitty Laurence, Ben's roving sales agent and timber buyer

Wisden acquired Dark & Son, and thus assumed the mantle of the first of the professionals, John Small Senior himself. But for how long Wisden continued to make bats at Lord's, if ever, is again not known. H. S. Dark, whose patents for cork-reinforced handles of 1886 and 1891 have already been noted, continued as manager of the Lord's shop till his death in 1930, when Wisden's association with it also ceased.

At about the same time as they took over Dark, Wisden bought a factory at 52 Richford Road, West Ham. The boom was in full swing. In November 1909 Stuart Surridge felled nine hundred willows at Clapham Park and many a thousand bats he would have made out of those. He invited keen players to visit his yard at Atkins Road and make a personal selection of a cleft in its rough state from the twenty-five thousand he had stacked there for seasoning. 'No bat is ready for use under 13 months from the date of felling trees.'

Lillywhite Frowd's Newington Causeway cricket bat factory was destroyed by a German flying bomb one night in 1943 after eighty years' non-stop activity, which by then included manufacturing a wide range of sports goods, particularly tennis racquets, as well as cricket bats and gymnasium equipment. The self-contained cricket bat shop, run by the much respected Mr Summers, was blown to smithereens, but work began anew as soon as possible underneath the arches of a nearby railway viaduct in Union Street off Blackfriars Road.

Between the wars Maurice Tate the famous English player who kept The Kings Arms at Rotherfield, not far from Tonbridge, was closely associated with Lillywhite Frowd who marketed both 'Maurice Tate' autograph cricket bats and cricket balls. In 1939 their 'J. Hardstaff' autograph bats sold for 45s retail, full size, Lillywhite Frowd Test Match ninety to ninety-five cricket balls for 14s 6d. At this time, too, they made Jippo Practice vellum covered bats. Chairman of the company was William Hartley who was also a director of the Van Heusen shirt and collar firm. Walter Frowd was managing director. He lived in Woking.

When the war ended more suitable London premises were acquired for cricket bat making than the temporary accommodation under the railway arches, and soon full production was resumed at a factory in Belvedere Place (now Belvedere Buildings), a quarter of a mile south of Union Street, off Southwark Bridge Road.

In 1946 R. H. Ellis, who had joined Lillywhite Frowd in 1929, in conjunction with an associate acquired the retail rights of all the products made at Belvedere Place, apart from the gymnasium equipment, and set up Lillywhite Frowd Sports Goods Ltd to operate shops in London and the provinces. Tom Barling, the Surrey opening bat, became one of his sales representatives in 1947. Walter Frowd died in 1948 at the age of seventy-two and left no heir to succeed him. In 1951 R. H. Ellis and his associate also purchased the Lillywhite Frowd manufacturing units in London and Tonbridge (again apart from the gymnasium equipment side which went to Roy Allen who runs it as an Olympic Gymnasium). Cricket ball business was expanding and by 1951 the little workshop on the north bank of the Medway was wholly inadequate, and the firm, with manufacture and marketing now consolidated under R. H. Ellis's management, acquired the big gas works

The Cricket Bat Maker in this 1934 etching by William Washington is shown in the classic position of the pod shaver

manager's house on the south bank of the river in Medway Wharf Road which was converted into the second Riverside Works cricket ball factory.

Cricket bat manufacture continued in London at Belvedere Place until 1964 when the works were closed; and cricket ball manufacture at Tonbridge till 1968. From that year Lillywhite Frowd operated as a marketing company for cricket bats and cricket balls made elsewhere to their own specification, as well as other sports equipment. In the early 1970s the firm was particularly associated with Kent and England player Brian Luckhurst who gave his name to their range.

In 1910 Aquila Clapshaw & Salmon Ltd, still producing cricket bats in large quantities on their five-acre site at New Southgate, was taken over by the father of Bernard Taylor who, after taking his degree at London University, himself joined the firm twenty years later. Output was some forty thousand cricket bats a year, as well as other wood products such as stumps, hockey sticks, tennis, squash and badminton racquets. Every year they exported many thousands of cricket bats to New Zealand, the West Indies and Australia. In the 1920s they took out a patent for a cricket bat handle with six springs named 'Invincible'. Bernard Taylor, well known in sporting circles, gave Aquila Clapshaw a new lease of life, and in 1934 he moved the enterprise to the works at 283–4 Chase Road, Southgate. Cricket bat making went on here right up to the 1970s but when it was stopped following Bernard Taylor's illness the firm continued to market bats made for them elsewhere under their old patents.

> As a firm who once had the Prince Consort's royal warrant [says Bernard Taylor] and heirs of what we believe to be the first family to make cricket bats *as a company*, we feel we have a responsibility for keeping alive a tradition in the craft which is part of cricket history. We are the standard bearers. Was not 'aquila' the Latin word for the eagle standards which the armies of imperial Rome carried into battle? How the first Clapshaw came to be called 'Aquila' we have no idea, but it is a name the family have never allowed to die. Two are still living: Ernest James Aquila Clapshaw, born in 1900, and his son Ernest Russell Aquila Clapshaw, born in 1943. But neither of them, alas, are cricket bat makers. Incidentally the Midlands firm of Clapshaw & Cleave have no connection with the family.

The first decade of the twentieth century was a time when many innovators who were not strictly cricket bat makers hastened to apply their inventive powers to a game that had obviously become 'commercial'. In 1909 three kinds of blade were patented. H. M. Edwards had an idea for bracing it with 'a stout textile band' (no 17,128); H. Iddon wanted to inlay the face with india-rubber and then vulcanise it under pressure to weld rubber and wood together (no 17,485); S. Brown conceived a blade which consisted of a frame of bent willow strip surrounding a central willow portion (no 21,632). In 1910 W. Wills-Moren patented a leather-faced cricket bat blade with leather or compressed felt glued to the face and secured by pegs (no 17,814); in 1911 P. R. Lange and W. H. Ludwig covered the blade with celluloid or xylonite (no 9,021); in 1914 J. Kelk covered it with aluminium 'or other

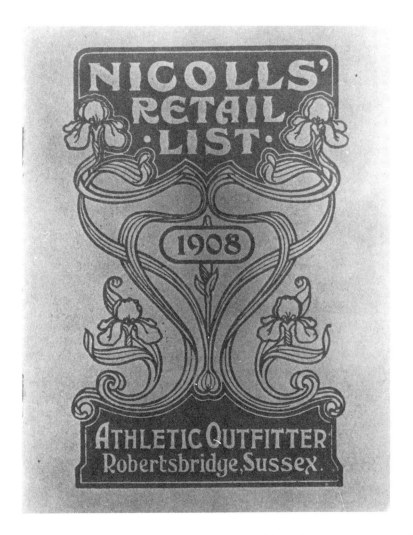

suitable metal' secured under pressure and heat by adhesive and if necessary nailed as well (no 13,559). 'The cover is coloured to resemble wood,' recommended Kelk in his specification, but apparently he could invent nothing to disguise the noise it made when it hit a Leathery Duke which must have been far from pleasant, or the extra weight. If weight was the problem Kelk's idea for an aluminium-faced blade could have been combined with P. G. E. Daniel's handle which had a slot at the top through which the player could insert and remove weights to vary the balance and make it heavier or lighter (no 17,579).

A more elaborate kind of blade was proposed by J. Harris in 1929 (no 327,513). It was made of a composition of rubber, granulated cork and/or wood shavings or sawdust, together with vulcanising ingredients such as sulphur or litharge to give hardness or resilience as required. The cane handle was to be coated with a rubber solution and placed in a mould, and the whole was to be vulcanised together under pressure.

Art nouveau helps to sell L. J. Nicolls cricket bats with this pleasing cover design on a retail price list of 1908

While the making of cricket balls, mostly bought by clubs and not players, was largely confined to London and Kent where there was the tradition of the skill and patience, the cricket bat makers tended to congregate wherever their main customers, the players, were to be found, or round the willow tree areas. One of the latter in 1924 was A. E. Trimmings. His workshop was on an island in the Great Ouse near St Neots in Huntingdonshire. He took out a patent in that year (no 242,103) for a handle with an intermediate lamination of resilient material parallel to the face of the bat and separated from the remainder of the handle by cork or rubber.

When journalist Helen Johnson paid the factory a visit thirty years later she found the business being run by Albert Trimmings and his son George – one of twenty firms making cricket bats in 1954 she reckoned. The Trimmings family, she said, owned three islands on which they grew willows. They employed eight men and made seven to eight thousand cricket bats a year. She described seeing the trunks of willows being split into clefts, sawn to size and skimmed with a draw knife to remove what they called the 'curf', which was the roughness left after the wood was sawn. This assisted drying, as the curf soaked up moisture. George Trimmings had no son, but his daughter Joyce (now Mrs Deacey) carried on the business with the aid of her husband, as County Sports St Neots Limited. Their distinguished list of customers has included Geoff Boycott, John Edrich, Mike Procter and Rod Marsh.

The 1930s was a time of handing down skills to a new generation of bat makers, just as it was a similar period for ball makers.

In 1935 Leslie Eade, the fifth generation of Eades, began to learn the craft as an apprentice (in the Duke cricket bat works at Chiddingstone Causeway) to his father, Cecil Eade, who up until 1931, when electricity came to the village, had used oil lamps and a treadle lathe. The ten craftsmen on the cricket bat side would fit and finish some eight dozen cricket bats a week.

A 1925 picture of Duke & Son's workshop which appeared in their 1936 catalogue. On the right is Cecil Eade, Leslie's father

Norman Hunt joined his father George Hunt at Benjamin Warsop in St John's Wood in 1930. In the 1929–30 season Patsy Hendren scored a thousand runs in ten innings in the West Indies with a 'B. Warsop' bat, and in 1936 Denis Compton also made a thousand runs with a B. Warsop bat. These two famous names became associated with the firm of 'B. Warsop, Makers, Marylebone, England' and 'Patsy Hendren' and 'Denis Compton' bats were sold all over the world. In addition B. Warsop made bats on an increasing scale for Gradidge, Wisden and Slazenger. The whole operation had been building up ever since the end of the First World War. In 1916 they had only purchased raw materials to the tune of £488, but in 1919 the figure had risen to £1,256 and by 1926 was up to £2,603 – of which £1,136 was on wood, £104 on cane, £51 on glue and string, £66 on leather and rubber. In that year they bought in goods from Clapshaw & Cleave Ltd. It was a peak year, for seven years later the total in the Bought Ledger was down to £2,183.

The chips fly as Norman Hunt turns a bat handle on a lathe at the B. Warsop cricket bat factory near Lord's where he joined his father George Hunt in 1930. The firm which Benjamin Warsop founded in 1870 was active until 1973

A degree of concentration took place in the cricket bat industry when in 1940 Grays of Cambridge took over Shaw & Shrewsbury of Nottingham. Alfred Shaw and Arthur Shrewsbury were two noted players of the Notts County Club which had had its headquarters at the famous Trent Bridge ground since 1838, though a Notts side had been challenging all who came against them since 1771. Shaw and Shrewsbury were in their prime in the 1880s. Neville Cardus speaks of Arthur Shrewsbury as 'the first modern batsman'. His influence on the future of batsmanship was as potent, he said, as Ranjitsinjhi's at a later date. The two craftsmen-players had their cricket bat workshop in Nottingham. A Shaw & Shrewsbury bat of 1909 is at Lord's.

Later in 1940 Grays ceased to make cricket bats at Cambridge when they formed a separate company for that purpose with L. J. Nicolls of Robertsbridge, Sussex. In 1941 Gray-Nicolls Ltd, as this was called, bought the cricket bat firm of S. M. Wainwright of Leeds, with the result that the cricket bat making activities of Grays, Nicolls, Shaw & Shrewsbury and Wainwright were concentrated at Robertsbridge. The maker of Ranji's second choice of bat, C. A. Odd & Sons of Croydon, one of three cricket bat makers of that name, also became part of the Gray-Nicolls group. A bat stamped 'Odd & Son' on top of the handle and 'Odd's Flexible Handle' on the blade is to be found in Hunter Tent at Winchester College – it belonged to J. R. Mason who was in the school 1887–93. Monty Odd is still to be found pursuing the family craft in West Street, Sutton.

In spite of its vulnerable position beside the railway and the canal, Warsop survived the Second World War without damage. The only cricket bat maker to be left at St John's Wood out of all the firms that had settled in the shadow of Lord's Cricket Ground in the Golden Age, it continued to maintain a small but steady output of twelve dozen bats a week. J. T. Ambridge went on turning bat handles at his lathe in the shop he had joined as a boy of fourteen – the photo shows him still at it at seventy-five in 1953. In the same year in another part of the building sixty-six-year-old F. Church, who had been with Warsop for fifty-one years, was carrying out the crucial finishing process. George Hunt, also seventy-five, was still very much in charge when those 1953 photos were taken, and not only in charge but at the bench; his son Norman likewise.

In 1959 Thomas Ives, the Tonbridge cricket ball maker, acquired Walter Warsop the Essex cricket bat maker which for a time continued at Little Baddow. But the following year the Essex factory closed and Ives began making bats as well as balls at Preston Road, Tonbridge. On the formation of Tonbridge Sports Industries in 1961 the cricket ball department of Ives at Preston Road, as noted, was closed, and the craftsmen moved to Chiddingstone Causeway – they had become part of TSI. The Ives company remained in being however as an independent operator, and retained the Preston Road works which became entirely devoted to cricket bat making – 'Strokemaster' was the brand – under the direction of Beverley Ives. A change of marketing policy came in 1970 with the decision to sell by mail order. When a serious fire destroyed the interior of the Preston Road bat works in 1971, leaving only the solid brick walls, Ives transferred their business to a wooden

J. T. Ambridge was seventy-five when he was photographed at the Park Road cricket bat factory of B. Warsop & Sons in North London in 1953; 12 dozen bats were completed there every week. He had then been with the firm sixty-one years, having started to learn the craft as a boy of fourteen

building beside Wisden at Chiddingstone Causeway. But in September 1972 this building, too, was totally destroyed by fire. The entire plant and stock including two thousand bats which the Test cricketer Basil D'Oliviera had signed only the night before, and all their files and order books, were lost in the flames. Undeterred, Beverley Ives moved the whole operation back to Tonbridge and carried on the mail order scheme with 'Avenger' bats and balls made by Gray-Nicolls and TSI.

A third fire occurred in June 1973 in the fifty-year-old Trimmings works at St Neots, doing great damage to County Sports' machinery and stock. The cricket bat making fraternity came to their rescue with commendable alacrity. Among those who helped out was Norman Hunt who was on the point of retirement. He closed the 103-year-old Ben Warsop factory in St John's Wood and sold his machinery and stock to County Sports – a move that completed an historical cycle. For Ben Warsop and Albert Trimmings had worked together at the end of the last century.

At Little Baddow, Danbury near Chelmsford, Max Warsop and Harry Stebbing formed an enterprising partnership which, in the tradition of Matilda Dark and Eleanor Page, was at one time joined by a lady cricket bat maker actively engaged in the craft, Sheila Warsop – the third of a distinguished contemporary trio with Joyce Deacey (née Trimmings) and Nellie Cochrane, who was making cricket bats at 66 South Street, Lewes, at least up to the end of the 1950s.

Unlike the cricket ball makers, the cricket bat makers who survived the Second World War had little to fear from overseas competition. For them (as indeed for the ball makers as well) it was the market itself, not their share of it, which caused the concern. Sailing, sub-aqua diving and other new sports of the affluent society had proved serious rivals, and in the 1950s the demand for cricket bats slackened off.

Dennis Howell's Sports Council, introduced by the Labour Government of which he was a member, helped to check the drift away from cricket, and the creation of the Cricket Council and the National Cricket Association (for other than 'first class' cricket) strengthened the informal control of cricket exercised by the MCC and the Test and County Cricket Board. It was a move welcomed by the cricket bat and cricket ball makers who saw in it a means of bringing the game and the trade closer together, and they were further encouraged in this view by the National Cricket Association setting up a Cricket Facilities Committee.

The 'revival' of cricket at the end of the 1960s through one-day and knock-out matches, the positive encouragement of school teachers to qualify as coaches, and subsidies from commercial interests like the Wrigley Foundation, made it more important than ever that the cricket authorities should not be caught on the wrong foot and be overtaken by events they deplored but could not reverse.

The cricket bat makers were not particularly well organised as a trade, but they were few in number. In the 1950s there were only some twenty of them. In 1956 they produced 157,490 cricket bats, and in 1957 160,508. Production then went steadily down – in 1963 it was 118,739. By 1965 it was slightly up, to 130,405, representing a net change in the decade of minus seventeen. Retail prices remained stable, but bats differed in weight, balance, pick-up and handle springing. Many big retailers commissioned bats to their own specifications which they sold under their own brand names. Others sent expert buyers round the bat makers to acquire the cream of their production. A popular sales promotion aid was to get famous players to autograph bats.

When Malcolm Goodman did research in 1965 for his thesis *The Cricket Bat and Ball Industries of Britain*, from which these statistics are taken, he found there were only twelve firms making cricket bats in Britain and that four of them made seventy-three per cent of the total annual output. Competition between the various firms was mild. Two of the leading four companies were headed by retired cricketers who tended to compete in a leisurely way. Competition, thought Goodman, was too slack for efficiency. The top four companies set the pace and there was little evidence of positive price leadership or of interdependence. Neither did he find any collusion between the other eight firms (which between them only made 35,000 bats a year) for the purpose of presenting a united front to the top four.

'Competition from abroad,' concluded Goodman, 'is hardly effective, the British firms having as far as is known a monopoly of the world market. The chief overseas markets are the cricket playing countries of the Commonwealth.' But orders had come from Holland, Denmark, California and Argentina. A third of the output of the leading firms went abroad. Only India and Pakistan had a cricket bat trade. They made them from Kashmir willow which was inferior to English willow.

There was no doubt cricket bat making belonged to England; to find it anywhere else seemed out of place.

6 Hands at Work

How much longer?

'From first to last this is a craftsman's job – and what craftsmen they are! Nobly they represent at the Court of King Willow the best and highest traditions of English craftsmanship. Here England leads the world.'

Richard Kent's reaction to a visit to Gunn & Moore's cricket bat factory in Nottingham.

He called the splitting of the trunks into clefts 'riving', and he saw it being done with a 'beetle' and an axe as 'Razor' Smith had been doing in Stuart Surridge's yard at Clapham Park. He then saw them taking off the bark with a five-pound side axe.

> These jobs of riving and barking call for a strong arm and a steady arm and a steady hand. An equable temper too, for the fine edge of the axe may sometimes come to grief through meeting some unexpected obstacle embedded in the wood. Pieces of wire are often found and so are various types of shot from sportsmen's guns. It is less easy to understand how bottles become encased in trees. On one occasion it is reported, a scent bottle was extracted intact.
> With a few deft strokes of his keen-edged knife the craftsman fashions the blade swiftly and with unerring accuracy – a masterly display of skill and judgement. The shaping of a bat calls for a high degree of skill and only after years of training can employees be entrusted with this vital task. The factory is staffed with men who have grown up with the firm. Some have been with Gunn & Moore for more than forty years and several for twenty and thirty. In this age of mechanical mass-production it is good to know that there are still a goodly number of stout English yeomen who take a delight in fashioning things by skill of eye and hand and feel a thrill of honest pride in the product of true craftsmanship. Certainly this shaping of the blade can never become a mere routine. The willow varies considerably in density and two clefts, even from the same parent butt, may require entirely different treatment. Yet these experts with the draw knife never niggle or hesitate. With swift sweeping cuts they pare off the unwanted wood, leaving a true and finely balanced blade.

Like Bussey, Gunn & Moore had their own design of pressing machine, invented by William Sherwin – the only piece of machinery Richard Kent encountered.

The way cricket bat makers obtain their willow has changed little through the years. Some rely on timber agents who specialise in cricket bat willow to deliver wood ready cut into clefts – like Edgar Watts Ltd of Bungay in Suffolk who describe themselves as 'Largest Producers and Exporters of English Willow Clefts For Cricket Bats in the World' and J. S. Wright & Sons Ltd of Great Leighs near Chelmsford who were established in 1894. Others buy standing willow trees from farmers and landowners and arrange to have them felled and delivered much as Ben Warsop was doing at the beginning of the century and George Bussey even earlier. Most, like Gray-Nicolls, do both. In the covered sheds in the woodland setting of their Robertsbridge factory are stacks of neatly cut clefts with both ends waxed which they have had from agents, and in the clearing opposite lie cuts from trees still with the bark on, which they have bought direct. A Gray-Nicolls buyer has inspected these trees and judged whether they had reached the right age for felling just by looking at them.

Today a willow with only twelve years' growth could be ripe for felling, but it is more likely to have fifteen. By the time it is twenty years old its wood would be too hard. Gray-Nicolls like a tree to be about forty feet high of which the central ten feet of the trunk, starting five feet from the ground, has been kept free of branches. It will be over four feet in circumference. This is sawn into four 'cuts' each two feet four inches long, from each of which will come six clefts – six embryo cricket bats. The top and bottom cuts yield the poorer grade wood; 'best' bats will come from the two middle cuts. But quality varies from tree to tree and it is up to the expert to detect where it lies. He negotiates a price before felling, as George Bussey had to do. He weighs up whether it is a tree

ESTABLISHED
1870

THE IMPORTANCE OF HAND MANUFACTURE
•

As every piece of willow has its own characteristics machines cannot make the best cricket bats. Only the experience and skill of the craftsmen is able to get the best out of the timber and ensure it is perfectly balanced.

All bats in the Ben Warsop Conqueror range are hand made and hand balanced from the best timbers. If you want the best that money can buy see the superb Conqueror Five Star. Craftsman made from the finest willow, it is expensive, but as perfect as a cricket bat can be.

Warsop's designs

The spacious cricket bat workshops of Gunn & Moore Limited at Nottingham in the 1930s

which has grown slowly and become 'woody', or one that has grown relatively fast and so 'well'. He encourages the farmer to grow more willows by providing him with 'setts' – a word that has collected a second 't' – to plant in the place of the axed tree. Willows resent regimentation and need plenty of light and air.

Cleaving the cleft from the cross-section, or cut, of the tree trunk is done with the grain by means of a beech wedge. The bark is then removed and the cleft sawn roughly into the shape of a cricket bat blade, graded according to its position in the trunk, and stacked with its fellows under cover in the drying yard for seasoning for between nine and twelve months.

In the 1920s some two hundred willow setts from Cowfold and Beltring were planted opposite the cricket field in Robertsbridge, but when the trees were felled towards the end of the Second World War they were found to be hard and of poor quality. More recently however a tree was cut in Robertsbridge which was fifty inches round the trunk after only nine years. Len Newbery, who was managing director of Gray-Nicolls until his death in 1976, might have differed from George Bussey about the worth of the lower cut, but he was at one with him over the significance of markings. 'The timber of the *salix alba caerulea* is distinguished by a bright orange stain which is known in the trade as "butterfly" stain,' he said. 'When these stains appear on the blades of bats, players often reject such bats thinking that the stains are faults or knots, whereas they are in fact the hallmark of the finest quality cricket bat willow.'

But it is all white willow now – some blades are even bleached, to make them whiter than white. But the various stages of production

The late Len Newbery, managing director of Gray-Nicolls (extreme right) supervises the felling of willows at Robertsbridge, Sussex – a photograph taken in February 1929. The top of the tree, useless for cricket bat making, has been discarded (right). The rest of the trunk is cut into four or five sections each one of which is axed into some five or so 'clefts' on the spot

have not changed since the days of William Pett and Aquila Clapshaw, though certain new techniques have taken over from the old ones.

When Bill Lucking, foreman of Gray-Nicolls in the 1970s, joined the firm in 1947 they had already mechanised the preliminary processes whereby the cleft was roughly shaped in the workshop they called The Mill – taking the ends off and a thin slice from each side, cutting the shoulders, chamfering the toe, incising a V at the top of the blade for the handle. When the man with the name which keeps recurring in this story, Joe Martin, was foreman in the mid-1920s – his son Brian Martin was still with the firm in the 1970s – all these processes were done by hand, but from 1925 onwards machines gradually took over, though of course mechanical saws have to be guided by experienced hands.

Every batmaker had his own version of a bat press where the rough casting of a blade went after milling. Not so long ago at Robertsbridge this was a single roller, a wooden affair through which the blade was pressed by hand four times, the weights having to be adjusted after each run. The press which superseded this has three rollers shaped like diabolos, the first giving light pressure and the other two pressing progressively more heavily. The weights adjust themselves automatically. The roughly shaped blade is drawn under the rollers in one direction and then reversed. What had had to be done four times by hand is now undertaken in a single mechanical operation. During the process of compression – two tons a square inch – the weight of the blade has been drastically reduced. The blade has to go through the press again at two other stages of the manufacture. By the end no area is capable of being compressed further, however fierce a battering it receives from a cricket ball.

Time was when the sticks of cane were clamped together into 'slips' with a glue made from boiled goat skins which took twenty-four hours to set, and the four slips making up a 'best' handle were glued to one another in the same clamp for another whole day. In the 1970s the whole process takes four minutes. It is as well that time is saved, for no one has found a way of not wasting half of the material – and Sarawak cane, which cost £200 a ton in 1973, cost £825 in 1978. These highly flexible wooden rods, which can be bent double without breaking, are of course circular in cross-section and have a hard smooth shiny skin, or bark. So that four rods can combine flush into a single slip and four slips can be glued together to form a handle, the faces which meet have to be shaved flat. The skin is removed so that the cross-section of the round cane becomes rectangular. In doing this, half of the wood goes on the floor. More goes to waste when the now straight-sided handle is turned on a lathe to restore the circular cross-section of the original cane. Best handles are made of sixteen slim Sarawak rods; boys' and cheaper bats from four of the thicker Manila cane.

For the highly skilled job of fitting the handle into the neck of the blade, Richard Saunders uses the light brown goatskin glue, which has been rejected in favour of the resin adhesive, for binding the *fasces* of canes for the handle. It is provided however in solid form, not actually boiled from skins in the yard, but it has lost none of its pungency. A modern marine glue is harder, but it has to be at the right temperature which would never give Richard time to get the splice in.

Many generations of craftsmen are represented in this 1950s group of those who made the cricket bats marked 'B. Warsop, Marylebone' in the Park Road factory beside the Regents Canal. On the left, front row, is Norman Hunt, and beside him his father George Hunt who died in 1969, aged ninety-one

Richard's work is entirely manual. His task is to make a tight fit between the handle's splice and the fissure in the blade without adhesive. His whole attention is concentrated on planing the opening and the splice over and over again, so that each has perfect surfaces. His skill and experience determines what wood to remove and how much. He has reduced the operation to a fine art. Each day he does it one hundred and fifty times. Tight at the top and loose at the bottom is the secret – and hammer in the splice tilted slightly forward, finally with the hot animal glue applied to the wood that will take twenty-four hours to set.

In the hands of sixty-year-old Ted Jolly who started in L. J. Nicolls' workshop in 1926, of Cecil Unsted and Norman Walters, the bats receive the treatment, first conceived in the workshops of John Small, which no machine has ever been able to emulate. Today's pod shavers use the tools the first masters used. Cecil Unsted takes the blade and handle which Richard Saunders has recently joined and puts it in a vice. He takes each shoulder off with a draw knife – they have been kept 'unshaved' till now – and proceeds to shave away surplus wood. He calls it 'drawing the back off'. He takes a plane to 'clean up the rough spots' on the face and over the splice, and smoothes the sides. He takes a surform rasp to the handle and rubs it up and down to make it not round, but oval in cross-section – it fits the hand better that way. He

finishes three-and-a-half dozen 'very best' bats a day – if that is the batch to hand – or five dozen 'best', six dozen lower grade or eight dozen boys'. He has been practising the craft for thirty years.

Once 'finished' the bats go for sanding on an endless moving belt of garnet cloth, and for 'buffing' (smoothing) on a fast rotating mop. Threequarters of Gray-Nicolls bats have a six inch long, millimetre thick, steel spring in the handle, wrapped in four widths of rubber, to aid recovery. The handles of these are wound with twine; those without the steel spring are taped. A girl coats the handles with glue and pulls on rubber grips at a rate of two a minute. Some players – particularly in the West Indies – like a bright shiny white surface, and for them Gray-Nicolls wrap half or three-quarters of the blade in linen on which they put a glossy, damp-resisting coating. Handles come short and long (standard). Their 'supershort' bat has a handle an inch shorter than a normal 'short' handle. Some blades are an inch shorter than standard; some have the shoulders cut away to aid weight distribution. One brand has a reinforced transparent fibre coating which is damp-proof and needs no oiling. There is the bat for the first-class player who does not mind slight blemishes in the blade, another with a reinforced fibre covering. For no extra charge certain models can be supplied auto-graphed by one of a list of thirty-three cricketers.

The moment of truth for a senior craftsman at the War-sop cricket bat works in North London when the accuracy of the hand splice, and the opening into which it has to fit, is put to the test

A pod shaver for over fifty years – Mr Church who finished bats for B. Warsop & Sons

In 1975 Gray-Nicolls introduced the perimeter weighted or 'scoop' bat made from a larger than normal cleft of willow. The object was to spread the weight towards the perimeter of the bat by scooping out the back. It gave it a larger playing area. The additional thickness meant the ball went as sweetly off the edge as off the centre. The idea was borrowed from the golf club makers. Jock Livingstone their sales director considered it 'the biggest innovation in bat making for years'.

The GN 100 (Scoop) has its place in the 1978 catalogue alongside the bat with the steel spring in its handle and the interwoven transparent fibre faced blade. In the five years 1973–78 the retail price range (men's) has gone up from about £12.45/£7.95 to £45/£20.

Choice of bat is not determined by price alone. The processes which give a bat its distinctive character are not stereotyped but directed by varying sets of human hands. The same models will therefore vary from bat to bat. This gives considerable scope for personal selection, not only of the right model but of a particular bat within a model range, to suit the player's own vital statistics and particular style of batting. Though one might have expected the problem to have lapsed when bats ceased to be curved, some makers of the 1970s still announce 'all models available for left-handed players on request'.

But that apart, ideas on what to look for in the selection of a bat vary even more than bats. In an article in their house magazine, Slazenger stated that the average weight of a bat in the 1970s was about 2lb 5½oz. 'But for club use it is advisable to select bats of a heavier weight. Indeed, some of the great strikers in cricket use, and have used, a bat even heavier than the 2lb 6oz average of a club cricket bat. Bob Barber used a

2lb 9oz bat and Graeme Pollock and Dennis Amiss both use a bat of 2lb 7oz.'

A hundred years ago W. G. Grace in a 'first rough article on cricket' gave as 'one last hint to the young beginner': 'Do not play with a bat too heavy for your strength. I think a bat should not exceed for any young batsman 2lb 3oz or even 2lb 2½oz. It is this overweight that cripples many a promising player and prevents him from doing justice not only in the present but mars his utility in the future.' It is largely a question of fashion. When Tony Greig, England's captain, began using a bat weighing three pounds, heavy bats became all the rage. At Danbury in 1977 Max Warsop produced a bat which was decidedly heavier than normal, but then it was double-sided. When one face was worn out you turned it round and used the other side. It cost £20 but, as his partner Harry Stebbing pointed out, it was two bats in one. This followed Warsop & Stebbing innovations such as replaceable edges, cut-away corners and bats with holes to reduce wind resistance.

The main selection is of course among the various manufacturers – among the products of Gunn & Moore from Nottingham, Gray-Nicolls from Robertsbridge, Slazenger from Horbury, Surridge from Witham, and of firms like G. K. Adams of London, S. M. Kennedy of Leeds, Walter Lambert of Nelson, Wade & Ellis of Barnsley, Monty Odd of Sutton, County Sports of St Neots. Small and big firms not only market their own range of models but make bats to the specification of wholesalers and dealers who sell them under *their* brand names.

Latest entrant to the ranks of craftsmen cricket bat makers is Duncan Fearnley. He learned his cricket and his craft in the West Riding of Yorkshire. He played first for Farsley, the club to which belonged Ray Illingworth who later became captain of England. Fearnley had ambitions to play for Yorkshire and he was once twelfth man in a 'Roses' match against Lancashire, and came on as substitute for Freddie Trueman when he injured himself. But it was Worcester which left-handed Duncan Fearnley eventually joined as a professional, and it was Worcester where in 1960 he first made a cricket bat. He made others and it became a hobby which rapidly became a business. He opened up a workshop in Sansome Place, Worcester, employing a number of craftsmen. Very shortly Test cricketers and county players like Glenn Turner, Barry Wood, Dennis Amiss and New Zealand's Bev Congdon, were buying his handiwork and showing his black wicket trade mark all over the world. Duncan Fearnley bats were soon in demand in Australia and New Zealand.

The blade lost its curve and gained a splice, the handle lost its sting and gained a welcome flexibility, but in two hundred years the cricket bat making craft remained basically the same. This is even more true of cricket ball making – the basic processes are still those which Joseph Farington saw at Redleaf in 1811.

The craft is practised by men who have learnt it in the workshops of Thomas Ives, Lillywhite Frowd, Wisden and Surridge in Tonbridge, Twort at Southborough, Duke at Chiddingstone Causeway, and Alfred Reader at Teston, and have practised it at several, going from one to the other. They belong to a single community of craftsmen with an entity separate from that of the employers for whom they work. There is no longer any cricket ball making in Tonbridge. All the cricket ball craftsmen are working for one of two firms.

Up until 1978 there were three centres, Teston, Chiddingstone Causeway and Southborough. But at the end of January that year Tonbridge Sports Industries closed the Twort works in Park Road, Southborough, where the finishing processes were carried out by veteran seamers like Brian Bartlett, George Vidler and Alec Brown who made sure the quilts they received from Chiddingstone Causeway were well and truly covered, and the covers securely joined. Bill Mepham became manager at Chiddingstone Causeway and administrative director of TSI based at Robertsbridge.

So hand-sewn cricket ball making in Britain is now confined to Teston and Chiddingstone Causeway. Six of the nine craftsmen at Southborough joined the seventeen quilt winders, stitchers, turners, closers and the rest at Chiddingstone Causeway. These twenty-three cricket ball makers who comprise the Duke workforce are back in the old building on the north of the road built in 1841 to house the operation when it moved from Red Leaf and, unlike the other workshops built for expansion, untouched by fire. Once again all under one roof, the entire process can be supervised by production manager Ken Munday who started making cricket balls for Gray-Nicolls at Hildenborough in 1947 under Bert Dyer, the last of the Duke all-round craftsmen – still in active retirement in 1978. Between 1966 and 1975 a shrinking staff gradually transferred to the 1841 building from the big factory across the road, as Duke/Wisden concentrated on high grade cricket balls. The low grade market was taken over by imported balls sold at a price with which Duke could not compete.

At Chiddingstone Causeway the oldest, and Teston the largest, operation, the old names have an obstinate way of persisting. It is unlikely that Harold Farington is a descendant of the diarist, who after

Ken Munday (centre) the production manager of Tonbridge Sports Industries Limited, which have taken over the old Duke & Son factory at Chiddingstone Causeway, with 14 of the remaining 23 craftsmen

all was only visiting the area from London, but it would be nice to think that the turner of that name who has been working for Duke for more than a quarter of a century, is somehow connected. Harold presides over the five-station press that gives the half cover of the ball its cup shape – which is what 'turning' is all about. Once he used to place it into a concave brass mould which formed the lower part of the hand press which still lies discarded in a corner of the shop. He would then twist the heavy handle on top of the press which screwed down the rubber and cork compound bung into the leather below, and blocked it out. But the pressure once supplied by Harold's muscle power has been replaced by compressed air – five tons a square inch – and the lower mould is heated electrically to help the bung do its work of turning the two soft leather 'closed' quarter pieces into a strong, cup-shaped cover for one half of a 'best' Duke cricket ball.

He lowers the bung and allows the pressure to do the initial forming for a couple of minutes, raises it, adjusts the false quarters which line the real ones so that they fit more snugly against the side, and after more poking and trimming, lowers the bung once more for another minute or two of heat and pressure – and so on until he is satisfied. He then places the rigid, fully shaped leather cup in a mould to rotate beneath a sharp, stationary knife set at an angle, which trims the leather round its edge. This gives the rim of each half cover the protruding bevelled lips which the seamer can sew together to form the whole cover. This bevelling is another part of the turning process which for twenty-five years or so Harold has done by hand – he joined Gray-Nicolls just after the Second World War.

Another craftsman of the turning department has to prepare the half covers before they come to the press. These arrive from the closing department inside out, so that the closers can more easily sew the quarters together; before going for shaping they have to be turned back again with the outer skin outside. A system is arranged whereby Harold can do a stint of preparing for a week or two while a colleague takes over the press; changing jobs in this way neither of them become bored. The half cover of a cheaper ball is one piece, so it by-passes the closing department which is solely concerned with closing two quarter pieces to form the half cover for the superior balls. But the one-piece half cover with its one-piece lining and button ('false half') is pressed into shape on the five-station press just as the one made of two quarters.

Turning is a part of cricket ball making which Roy Hunt knows as well as closing. He is a closer, but he began as a stitcher at Lillywhite Frowd in Tonbridge and has done quilt making as well. Doing his stint as closer, he demonstrates his mastery of making up the length of thread with which he is going to close the two quarters. He measures six strands of hemp by a stretch of his arm plus a half, and pulls the end of each strand to a fine point; 'waxes' the strands with a lump of what is in fact a mixture of resin and lard inside a hard leather, binding them to a nail and rubbing up and down with the 'wax'. He twists them on a leather apron to form a single thread, having rubbed white chalk on his hands to give a grip. One end he twists into a fine tail with which he entwines a nylon bristle, strong enough to make the initial penetration of the holes and pull the thread through with it.

Eric Card, a quilt winder, at the Duke & Son factory at Chiddingstone Causeway, Kent, is about to wrap a thin layer of cork around the cork cube which he holds firmly in his left hand. He will then bind it on with wet worsted thread to make the heart of a hand-made cricket ball

Another layer of cork is wrapped round the core

Bob Burkett came to Wisden at Baltic Road in 1947, when it opened at the end of the Second World War. He used to carry out the closing process by stretching the quarters over a wooden block, a 'tamping pin' on a bracket, which whilst seated he held between his legs. But now he sits at a bench of his own devising and sets the block on that. 'Rounding a quarter' by hand used to be part of closing – cutting the quarter shape with a sharp knife held in the right hand round a metal pattern placed on the leather and held in the left hand. But now quarters come to him from the leather department where they are stamped out by a mechanical hammer beating down on the top of a quarter-shaped, two inch high steel cutter. Moreover the quarters come to him rounded out and 'skived' to the right thickness. Skiving, too, was once the job of the closer, who would taper the quarter manually with a knife.

One quarter is sewn to its mate with eighteen stitches, and to do this nineteen holes have to be made in the bevelled edge of each quarter. Not many years before there had been three 'grades' of closing; the quarters of a best ball would be closed with twenty-eight stitches; a second best ball with twenty-four stitches; and the cheapest with twenty-one. But now they are standardised at Chiddingstone Causeway on eighteen stitches for all quarters. The equidistant points of the nineteen holes are marked round the lips of the two quarters with a mica marking comb dipped in dye. Each marks the end of a tunnel in the thickness of the leather which the closer is going to make with his fine curved holing awl, starting at a point half an inch from the edge. When Bob first started on the job he marked these start points with the aid of dividers, but after thirty years he has come to judge it well enough by eye. He

keeps his awls, which only last some three or four weeks, razor sharp on
emery cloth. A blunt sewing awl comes in useful however for opening
up the holes again just before he starts to do the sewing. This begins
with pushing the home-made, six-ply hemp thread into the tunnel with
the aid of the nylon bristle, which in a sense acts as a needle. In earlier
days a hog bristle from Russia was used. The sewing-closing takes place
right to left and left to right simultaneously, six-ply in each direction.
The thread is pulled through by hand, so that twelve-ply goes through
the holes. The quarters are closed with a continuous thread.

Once the quarters have been closed, the halves which they become
are seamed together to make a 'whole', but only after the stuffing has
been put into them. At Reader Percy Lambert, who was born in the
village of Teston, learnt how to make the stuffing – the 'quilts' – in one
of the huts which Tom Martin erected in the garden behind the post
office as an annexe to the main workshop. Percy joined Alfred Reader &
Co in 1919 after being discharged from the army.

Today he sits at his bench taking the corners off a cube of cork with
his knife and, holding it tightly in his left hand, wrapping layers of thin
cork on to it and binding them with wet worsted thread. He protects the

Craftsmen at benches by windows to catch maximum light at Alfred Reader's Teston cricket ball works in 1947

flesh of his fingers from the searing cord with pads of paper fibre. All the time he taps the quilt with the venerable four pound hammer with the short wooden handle, worn half through underneath where his thumb had been clutching it so firmly for so long. After five layers of cork, each wrapped round with wet thread, the half-finished quilt is taken away and put into an oven where the heat dries the thread so that it contracts round the cork which shrinks to half its size and weight. Back comes the reduced quilt to Percy Lambert who wraps another two layers of cork sheet on to it. The inner cube of cork, the seven layers of thin cork sheet and the yards of thread then go into an oven once again for a final baking. Alongside Percy, Gordon King and several others are making quilts for other grades of ball which require different combinations of materials.

At Chiddingstone Causeway, no longer in the hush-hush quilt shop which was demolished in 1949, the man with the Teston name goes through roughly the same procedures, sitting on the seat his grandfather had sat on doing precisely the same job. When Ken Martin's grandfather Walter Martin died at the age of ninety-six in the 1950s, Ken inherited the black wooden seat which the old quilt maker had built for himself, and sat on throughout his working life. He had started his career, not surprisingly, at Reader (at Teston) which he left to join the Baltic Road works of Wisden in Tonbridge. He retired in the 1930s when he was seventy-six.

Walter Martin had two sons, Frederick and Frank. Ken's father was Frederick and a stitcher at 'Quarry Hill' (Baltic Road), but it was Uncle Frank who taught Ken how to make a quilt. Frank Martin had been at Quarry Hill and at Chiddingstone Causeway where Pat Lee, as has been seen, took over from him as foreman. In 1938 Frank went to Surridge, in Salford Terrace, which Ken joined in 1943. In those days Ken had to cut the layers of cork out of big sheets himself, but at Duke today they come to him ready cut. He uses his knife however to cut the central cube of cork from the big slab, once the bark of a tree in Portugal, he keeps beside him on the shelf. If he feels the cork is soft he cuts a bigger cube than usual. He then gives it a number of extra faces. The thin sheet of ready-cut cork he divides into six squares, and after winding a preliminary length of thread on the bare hunk of cork, he places one square on either side of it, winds them with thread; places two more and winds; places the final two and winds – tapping the expanding orb after every new addition. He puts on another six squares in the same fashion, twisting and rotating the quilt with his left hand and winding round the wet worsted at incredible speed. This constitutes the first stage of a 'best' ball; for a cheaper ball he wraps a strip of cork round the inner core, winds it with thread, puts a cork cap at either end, taps it and winds more thread until the cork is covered up – an altogether quicker and more superficial procedure.

To protect his fingers Ken will have nothing less than old, hard leather, and he spends a considerable time scouring likely places for discarded farmers' boots and leggings which have lain long in the open and become perished. So much footwear is now made of synthetic material that this is hard to come by, but Ken finds Deal beach a fruitful source of finger protection material. He frequently combs the beach for old fishermen's boots which have been washed up after long soaking in the sea has made them hard and shiny. On a shelf in a basket are the prizes of these scavenging trips, and they are more worth to him than gold. Similar hoards are closely guarded by his fellow quilt winders, Ernest Grayland, who has been in the business for thirty-one years, and Bert Hunt who began at Lillywhite Frowd in 1946 when a youth of sixteen. They cut the pieces of old leather into small bits, which they tie round the parts of the fingers which have to take the strain of the wet thread as they stretch it before winding on to the growing quilt.

For the best ball he is making Ken wraps a long strip of thin cork over the two layers of six squares he has already put on the inner core, followed by a cork cap at top and bottom, all wound on with thread with Ken tapping all the while. This constitutes the third layer, and at this point it is taken away and put into a warm oven for a period. When he gets it back Ken notes the extent to which it has shrunk and the new shape and size it has assumed – no quilt comes out the same at this stage – and adds a thick or thin fourth layer of cork strip accordingly. He puts it through a ring gauge made to the circumference which the quilt of that particular grade of ball should have at this stage. The leather of a cheaper, half cover cricket ball is thinner than the better quality product, so the quilt has to be bigger. He also has to concern himself about weight, and weighs it on the hand scales on the bench beside him. If it is less than the two-and-threequarter ounces required of a best ball on coming out of the oven after its third layer, he will see that the fourth layer restores the lost weight. The same process is repeated for a fifth layer. The finished quilt of a best ball is required to weigh three-and-a-quarter ounces. The fashion was once to put small white feathers on after the fifth layer, but Ken has stopped doing that for many a year. If the quilt comes out too heavy at the last stage, then it can go back into the oven until its weight is as it should be.

In the days of the old quilt shop in the cottage where Eric Card took over quilt making from Pat Lee, after having been taught by Percy Wells, the oven was built round a coal fire with trays all round for holding the half-finished quilts. Eric was a quilt maker for twenty-five years. He now works on the final stages of ball making in the same shop as twenty-year-old Ken King, who joined five years before. Representative of the eighth generation of Duke cricket ball makers, Ken will be able to hand down the secrets of the craft to coming generations as those have done before him who have worked on a site which has seen the craft practised for 138 years, having been brought there from Penshurst, where it was practised for 80 years.

From one corner of the quilt department at Chiddingstone Causeway come instant quilts, which would never have been tolerated in quilt shop days – 'squabs' (the dictionary gives 'squab' as a verb meaning to stuff, 1819). Bert Hunt mixes small cork granules with latex rubber which is totally absorbed by the cork after twenty minutes. He then pours three ounces of dry cork granules into an upright cylindrical canister, the bottom and top of which are cup shaped. The top cup presses on to the lower cup with a pressure of 2,500lb per square inch, and the granules come together in the shape of a ball. Bert takes the canister out and stands it in an oven for a quarter of an hour. The result is a smooth, shiny, perfectly round squab ready for immediate covering. It is the heart of a cheaper ball.

Hides for English leather cricket balls come mostly from Scotland and Switzerland. In the alpine pastures of these countries cows wander freely without knocking into prickly hedges and sharp walls, or cutting their sides on barbed wire. Best cricket balls can only be made from cow hide which has minimal scratches on it. Hides come to the cricket ball maker having been tanned in Derbyshire, Yorkshire, Northumberland and elsewhere – or rather, having been treated with a salt and alum dressing. A hide is graded amongst other things for the extent to which it is scratched; a 'first' has a few superficial barbed wire scratches (no cow wanders completely scar-free), a 'second' has more and deeper scratches. The belly of course has the softest skin, and a cricket ball maker who buys a 'back' gets the tanner to induce 'fat liquor' to make it more pliable. Joseph Farington noted (perhaps mistakenly) that Duke was making his cricket balls from bullhide – which some have transcribed as 'ballhide'. The skin of a bull is coarser than a cow's and less pliable, but perhaps it was considered more 'manly'.

In the 1970s undyed hide is sold by the pound; dyed leather by the square foot. Cricket ball makers buy both. The alum-dressed but undyed hide which comes to Dennis Bartlett, foreman of the leather department at Chiddingstone Causeway, still has the shape of the animal it has recently covered, and is milky white in colour both on the outside and the rougher inside. Dennis has been in the trade twenty-five years, starting at the ex-Hitchcock works in Hildenborough when Gray–Nicolls were making cricket balls there, and working both for Surridge and Lillywhite Frowd. He takes in twenty hides a week. He has each cut into strips five-and-threequarter inches wide, and made into bundles of eight. Sixteen of these bundles weighing two hundred pounds are put into a big wooden drum containing eighty gallons of water with a red dye in it. Only twelve years previously dyeing had been done by putting the strips of hide into vats where they stayed for two weeks. Now they churn around in the drum, rotated by an electric motor, for only two-and-a-half hours.

In fine weather the strips dry gradually outside in the sun and air, which is the best way, with someone constantly shifting their position on the line by hand. Otherwise they are put in a drying cupboard inside the leather department, which dries them more swiftly but more harshly. Once dry, the leather undergoes the first of many stretching processes to make it supple. This is done first by a 'strake' machine extending the strip longitudinally, and then by a stretching machine which simulates a man pulling its sides over a wooden block with claw pinchers – the first machine to be used in the leather department.

Cowhide in its natural state is too thick for a cricket ball cover and it has to be 'split'. This also used to be done by hand with a blade like the old spoke shave, but at Chiddingstone Causeway Sid Wickens, who has been a cricket ball craftsman for thirty-two years, and worked for a time at Ives in Tonbridge, does the job on a splitting machine which reduces the thickness of the leather from the underside with a mechanical knife and deposits the unwanted shavings in the waste bin. The thinned leather strip goes to Hilda Furminger who cuts from it some thirty leaf-shaped quarter covers on the clicking press in the way already described. She avoids the places where there are scratches and cuts none from the ends which are of poorer quality. From these she cuts the 'false quarters' which act as reinforcing linings glued inside the 'real' quarters. With another shaped cutter she cuts the circular linings for the half covers. Both these and the false quarters are mechanically tapered to make them thinner at one edge.

Quilts and covers of the same grade meet for the first time in the seaming department. The problem is to push the bevelled edges of the two half covers over the apparently over-sized quilt so forcibly that they rise like a circular blister round the ball's circumference. Then the seamer can pierce the holes through them with his curved awls and the eight strands of flax, waxed and twisted into a single thread, will bind the two halves together. For the twenty-six years that Fred Rand was a seamer at Teston – he died in 1929 aged forty-six – it was a question of

A study in concentration. Hand-stitching the leather cover of a cricket ball demands total attention every time, even when you have been doing it as long as Percy Phipps of the Duke/Wisden factory at Chiddingstone Causeway, Kent

doing as best he could with a wooden hand vice which clamped the ball in brass cups; but at Reader where his son Cecil Rand has been working for forty-eight years an ingenious piece of apparatus has been devised which enlists the help of a car jack. The sewing is done as for closing, leading the thread through the holes in two directions simultaneously with the nylon bristle, which of course is finally jettisoned. Best balls are seamed with pure flax thread, resin and lard waxed. This 'lard' was once deer fat, traditionally from Scotland, but rendering it down has become too expensive and complicated. The cheaper balls are seamed with waxed terylene by some, though not by all. But quality is determined not only by the kind of seaming thread but by the number of stitches – sixty, seventy, eighty or ninety – the higher the number, of course, the higher the grade. In the end the stitches of the seam are hammered flat.

Seaming is a critical process and those who do it are proudly aware of this. For seamers at Teston, and for men like Brian Bartlett and George Vidler on the top floor of the little factory at Chiddingstone Causeway, it is a matter of performing a precision job with the same sense of responsibility which has animated the long line of craftsmen who have sat there before them seeing the emergence between their hands of something which, for the first time, could properly be called a cricket ball.

There is a role for buckfat (or buckfat substitute) in cricket ball making – as the grease in which the ball is dipped after seaming. This gives the leather a deeper colour and waterproofs it. It also enables markings to be made on the cover for purposes of grading and identification which could be removed at the end of the day without having scratched the surface.

Up to the time of Tipper's Patent every English *leather* match cricket ball was hand-stitched. As stitcher John Munday will tell you, looking back on thirty-one years in the craft, hand-stitching has defied mechanisation. Machine sewn straight stitches had never provided the same grip for the bowler's fingers as hand-sewn diagonal ones, and providing such a grip is the principal purpose of stitching, in addition to seaming, a cricket ball. John started with Gray-Nicolls at Hildenborough and then went to Ives at Tonbridge before coming to Duke; and for him, putting on dummy stitches, which are purely decorative, with a sewing machine was never a substitute for sewing by hand. Bert Dyer, who still did stitching mornings at Twort when they were at Southborough and had been manager of Hildenborough, is of the same opinion.

As Tom Humphrey who has been in the trade for thirty-four years, and Harry Butter for forty-nine years, both point out: at Teston every stitch is an individual lock. If the seam breaks the stitching imposed on the ball after seaming will hold the ball together. As Tom sews the thread through the holes by means of the nylon bristle, after the manner of the closers and seamers, he gives it a twist. Most cricket balls have two rows of stitching; some may have three.

To correct the distortion – the 'proudness' – which hand-stitching gives to the shape of the ball, it is placed in a press and squeezed until it has resumed spherical form. In the finishing department a critical eye checks that its proper shape has in fact been restored and the stitches are

Archibald Reader sizes up a tray of Reader cricket balls of 1948

as they should be. Those that pass inspection have their colour brought back over a bunsen burner. Excess grease is rubbed off to make way for a varnish applied by hand, and the surface is polished by hand, one side at a time. The varying grades are finished in different ways. The Test and County Cricket Board and the MCC frown on a polyurethane finish which gives the ball a too lasting shine. The shine, they say, has to be allowed to wear off. If the bowler wants to have the ball's movement in the air affected by a shine on its surface, then he has to induce it by rubbing it on the side of his trouser leg.

Best balls are branded with gold leaf before polishing – the grade ('Special County', etc), a crest perhaps, the weight (5½oz), and of course 'Made in England'. The cheaper ball, known as a 'scuffer', has its marking stamped on after polishing. Whether done before or after polishing, stamping tends to distort the shape, and pressure is once again brought to bear to take the elongated grin off its face and make it less 'proud' by further milling.

Perhaps the experiments which Tonbridge Sports Industries conducted at the end of 1978 in collaboration with Professor W. A. Mair, head of the Department of Engineering at Cambridge University, and Professor V. Stephens, in the department's wind tunnel (which led to their building a smaller version at Chiddingstone Causeway) will help discover if a ball's swing is caused not by shine but by some other feature hitherto unsuspected. William Gray, great grandson of H. J. Gray, chief executive of Grays of Cambridge (International) Limited, the parent company of TSI, has instituted this pioneering piece of research as part of a campaign to bring the more meaningful British Standard Institution's 'kite-mark' to every English-made, grade 'A' cricket ball. Then those who buy cricket balls will know that such an article has reached a standard set not by the industry but by the independent BSI who will impose their own tests for wear, deformation, hardness, etc. Today any Indian manufacturer can stamp a meaningless letter 'A' on his product knowing he will receive orders from unsuspecting leagues who specify an 'A' ball for their matches and leave it at that, in the belief that every cricket ball with an 'A' on it is of the same quality. But unscrupulous Indian manufacturers will print a counterfeit kitemark on their cricket balls at the risk of prosecution. The additional claim that the ball conforms to the requirements of 'Law 5' is limited to tolerances of weight and size. There is no requirement for material. It can conform without being either of leather, or red. Bill Gray's drive for a greater degree of uniformity has the full support of the MCC and the TCCB. If he achieves it, it will in no way detract from the excellence associated with something that is hand-made. Science, in the form of the BSI tests at Hemel Hempstead and the wind tunnel experiments at Cambridge and Chiddingstone Causeway, will guide the hand not supplant it. The result should be a welcome piece of consumer protection long deferred.

While Duke have been concerned about swing, Reader have been looking into bounce. This is measured by dropping the ball from a height of seven feet on to a concrete floor and measuring the percentage recovery. Traditional grade 'A' English-made cricket balls have a twenty-five to thirty per cent bounce; recent Australian balls have a forty per cent bounce. Reader, who are as much interested in attaining a standard specification as Duke, consulted the MCC who agreed that the optimum bounce figure should be thirty-five per cent. To meet this the Teston firm produced what they called the Alfred Reader Quiltmaster Grade A cricket ball with a centre composed of a hand-wrapped lamination of cork, rubber and Terylene fibre, with a fabric retaining strip which is machine-finished and cured under intense pressure. The centre is then fitted into the leather covers and hand-stitched by their craftsmen in the traditional way. Each ball has eighty stitches in the seam. They claim the centre cannot lose its shape or its resilience. Donald Reader regards it as 'the most significant advance in cricket ball manufacture this century'.

'Indoor cricket', introduced in 1974 with the aid of the Wrigley Foundation and adopted by the National Cricket Association, has its own rules and its own tools. Reader produced an approved indoor cricket ball to the required four ounce weight but of the same size as a 'regular' cricket ball. It is all-plastic and designed to rise from the matting on the floor, bounce off the walls and hit the wickets on springs in the way that makes the game attractive to the mounting numbers of indoor cricket fans.

Readers make some 65,000 leather cricket balls of all grades a year and about 300,000 plastic balls which, if painted white, find their way onto a hockey field, if red onto a cricket pitch. The vast majority become hockey balls. Duke make some 25,000 leather cricket balls a year – or 2,000 dozen as they still like to say (metrication is still far away) – and no plastic cricket balls (outdoor or indoor).

Both make Ladies' Cricket Balls and Youths' Cricket Balls which are made in the same way only lighter in weight – five ounces for the ladies and four-and-threequarter ounces for the youths. In 1974 the retail price

The present generation of Readers in charge at Teston in 1979; D. V. N. Reader (left) and John V. Reader. Dennis Lillee separates them, clutching samples of the only other hand-stitched leather cricket balls to be made in England apart from the products of the Tonbridge Sports Industries group at Chiddingstone Causeway

of a Men's or Ladies' Grade A, hand-stitched, leather cricket ball was creeping up to £7. Five years later the top price was more like £17, with the cheapest ball £7.30.

It is a tribute to players of cricket that they have continued for so long to delight in the difficult-to-identify satisfaction of using something that is hand-made. When the game began, as this story shows, it was the only way cricket bats and cricket balls could be made, and so a tradition was established which carried over into an age in which it has been maintained other than for tradition's sake.

There was the feeling that an old cricket bat was a good cricket bat; that, unlike a golf club or tennis racquet, it matured; that well kept and well oiled it became better and better. Playing with a hand-made cricket bat and a hand-made cricket ball has been part of the pleasure which has kept cricket high in the league of national pastimes. Both are basically simple in form and can be made in fair quantity by hand. Production of a more sophisticated article in large quantities would have defeated the hands. No drastic change has overtaken them comparable to the introduction of steel shafts for golf clubs which made Tom Auchterlonie and the rest of the St Andrew's craftsmen 'old-fashioned' overnight.

The relationship between fingers and cricket ball which has never existed with a golf ball or tennis ball, accounts much for a continuing demand for the leather, hand-stitches, four quarters and quality finish of the 'best' ball. To many, a tennis ball seems to fly away from a tennis racquet, a golf ball from a golf club, with the aid of an outside agency which somehow does not belong to the racquet or club, or the arms that direct them. The stocky cricket bat, held firmly in the two hands close to the body, however, seems solely and directly responsible for the flight of the ball to the boundary. It is a much closer, more intimate relationship than club and golfer, racquet and tennis player.

To seek an explanation for why the cricketing fraternity has not been

prepared to make do with cricket bats and cricket balls made on con-
veyor belts by mass production methods is perhaps superfluous; suffice
it that such is the case. But standards have been slipping, compromises
have been made to meet the demands of mechanisation, if not automa-
tion. There is a trend to make all best cricket balls with seventy stitches
instead of offering a range of between sixty and ninety (ninety-five
went out long ago). Less and less players care for niceties such as this,
and makers must naturally feel it profitless to make a product which no
one appreciates.

Yet events at Lord's in 1973, when umpire Arthur Fagg complained
of leather cricket balls losing their shape after five or six overs, made
many reflect that the trouble may not only lie in the unawareness of the
players of the game but in craftsmen allowing well-tried disciplines to
matter less. Perhaps they no longer hammer enough, nor bind tightly
enough, nor stretch the worsted enough – with the result that the inner
core and its layers fails to reduce enough in the oven and the quilt swells
so that the ball, on being played, assumes the shape of a lemon or an egg.
It may become a temptation for the craftsman on piece-work, conscious
of his kind being in shorter and shorter supply, to take short cuts and
disregard the routines on which his craft has been founded, in an effort
to increase his output for a market which he knows can never take
enough of his handiwork. When that happens his customers will think
of ways of by-passing him in order to be certain that in Tests and
County matches at least, the ball remains round for all of the overs for
which it must remain in continuous play. There will then emerge the
William Lee of cricket who, like the sixteenth-century parson of Nottingham who devised a machine for simulating the movements of the
hand knitter, will invent automated plant for turning out permanently
circular, leather, cork-quilted cricket balls in large quantities which no
one will fault and no one regret. No one will care, for most will have
forgotten what it is they are meant to care for; few will be left who knew
what Cricket was.

The game is in danger of sliding. Apart from a few tolerances regarding the circumference and weight of a ball, and the width and length of a
bat, the MCC and TCCB has never attempted to draw up complete
specifications for the tools of cricket or set up machinery to see they are
carried out, as the Lawn Tennis Association and the Royal and Ancient
have done for tennis and golf. The Federation of British Manufacturers
of Sports and Games would like the Cricket Council to lay down a
specification for a cricket bat before an enterprising manufacturer
introduces, say, an all-plastic bat which changes the whole character of
the game. Before the MCC and other authorities became aware of what
had occurred, the new bat could have become universally adopted and
impossible to dislodge. It would be too late to introduce a retrospective
specification to pull it back to the implement with which people once
played what used to be cricket. The plastic pole changed the character of
pole vaulting before anyone could do anything about it. It could happen
to cricket – perhaps for the better. But it is difficult to disagree with the
late A. H. Spink, secretary of the Federation, that it is not a change
which should be allowed to creep up on the game unawares, but be the
expression of the will of those who play it and be determined by them

after they have acquainted themselves with the implications. In other words, they should do a bit of thinking about what sort of game they want, and then lay down a specification of the kind of bat and ball (and other equipment) which they see as best making that game possible, and not only in terms of shape and size and weight but also in terms of material. Even a film of plastic on a blade makes a difference to hitting; if it is more than $\frac{1}{32}$ of an inch thick it affects the characteristic of a bat, doing very much more than merely protecting and waterproofing it. Small modifications of this kind when multiplied could slowly distort the nature of cricket and turn it into something which players realise, too late, is very much less satisfying than the game they once knew.

Whatever face may be put on them, at least the pods of most cricket bats, and not only those made in England, are still English willow. Carlton Wright of Chelmsford, doyen of willow suppliers, supplies the cricket bat industry with 180,000 clefts a year from *salix alba caerulea* willow planted thirty-five to forty to an acre and materialising in twelve to sixteen years. It is the wood which gets its name from the sky bluish white tinge seen on its surface immediately the bark is removed which sadly turns to brown (oxidising) within five minutes. Makers of cricket bats in Australia may have acquired something of the technique of cricket bat making, but they have to send to Essex for the raw material.

Cricket bat blades have changed as cricket balls have changed. English-made, hand-stitched cricket balls have become too expensive for those – the majority – not involved in first-class cricket. They are also in short supply. Clubs have been forced to use imported balls not only for practice at the nets but in matches. These are very much harder on hands and bats, and have led bat makers to think up ways of making blades less vulnerable to the damage they can inflict. They have covered them with vellum; had resort to 'polyarmouring' (covering with a liquid casing) and to what they call the non-oil process by which they impregnate the wood to give it additional strength and a silky texture which requires no oil. All three have proved useful answers to a situation, well entrenched in the 1970s, which presumably the bat makers, not prone to introducing gimmicks solely for the sake of sales promotion, would have preferred never to have arisen.

How sad it would be if the methods of the hand-craftsmen of Teston and Chiddingstone Causeway, Witham and Robertsbridge, Nottingham and St Neots became olde worlde ways of doing the job, patronisingly kept alive by trendy folklorists and antiquarians for their 'quaintness'! The craft of cricket ball and cricket bat making has been part of the living tissue of the very healthy game of regulation cricket for two hundred years and, with player and craftsman aware of the alternatives, there is no reason to think it cannot continue to be for another two hundred; for the game played with anything other than their handiwork is just not cricket.

Street Plan of Southborough showing location of bat and ball craftsmen

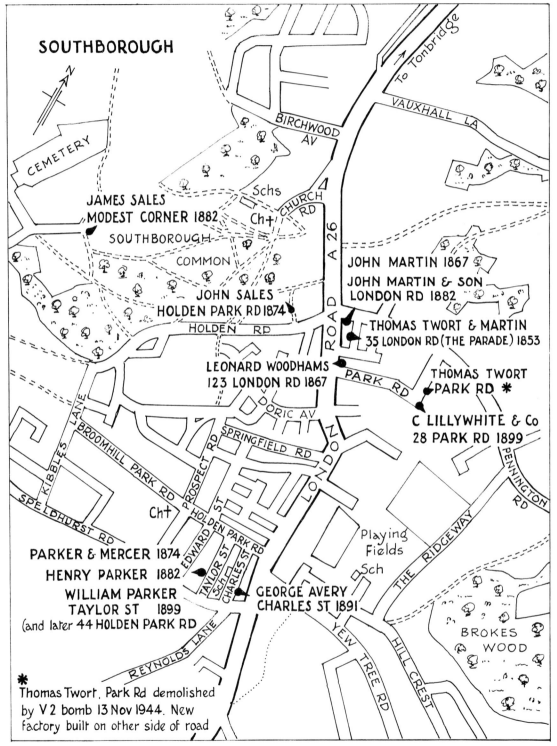

SOUTHBOROUGH

CEMETERY

BIRCHWOOD AV

To Tonbridge

VAUXHALL LA

Schs

Ch†

CHURCH RD

JAMES SALES
MODEST CORNER 1882

SOUTHBOROUGH
COMMON

ROAD A 26

JOHN MARTIN 1867
JOHN MARTIN & SON
LONDON RD 1882

JOHN SALES
HOLDEN PARK RD 1874

HOLDEN RD

THOMAS TWORT & MARTIN
35 LONDON RD (THE PARADE) 1853

LEONARD WOODHAMS
123 LONDON RD 1867

PARK RD

THOMAS TWORT
PARK RD *

DORIC AV

C LILLYWHITE & Co
28 PARK RD 1899

KIBBLES LANE

BROOMHILL PARK RD

SPRINGFIELD RD

PROSPECT RD

LONDON

PENNINGTON RD

SPELDHURST RD

Ch†

HOLDEN PARK RD

EDWARD ST

TAYLOR ST

Sch

CHARLES ST

Playing
Fields

Sch

THE RIDGEWAY

PARKER & MERCER 1874
HENRY PARKER 1882
WILLIAM PARKER
TAYLOR ST   1899
(and later 44 HOLDEN PARK RD

GEORGE AVERY
CHARLES ST 1891

REYNOLDS LANE

YEW TREE RD

HILL CREST RD

BROKES
WOOD

*
Thomas Twort, Park Rd demolished
by V2 bomb 13 Nov 1944. New
factory built on other side of road

Street Plan of Tonbridge showing location of bat and ball craftsmen

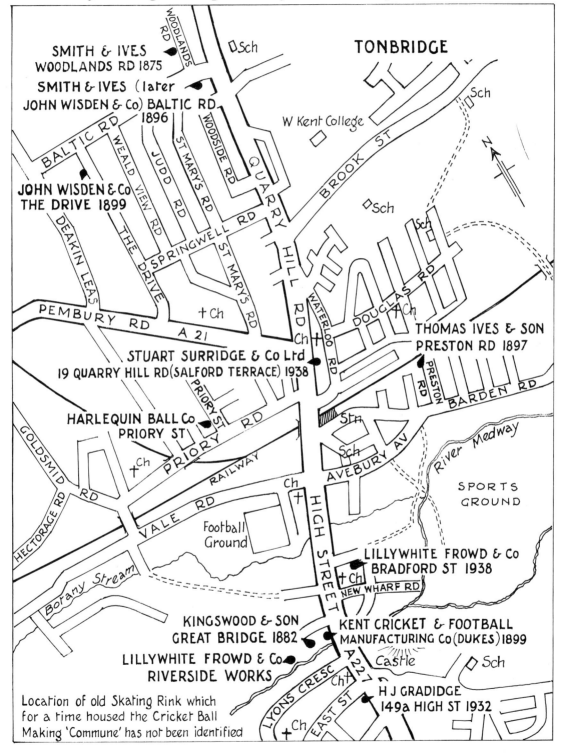

SMITH & IVES
WOODLANDS RD 1875

SMITH & IVES (later
JOHN WISDEN & Co) BALTIC RD
1896

JOHN WISDEN & Co
THE DRIVE 1899

TONBRIDGE

□ Sch

W Kent College

□ Sch

□ Sch

Sch

N

WOODLANDS RD

BALTIC RD

WEALD VIEW RD

JUDD RD

ST MARYS RD

WOODSIDE RD

SPRINGWELL RD

ST MARY'S RD

THE DRIVE

DEAKIN LEAS

QUARRY HILL

BROOK ST

PEMBURY RD
A 21

† Ch

QUARRY HILL RD

WATERLOO RD

DOUGLAS RD

† Ch

Ch †

THOMAS IVES & SON
PRESTON RD 1897

STUART SURRIDGE & Co Ltd
19 QUARRY HILL RD (SALFORD TERRACE) 1938

PRESTON RD

BARDEN RD

HARLEQUIN BALL Co
PRIORY ST

PRIORY ST

PRIORY RD

×Ch

Sch

Sch

AVEBURY AV

River Medway

SPORTS
GROUND

GOLDSMID RD

HECTORAGE RD

RAILWAY RD

VALE RD

Ch †

Football
Ground

HIGH STREET

LILLYWHITE FROWD & Co
BRADFORD ST 1938

† Ch
NEW WHARF RD

Botany Stream

KINGSWOOD & SON
GREAT BRIDGE 1882

LILLYWHITE FROWD & Co
RIVERSIDE WORKS

KENT CRICKET & FOOTBALL
MANUFACTURING Co (DUKES) 1899

Castle

□ Sch

LYONS CRESC

A 227

Ch †

EAST ST

† Ch

H J GRADIDGE
149a HIGH ST 1932

Location of old Skating Rink which
for a time housed the Cricket Ball
Making 'Commune' has not been identified

Cricket Bat and Ball Makers

Names mentioned in the text of individuals who established, or became proprietors of, workshops; and of partnerships and companies which established or acquired cricket ball and cricket bat making businesses.

CRICKET BALL MAKERS

Timothy Duke
Duke & Son
John Small senior
John Small junior
Stonyhurst College boys
Robert Dark
Thomas Rhodes
William Martin
Thomas Twort
Martin & Twort
Leonard Woodham(s)
John Martin
John Sales
Parker & Mercer
Henry Parker
William Parker
James Sales
George Avery
James Clout
Kingswood & Son
Thomas Twort & Sons
John Wisden & Co
Henry Luff
Luff & Week
Thomas Ives
Charles Smith
Smith & Ives
Thomas Ives & Son
Kent Cricket & Football Manufacturing Co
H. H. Hitchcock

E. H. (Ned) Hitchcock
Harry Martin
H. Martin & Son
W. Martin
Edward Martin
Thomas Martin
Alfred Valentine Reader
Benjamin Harse
Harse Brothers
Fuller Pilch & Martin
Archibald Alfred Reader
Joseph Villiers Reader
Alfred Reader & Co
Eleanor Page
William Thomas Page
Edward James Page
J. T. Finney
W. E. Bussey
J. S. Pinder
F. H. Ayres
G. F. Evans
Tonbridge Workmen's Guild
Lillywhite Frowd & Co
Harry Gradidge
Colonel Arkwright
Gray-Nicolls Ltd
Stuart Surridge
Co-operative Wholesale Society
Grays of Cambridge (International) Ltd
Tonbridge Sports Industries Ltd

CRICKET BAT MAKERS

Stonyhurst College boys
John Small senior
John Small junior
William Pett
Thomas Pett
William Staples
Charles Budd

Thomas Nixon
White & Helyer
Joseph Feltham
Charles Armstrong
Thomas Mayo
Peacock & Graham
Henry Day

J. B. Bentley
Nellie Cochrane
Aquila Clapshaw I
Christopher Thorn
George Wheeler
Thomas Edmonds
W. Pawley
Durtnall
E. Bagot
Fred Lillywhite
John Lillywhite
James Lillywhite
James Lillywhite & Frowd
Duke & Son
Eleanor Page
Mrs E. Page & Son
Edward Ayres
Fuller Pilch
Edward Martin
Fuller Pilch & Martin
James Cobbett
Aquila Clapshaw II
Charles Clapshaw
Samuel Clapshaw
Ben Dark
Matilda Dark
Frank Dark
John Crane
George White
Mark Clapshaw
Albert Clapshaw
Aquila Clapshaw & Salmon Ltd
W. H. Caldecourt
William Dibb
William Gladman
Thomas Couchman
Richard Allen
John Bartlett
Charles Bentley
Edward Block
John Hulme
John Ross
Alfred Clark
Frank Ogden
William Lambley
Luke Eade
Frederick Eade
Alfred (Sixer) Eade
Benjamin Warsop & Sons
George Bussey
E & W Page
E. J. Page & Co
Thomas Eaton
John Grimwood

William Mortlake
John Peters
John Fensom
Lambert & Hammond
William Gunn
T. J. Moore
Gunn & Moore
William Sherwin
H. C. Crawford
J. Browning
H. S. Dark
William Page
W. T. Page & Co
John Wisden & Co
L. J. Nicolls
Stuart Surridge
John Thompson
Henry Pettifer
Harry Gradidge
G. W. Frowd
W. G. Frowd
F. H. Ayres
Davenport
Robert Henderson & Sons
John Bryan
Frank Bryan
R. G. Barlow
Frank Sugg
Walter Lambert & Sons
H. J. Gray
H. J. Gray & Sons
Richard Daft
Harry Hayley Ltd
Gray-Nicolls Ltd
A. E. Trimmings
George Trimmings
Joyce Trimmings (Mrs Deacey)
Lillywhite Frowd
Shaw & Shrewsbury
S. M. Wainwright
C. A. Odd & Sons
Monty Odd
County Sports St Neots Ltd
Walter Warsop
Max Warsop
Harry Stebbing
Warsop & Stebbing
Slazengers Ltd
G. K. Adams
S. M. Kennedy
Wade & Ellis
Duncan Fearnley
Tonbridge Sports Industries Ltd
Grays of Cambridge (International) Ltd

Chronology

1568   William Allen opens English College at Douai

1582   Father Robert Parsons founds English Grammar School at Eu and takes sixteenth century cricket with him

1683   Cricket pitch becomes twenty-two yards long, according to John Nyren

1709   William Pett born in Sevenoaks

1723   Old Pretender receives imported Batts for Cricketing to enliven exile in Rome

1729   Date on bat of James Chitty of Knaphill at The Oval – oldest in existence?

1737   John Small born

1743   Surmised date of bat marked 'J.O.' (Miles) at Winchester College

1750   Vine Cricket Club formed at Sevenoaks?

1756   First reference in Press to Hambledon Club

1760   Richard or John Duke, leather boot maker of Penshurst, diversifies into leather cricket ball making?

1762   Timothy Duke I born; Duke & Son formed?

1771   Thomas 'Shock' White of Reigate uses bat wider than wicket; and Hambledon Club limit width to four-and-a-half inches, a rule adopted by the Five Counties in 1774

1775   Wicket increased from two to three stumps

Duke & Son present thirteen-year-old George Prince of Wales with first treble sewn cricket ball

1780   Aquila Clapshaw opens bat workshop in Turnham Green

1785   Luke Eade born

1786   William Pett died.

1794   English Catholic schoolboys return from Liège, bringing sixteenth century cricket, and settle at Stonyhurst College

1800   Timothy Duke II born

1802   Robert Dark born

1808   William Martin starts making bats at Hadlow

1811   Joseph Farington describes visit to Duke's cricket ball workshop at Penshurst in his diary

1814   Thomas Lord moves cricket ground to present site

1826   John Small senior dies

John Wisden born

1828   MCC legalise round arm bowling

Thomas Twort born

1835   Length of bat limited to thirty-five inches

Spliced bat becomes norm?

MCC allow hand delivering ball to be raised as high as shoulder

1838   Circumference of ball limited to between nine and nine-and-a-quarter inches

1840   Eleanor Page sets up bat factory in Kennington

1841   Duke & Son move from The Paddocks, Penshurst, to Chiddingstone Causeway

1842   James Cobbett dies

Luke Eade dies

1848   Duke & Son start making bats as well as cricket balls

1851   Thomas Twort starts making cricket balls at Southborough

Pages start making cricket balls as well as bats at Kennington

1853   Martin & Twort formed at Southborough

Thomas Nixon introduces cane handles with a built-in springiness

1855   Thomas Ives born

1858   Timothy Duke II dies

Fred Lillywhite sets up bat making business with brother John in London

1860   H. H. Hitchcock opens ball factory at Hildenborough

1861   Martin & Twort partnership dissolved

1863   James Lillywhite & Frowd open bat factory at Newington Causeway

H. J. Gray, English Raquets Champion

1870   Benjamin Warsop opens bat workshop in Charles Street, St Johns Wood

1871   Alfred Reader takes over Martin cricket ball factory at Teston

1874	Thomas Twort & Sons begin operating in Southborough	1925	John Wisden/Duke & Son withdraw from ECBMA
1875	Smith & Ives formed in Tonbridge	1927	MCC reduce size of cricket ball
1876	Aquila Clapshaw & Salmon formed	1928	Alfred Reader move into bigger works at Teston
	L. J. Nicolls starts making bats full time at Robertsbridge	1932	Tipper's Patent
1884	John Wisden dies	1936	Thomas Ives dies
1885	Gunn & Moore formed in Nottingham	1940	Grays of Cambridge take over Shaw & Shrewsbury
1893	Stuart Surridge starts making bats at Clapham	1941	Gray-Nicolls Ltd, Robertsbridge, formed
1894	Henry Luff of Wisden's starts making cricket balls on own account	1943	Lillywhite Frowd bat factory at Newington Causeway destroyed by bomb
1896	Smith & Ives build Baltic Road cricket ball works in Tonbridge	1944	Twort works at Southborough destroyed by V2; but manufacture continues.
1897	John Wisden & Co buy Smith & Ives Baltic Road works.		Co-operative Wholesale Society of Manchester buy John Wisden & Co
	Thomas Ives forms own company, Thomas Ives & Son at Preston Road, Tonbridge	1961	Baltic Road, Tonbridge, works closed
	Amalgamated Society of Cricket Ball Makers trade union formed in Tonbridge		Cricket Ball departments of Surridge, Ives and Gray-Nicolls closed, and craftsmen moved to Chiddingstone Causeway.
1900	Benjamin Warsop & Sons incorporated, and move from Charles Street to Park Road		Tonbridge Sports Industries Ltd formed
1901	Lillywhite Frowd Medway Works, Tonbridge, opened?	1966	Thomas Twort joins TSI
1910	Aquila Clapshaw & Salmon taken over by father of Bernard Taylor	1970	Grays of Cambridge acquire John Wisden & Co from CWS
1911	John Wisden & Co acquire Dark & Son (?), and buy factory in West Ham	1971	Fire destroys Ives factory in Preston Road, Tonbridge
1913	W. H. Duke dies	1972	Fire destroys new workshops at Chiddingstone Causeway
1920	John Wisden & Co acquire Duke & Son	1973	Fire at County Sports St Neots; acquire machinery etc of Benjamin Warsop whose works at Park Road close; activities under Mrs Deacey, granddaughter of A. E. Trimmings, continue
	Formation of Workmen's Guild at Tonbridge?		
1923	Harry Duke dies		
	Cricket Ball Manufacturers Association formed by employers before the Great War, is re-formed as English Cricket Ball Manufacturers Association		
1924	Arthur Duke dies – the last of the Dukes; Harold Tipper takes over.	1975	All cricket ball craftsmen of TSI now concentrated at old (1841) factory at Chiddingstone Causeway, and Twort works at Southborough
	A. E. Trimmings sets up bat factory at St Neots	1978	Twort works at Southborough closed, and men moved to Chiddingstone Causeway.

Bibliography

Alison Adburgham *A Century in the Service of Sport 1863–1963* (Lillywhites of Piccadilly Circus), London, 1963

H. S. Altham *History of Cricket*, London, 1926

Anon 'From Willow to Wicket', *The Sportsman*, 16 April 1910

F. S. Ashley-Cooper 'The Ball', *The Cricketer*, vol V 'Laws of Cricket', album of notes and cuttings, MCC Library, Lord's

'Bat' *The Cricketer's Manual*, London, 1851

Sir Norman Birkett *The Game of Cricket*, London, 1955

William Bolland *Cricket Notes*, London, 1851

Thomas Boxall *New Articles on the Game of Cricket*, Maidstone, 1774

G. B. Buckley 'Duke & Son', *Cricketer*, 31 May 1952
'Historical Gleanings', unpublished MS, MCC Library, Lord's
Fresh Light on 18th Century Cricket, London, 1935

C. G. Bussey *A Popular Treatise entitled The Bat of the Victorian Era or the Evolution of the Demon Driver*, London, 1897

Neville Cardus *English Cricket*, London, 1945

A. K. Cook 'Hills, Meads and Games', *Winchester College 1393–1893*, 1894

A Correspondent (Father Herbert Thurston) 'Little Cricket', the Stonyhurst Game, Memories of an old performer, *The Times*, 12 September, 1936

A. Craig 'Ayres International Bat' (advertising card)

A. E. Crawley *The Book of the Ball*, London, 1913

Richard Daft *Kings of Cricket*, London, 1893

Sir John Dunlop *The Pleasant Town of Sevenoaks*, Sevenoaks, 1970

Pierce Egan *Sporting Anecdotes*, London, 1825

F. G. (Frederick Gale) 'About An Old Cricket Ball' *Baily's Monthly Magazine*, November, 1882

Joseph Farington *The Farington Diary* (ed James Greig), vol VII, 10 June 1811 to 18 December 1814, Chapter XVII, 'A Holiday in Kent'; (1st ed) London, 1927

'Felix' (Nicholas Wanostrocht) *Felix on the Bat*, London, 1845

Frederick Gale *The Game of Cricket*, London, 1887
Echoes From Old Cricket Fields, London, 1896

Father J. Gerard SJ 'Its Life Beyond the Seas' etc, *Stonyhurst College 1592–1894*, London, 1894

Malcolm R. V. Goodman The Cricket Bat and Ball Industries, a glance at some economic aspects, a thesis in MS, 1966; MCC Library, Lord's

W. G. Grace 'Batting', *Cricketers Annual*, 1872
Cricket, London, 1891

H. P-T (P. F. Thomas) *Early Cricket*, Nottingham, 1923
Cricket's Cradle, Nottingham, 1923
Old English Cricket, Nottingham, 1929

John Hadfield *A Wisden Century 1850–1950*, London, 1950

Lord Harris (ed) *The History of Kent County Cricket*, London, 1907

Arthur Haygarth *Memoirs of the Old Cricketers* (Lillywhites) *Scores and Biographies* 1877–1878, vol 14; 1841–1848, vol 3

Sir Ambrose Heal article on London woodworkers, *The Field*, 23 December 1933

H. J. Henley 'Implements of Cricket', *Times MCC Number*, 25 May 1937

Rev R. S. Holmes 'Cricket Notches', *Cricket*, A Weekly Record of the Game, 27 April 1893

Helen Johnson 'The Craft of the Cricket Bat', *The Countryman*, Vol XLIX, no 2, Summer, 1954

Pamela La Fane 'A Story of Skill and Care', *Cricketer*, 25 June 1949

W. Lambert *A Concise Treatise on the Noble Game of Cricket*, Lewes (3rd ed) 1816

W. J. Lewis *The Language of Cricket*, London, 1934

F. W. Lillywhite *Illustrated Handbook of Cricket*, London, 1844
Frederick Lillywhite's Cricket Scores and Biographies of Celebrated Cricketers from 1744 to 1826, London, 1862

John Lillywhite *Cricketer's Companion*, London, 1865

Norman and Jeanne Mackenzie *The Time Traveller, the Life of H. G. Wells*, London, 1973

Man of Kent 'How Cricket Balls Are Made', *Cricketer Spring Annual*, 1928

G. D. Martineau *Bat, Ball, Wicket and All*, London, 1950

Rev J. Mitford *The Rev John Mitford on Cricket*, Papers to the 'Gentleman's Magazine', London, 1921

John Nyren *Nyren's Cricketer's Guide* (7th ed) 1888
The Hambledon Men (new edition of *Young Cricketer's Tutor*), London, 1907

An Old Cricketer *The Cricket Bat*, London, 1861
Cricketer's Notebook, London, 1881

Eric Parker *The History of Cricket*, London, 1950

James Pycroft *The Cricket Field*, London, 1851
The Cricket Tutor, London, 1862
Oxford Memories, London, 1886

R. S. Rait-Kerr *The Laws of Cricket, Their History and Growth*, London, 1950

Prince Ranjitsinjhi *The Jubilee Book of Cricket*, London, 1897

K. J. Smart *Sevenoaks and Vine Cricket 1731–1959*, Sevenoaks, 1958

A Spectator Esq *Facts and Feats appertaining to Cricket*, London, 1862

Alfred T. Story 'The Evolution of Cricket', *The Strand Magazine*, September 1895

Joseph Strutt *Sports and Pastimes of the English People*, London, 1801

Alfred D. Taylor *Famous Sussex Cricketers Past and Present*, Penshurst, 1898

Dr Gordon Ward *Sevenoaks Essays*, Sevenoaks, 1931

Joseph Wright (ed) *The English Dialect Dictionary*, London, 1897

Bell's Life in London and Sporting Chronicle 'Cricket on Skates', 5 January 1845

Cricket, Badminton Library, London, 1920

Cricketana, London, 1865, The Author of 'The Cricket Field'

Cricket Bat and Ball Making, scrapbook album in MCC Library, Lord's

De L'Isle and Dudley Manuscripts Vol V, Historical MSS Commission 77, HMSO 1961

Gordon Ward Collection (U442), Kent Record Office, Maidstone

The extracts from Neville Cardus' *English Cricket* are reproduced by kind permission of Mrs Else Mayer-Lisman.

Picture Acknowledgements

Acknowledgements are made to: the Marylebone Cricket Club, pages 12, 13, 15, 29, 33, 39, 41, 42, 43, 48, 50, 52, 55, 59, 75, 86, 89, 90, 93, 94, 95, 113, 125, 167; Stonyhurst College, pages 18, 21, 22; Mr K. J. Smart and the Vine Cricket Club, pages 45 & 47; Mr R. J. L. Altham, page 46; Mr G. K. Medlock, page 49; Mr Leslie Eade, pages 62 & 98; Mr John Tipper, pages 63, 77, 78, 123, 130, 133, 141; Mr Bill Mepham, pages 68, 70 & 73; *Sports Trader* and Loughborough University, page 66; Mr John Reader, pages 83, 85, 135, 136, 137, 144, 145, 149, 150, 187, 193, 195; Mr Norman Hunt, pages 105, 111, 156, 157, 158, 159, 160, 162, 163, 164, 165, 171, 172, 177, 180, 181, 182; Gray-Nicolls Ltd, pages 114, 115, 116, 169, 178; Grays of Cambridge (International) Ltd, page 121; The Labour Party Library and Archives, page 129; Tonbridge Sports Industries Ltd, pages 81, 131, 139, 170, 186, 191; Southborough Town Council, page 154; Gunn & Moore, page 177. The photos by John Kay on pages 24 & 25 are by courtesy of Mr and Mrs Warren and Viscount De L'Isle. John Kay also took the photos on pages 101, 114, 118 & 181. The photo by Frank Manning on page 37 is reproduced by permission of the Surrey County Cricket Club; those by E. A. Sollars on pages 38 & 102 were arranged by Mr A. H. Brodhurst and are reproduced by permission of the Warden and Fellows of Winchester College; that on page 45 is a document from the Sackville MSS in the Kent Archives Office and is reproduced by permission of Lord Sackville and of the Kent County Council; those on pages 51 & 61 are from the Heal Collection of Trade Cards and are reproduced by permission of the Trustees of the British Museum; those on pages 65 & 108 by permission of the British Library. The photo on page 31 is by Don Eades; on page 49 by the Mercury Press Agency.

Index